Mastering Web Application Development with Express

A comprehensive guide to developing production-ready web applications with Express

Alexandru Vlăduțu

BIRMINGHAM - MUMBAI

Mastering Web Application Development with Express

First published: September 2014

Production reference: 1180914

Published by Packt Publishing Ltd.
Livery Place
35 Livery Street
Birmingham B3 2PB, UK.

ISBN 978-1-78398-108-3

www.packtpub.com

Cover image by Goldie Jason (goldie.jason@gmail.com)

Credits

Author

Alexandru Vlăduțu

Reviewers

Johan Borestad

Mohit Goenka

Arjunkumar Krishnamoorthy

Dave Poon

Commissioning Editor

Ashwin Nair

Acquisition Editor

James Jones

Content Development Editors

Nadeem N. Bagban

Poonam Jain

Technical Editors

Novina Kewalramani

Pratik More

Copy Editors

Mradula Hegde

Dipti Kapadia

Insiya Morbiwala

Alfida Paiva

Stuti Srivastava

Project Coordinator

Swati Kumari

Proofreaders

Ameesha Green

Maria Gould

Paul Hindle

Jonathan Todd

Indexers

Rekha Nair

Priya Sane

Graphics

Abhinash Sahu

Production Coordinator

Conidon Miranda

Cover Work

Conidon Miranda

About the Author

Alexandru Vlăduțu is a full-time JavaScript developer based in Bucharest, Romania. He started creating applications with PHP about 5 years ago, but after finding out about server-side JavaScript with Node.js, he has never had to switch technologies again. You may have seen him answering questions on Stack Overflow under the nickname `alessioalex`, where he is among the top three overall answerers for tags such as Node.js, Express, Mongoose, and Socket.IO. By day, he battles cross-browser compatibility issues, but by night, he brings together embedded databases, servers, and caching layers in single applications using the good parts of JavaScript. Apart from the geeky stuff, he enjoys spending time with his wife.

The first time I saw the video of Ryan Dahl presenting Node at JS Conf 2009, I was amazed. I have been fanatically working with Node ever since, and Ryan deserves credit for this.

I would like to thank TJ Holowaychuk for authoring Express, and the Node community for being friendly, helpful, and extremely active.

While writing this book, I had invaluable feedback from the reviewers as well as the Packt Publishing team; so thanks a lot everybody!

Most importantly, I would like to thank my wife, Diana, for her support, encouragement, and patience.

About the Reviewers

Johan Borestad lives and works in Stockholm, Sweden. With 10 years of experience in several successful start-ups, he has built up a deep knowledge of the industry. As a very outgoing and pragmatic perfectionist, he is constantly seeking new ways to improve himself and his team members. While always striving to deliver world-class products, Johan also enjoys telling bad jokes and drinking way too much coffee.

He is currently working at Klarna, building the Klarna Checkout. It is a multimarket, single-page application that is revolutionizing the e-commerce business currently. Its strong focus on usability and simplifying the buying process has made it a huge success in the Nordics and Germany. He has previously also reviewed *Express Web Application Development*, *Packt Publishing*.

> I'd like to give my warmest thank-you to my lovely family as well as to Klarna and my teammates who helped me during tough times.

Mohit Goenka is a Software Developer in the Yahoo! Mail team. He graduated from the University of Southern California (USC) with a Master of Science degree in Computer Science. His thesis emphasized game theory and human behavior concepts as applied in real-world security games. He also received an award for academic excellence from the Office of International Services at the University of Southern California. He has showcased his presence in various realms of computers, including artificial intelligence, machine learning, path planning, multiagent systems, neural networks, computer vision, computer networks, and operating systems.

During his tenure as a student, Mohit won multiple competitions, cracked codes, and presented his work on the *Detection of Untouched UFOs* to a wide range of audiences. Not only is he a software developer by profession but coding is also his hobby. He spends most of his spare time learning about emerging trends and grooming his technical skills.

What adds a feather to his cap are Mohit's poetic skills. Some of his poems are part of the University of Southern California Libraries archive under the cover of *The Lewis Carroll Collection*. In addition to this, he has made significant contributions by volunteering his time to serve the community.

Arjunkumar Krishnamoorthy is a Principal Engineer with Causeway Technologies in Bengaluru, India. He is well-versed in Java, JavaScript, Node.js, and Angular.js, among others. He has contributed to open source projects. He is passionate about programming, research, and open source technologies.

Dave Poon is a UX/UI designer, web developer, and entrepreneur based in Sydney. He started his career as a freelance graphic designer and web designer in 1998 and worked with web development agencies and medium-size enterprises. After graduating from Central Queensland University with a degree in Multimedia Studies and a Master's degree in IT, he began his love affair with Drupal and works for a variety of companies that use Drupal. Now, he is evangelizing good user experience and interaction design practices to start-ups and enterprises.

Currently, he is a Design Lead at Suncorp, one of the biggest financial institutions in Australia. He is also the cofounder of Erlango (`http://erlango.com`), a digital product development and design start-up, located in Sydney and Hong Kong, that creates user-centered digital products and tools for designers and users.

He is the author of *Drupal 7 Fields/CCK Beginner's Guide*, *Packt Publishing*. He is also the technical reviewer of *Drupal Intranets with Open Atrium*, *Tracy Smith*, *Packt Publishing*, and *Advanced Express Web Application Development*, *Andrew Keig*, *Packt Publishing*.

I would like to thank my wife, Rita, for her endless patience and support. Without her, whatever I do would be meaningless.

I would also like to thank my father for his continued encouragement.

www.PacktPub.com

Support files, eBooks, discount offers, and more

You might want to visit www.PacktPub.com for support files and downloads related to your book.

Did you know that Packt offers eBook versions of every book published, with PDF and ePub files available? You can upgrade to the eBook version at www.PacktPub.com and as a print book customer, you are entitled to a discount on the eBook copy. Get in touch with us at service@packtpub.com for more details.

At www.PacktPub.com, you can also read a collection of free technical articles, sign up for a range of free newsletters and receive exclusive discounts and offers on Packt books and eBooks.

http://PacktLib.PacktPub.com

Do you need instant solutions to your IT questions? PacktLib is Packt's online digital book library. Here, you can access, read and search across Packt's entire library of books.

Why subscribe?

- Fully searchable across every book published by Packt
- Copy and paste, print and bookmark content
- On demand and accessible via web browser

Free access for Packt account holders

If you have an account with Packt at www.PacktPub.com, you can use this to access PacktLib today and view nine entirely free books. Simply use your login credentials for immediate access.

Table of Contents

Preface

Express is a battle-tested web framework for Node.js, and is used in production in companies such as Paypal or MySpace. It has come a long way since its initial release back in 2009, with more than a hundred contributors and an active community of developers.

The simplicity of Express has even enabled people to build more complex applications on top of it, such as Kraken.js or Sails.js.

This book is aimed at developers who want to learn more about delivering real-world applications with Express 4 by taking advantage of the advanced features it provides and also benefiting from the great ecosystem of existing modules from NPM.

You will find a lot of practical examples along with different tips and tricks that will help you develop a better application at a faster pace. Even if you decide to use another framework in the future or create your own, the things you have learned here will be useful in the future.

What this book covers

Chapter 1, Diving into Express, covers the fundamentals of the framework, its use cases, how it compares to other web frameworks, and how to structure Express applications.

Chapter 2, Component Modularity Using Middleware, explains the concept of middleware in great detail while using practical examples so you will be able to create and use middleware based on the application's needs.

Chapter 3, Creating RESTful APIs, is a practical introduction to creating a RESTful API using Express. You will learn about general REST API design as well as tips and tricks provided by the framework while creating a practical application.

Chapter 4, Leveraging the Power of Template Engines, shows you how to use different template engines and techniques to organize applications as well as create a custom engine and integrate it into an existing application.

Chapter 5, Reusable Patterns for a DRY Code Base, covers how to avoid writing repeatable code in Express applications by using existing Node.js modules. Throughout this chapter, an app will be enhanced step-by-step to use such modules until we get a DRY code base, where DRY stands for Don't Repeat Yourself.

Chapter 6, Error Handling, covers the various ways of dealing with error handling in an Express app, explaining how to react to errors, how to throw custom errors, and other tips and tricks.

Chapter 7, Improving the Application's Performance, covers different optimization techniques that can be used to speed up an application, both frontend and backend. You will learn how to apply these best practices into an application.

Chapter 8, Monitoring Live Applications, explains how to effectively monitor an application so that it detects anomalies and makes the user aware of them. You will learn how to integrate metrics from multiple live applications into a dashboard.

Chapter 9, Debugging, covers how to debug an application in a live production environment, or locally when things go wrong. We will be using node-inspector and exploring how to add a REPL to the application, among other things.

Chapter 10, Application Security, covers the common security countermeasures that you can take to prevent certain incidents, and also covers how to integrate them into an Express application.

Chapter 11, Testing and Improving Code Quality, covers how to write tests while creating an application as well as triggering them before committing the code along with other tools to improve code quality.

What you need for this book

Before diving in, you should be familiar with JavaScript, Node.js, and Express. To run the examples, you need to have Node.js installed on your system. Some of the chapters require a database engine, so you should also have MongoDB installed.

Who this book is for

This book is ideal if you are a Node.js developer who wants to take your Express skills to the next level and develop high-performing, reliable web applications using best practices. This book assumes that you have experience with Express. It does not attempt to teach the basics of the framework, but instead focuses on advanced topics that need to be addressed by real-world applications.

Conventions

In this book, you will find a number of styles of text that distinguish between different kinds of information. Here are some examples of these styles and an explanation of their meaning.

Code words in text, database table names, folder names, filenames, file extensions, pathnames, dummy URLs, user input, and Twitter handles are shown as follows: "The layout.jade file will be created inside the views folder."

A block of code is set as follows:

```
exports.main = require('./main');
exports.users = require('./users');
exports.sessions = require('./sessions');
exports.files = require('./files');
```

Any command-line input or output is written as follows:

```
$ cd FileManager
$ mkdir {models,helpers,files,lib}
```

New terms and **important words** are shown in bold. Words that you see on the screen, in menus or dialog boxes for example, appear in the text like this: "The CSRF check was to ensure that the user actually clicked on the **Submit** button."

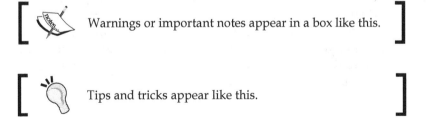

Warnings or important notes appear in a box like this.

Tips and tricks appear like this.

Reader feedback

Feedback from our readers is always welcome. Let us know what you think about this book—what you liked or may have disliked. Reader feedback is important for us to develop titles that you really get the most out of.

To send us general feedback, simply send an e-mail to feedback@packtpub.com, and mention the book title through the subject of your message.

If there is a topic that you have expertise in and you are interested in either writing or contributing to a book, see our author guide on www.packtpub.com/authors.

Customer support

Now that you are the proud owner of a Packt book, we have a number of things to help you to get the most from your purchase.

Downloading the example code

You can download the example code files for all Packt books you have purchased from your account at http://www.packtpub.com. If you purchased this book elsewhere, you can visit http://www.packtpub.com/support and register to have the files e-mailed directly to you.

You can also download the example code files for the book from GitHub at https://github.com/alessioalex/mastering_express_code.

Errata

Although we have taken every care to ensure the accuracy of our content, mistakes do happen. If you find a mistake in one of our books—maybe a mistake in the text or the code—we would be grateful if you would report this to us. By doing so, you can save other readers from frustration and help us improve subsequent versions of this book. If you find any errata, please report them by visiting http://www.packtpub.com/support, selecting your book, clicking on the **errata submission form** link, and entering the details of your errata. Once your errata are verified, your submission will be accepted and the errata will be uploaded to our website, or added to any list of existing errata, under the Errata section of that title.

Piracy

Piracy of copyright material on the Internet is an ongoing problem across all media. At Packt, we take the protection of our copyright and licenses very seriously. If you come across any illegal copies of our works, in any form, on the Internet, please provide us with the location address or website name immediately so that we can pursue a remedy.

Please contact us at copyright@packtpub.com with a link to the suspected pirated material.

We appreciate your help in protecting our authors, and our ability to bring you valuable content.

Questions

You can contact us at questions@packtpub.com if you are having a problem with any aspect of the book, and we will do our best to address it.

1
Diving into Express

Express is the de facto web application framework for Node.js and one of the most depended-upon modules, according to the NPM registry.

In this chapter, we will cover the following topics:

- The main features of the framework
- The comparison of Express with other web application frameworks
- Using the right tool for the right job
- The important companies that use Express in production
- How to structure applications with Express

The best parts of Express

When searching the Web for information on Express, we find that it is a minimal and flexible web framework that adds the essential bits and pieces needed to create powerful web applications.

It is minimal because it provides the basic features we need to create web applications, such as routing based on URL paths (it has DSL to describe routes), support for template engines, cookie and session management, the parsing of incoming requests, and so on. Without these built-in features, we need to create our own custom solutions on top of the Node HTTP. The source code for Express is just a few thousand lines of code, enabling us to easily dig deeper for a better understanding of how things work internally.

The flexibility comes from the fact that this framework does not impose things such as a certain application structure or database layer. Furthermore, not every middleware available is included by default when creating an application (unlike other big, monolithic frameworks); we have to explicitly include what we want. Even though Express is not a typical **Model-View-Controller** (**MVC**) framework, there's nothing stopping us from customizing it to be one if our requirements dictate it.

We can build different kinds of applications with Express, such as REST APIs, single-page and multipage applications, real-time applications, applications that spawn external processes and output their result, and many others. Due to its intuitive API and flexibility, Express makes it easy for newcomers to get started with the framework and use it for rapid prototyping when needed. Although there are methods to facilitate certain actions (such as redirecting the user to another page or serving JSON data), the functions built into Node are also available for this purpose.

The out-of-the-box performance of Express is really good; it can handle thousands of concurrent connections per second (the results are dependent on the concrete use case). An application can always be improved through caching, scaling to multiple processes, or other techniques, but it's good to know that Express won't be our bottleneck.

Comparing Express with other frameworks

When comparing a web framework to another, we first need to ask ourselves what problems each framework is trying to solve. After that, we can move on to compare their functionality and choose the one that suits our projects best.

Goal

Express was built to help developers with HTTP, not to be a full-stack framework that's packed with features. The framework gives us all the primitives to create all kinds of applications, from simple web applications to hybrid and real-time ones. Unlike big, monolithic frameworks, Express is not packed with things such as ORMs, view helpers, or other complex features. This means that we have the flexibility to plug in whatever we want to.

Conventions

When starting out with opinionated frameworks such as Rails, we need to learn about their conventions; a few examples of what we need to know are as follows:

- Where things go inside the application folder
- The naming conventions
- How to define data relationships

These conventions can be an advantage for teams with many developers (to keep everybody on the same page), but if we need to create smaller applications or want to avoid the steep learning curve, Express is a better option.

The fact that Express isn't opinionated can be viewed as a good thing or a disadvantage depending on the use case. It's flexible enough that we can create our own conventions, but at the same time, we might not want or have time to do that.

Databases

Some frameworks are tied into a particular database or **Object Relational Mapper (ORM)**, but that isn't the case with Express. It doesn't care about how we manage our data, so it doesn't tie us to a database, nor does it include drivers for any.

If we decide to add a database or an ORM to our application, we need to manually include it.

Views

There are a lot of templating engines available for Express, and it's very simple to integrate new ones. Some of them handle layouts and partials so we can reuse code and provide other features.

Express has support for view helpers, but the framework doesn't provide any out-of-the-box support.

Overall

Express is a good choice if we want as much control over our applications as possible, without having to recreate basic, HTTP-related functionality over and over again. It adds the bare minimum sugar syntax to create web applications and doesn't force us into using a certain database, ORM, or templating engine.

Since it's a minimalist framework, we can't expect it to have as many features as the more complex frameworks such as Rails, Django, or CakePHP.

Use cases

Before diving into the code, we need to consider whether Express is a good choice for the application we need to create. Next, we will check out a couple of good use cases for the framework.

Complex applications with heavy I/O bound operations

The Web is constantly evolving, and nowadays, applications do more than talk to a single database and send HTML over the wire. An application could use an in-memory database for session storage and caching, a message queue for background processing, at least one relational/NoSQL database, and external services to store files, stream logs, and monitor application health. The handling of I/O bound operations is a great use case for Node because of its nonblocking nature, and this applies to Express as well. This means that we can easily integrate all these components into our project, and it will still have a solid performance.

Single-page applications

Single-page applications represent web applications that don't reload the page when we use them. They update parts of their interface to provide a more native-like experience to end users.

There are many arguments for writing single-page applications in Express, which include the following:

- It has the ability to handle a lot of concurrent requests per second
- It's not a bloated framework; it has the bare minimum glue needed to write web applications
- It has a lovely DSL syntax to describe routes
- It can perform content negotiation, so we can have the same endpoint for our data but deliver different representations based on the client's request (JSON, XML, or others)
- It has a lot of small functions that make our lives easier, such as `res. sendfile`, which transfers a file to the client and sets the proper headers, and `req.xhr`, which checks whether the current request has been transmitted using Ajax, and many others

Reusable applications

Any Express application can be mounted onto another parent one, enabling us to create modular components that can be included in multiple applications. For example, we can create a user authentication system and reuse it for all our projects. Another situation where this can come in handy is when multiple people are working on the same project but each has different responsibilities; somebody could work on an API while a different person creates the multipage website, and each of them could use separate repositories for source control management. When a child application is finished, the master one can include it by adding a single line of code (okay, maybe two if we're declaring the first one as a dependency in the `package.json` file).

Code sharing between the server and the client

Writing application code that runs both on the server and on the client is a very hot topic right now, and has often been referred to as "The Holy Grail of Web Development". Besides eliminating code duplication, there is one other big advantage of using this approach with single-page applications: we can render the first page on the server and all the subsequent ones on the client. This improves the speed of the initial page load (so users don't have to wait until all the JavaScript code is loaded and executed) and is also SEO friendly and doesn't require us to resort to tricks such as proxying to a headless browser for crawlers. There have been several attempts to create frameworks that use the Backbone.js client-side API on top of Express, one of the most popular being **Rendr** (`https://github.com/airbnb/rendr`).

A base to create more complex frameworks

Since Express is a minimalist framework, we can use it to build more complex and opinionated solutions. In fact, there are lots of such MVC and real-time frameworks in the Node ecosystem. They offer advanced features that are packed into a single application, such as an ORM, middleware that boosts security, internationalization/localization, application life cycle middleware, a custom routing library, built-in view helpers, and so on. Another aspect to take into consideration is that these frameworks also impose certain conventions that we need to adhere to, the most notable being the application structure.

Bad use cases

If there is any CPU-intensive task that is blocking the event-loop, it means that every single client making a request to the Express application will just hang until that task has finished. This happens because, unlike the Apache web server that spawns a thread per connection, Node uses an event loop, so all the requests run in the same thread.

If we want to create a regular CRUD-based application that has complex database relationships—and scaling thousands of concurrent requests isn't the primary goal—then using a full-stack framework is a better option (for example, Rails, Django, and CakePHP). That's not to say that we cannot achieve the same end result with Express, but we would have to include all the components ourselves.

Express into the wild

Whether we are trying to introduce a new tool into a technology stack at our company or simply want to experiment with new stuff once in a while, we need to ask ourselves the following questions before diving straight in:

- Is it still an active project or has it been abandoned?
- Is it mature enough or do I have to battle-test it myself?
- Which companies are using it in production?

Express is the most popular web framework for Node, with more than a hundred contributors and thousands of commits, the first commit dating back to June 2009. Its repository is one of the most watched on GitHub. These facts answer the first two questions, so next, we'll talk about who is using it in production.

Popular companies such as MySpace, eBay, Uber, and Mozilla use Express in production, and others have made their own framework/project on top of it; here's a list of them:

- Yahoo! created an MVC framework called Mojito that can run on both the client side and server side
- PayPal released Kraken.js, an opinionated kind of Express with support for localization, application security, environment-based configuration, and other features baked in
- Airbnb's Rendr library allows us to run Backbone.js both on the client and on the server
- Ghost is a popular open source blogging platform with an elegant UI that can be used either as a standalone or by being attached to an existing Express application

- Sails.js is a real-time MVC framework based on Express and Socket.IO that has a lot of advanced features, such as automatic JSON API generation, role-based access control, and a database agnostic ORM

- Compound.js is an MVC framework that highly resembles Rails: it has scaffolding, a similar application structure, a lot of custom helpers, an ORM with relations support, and built-in validation as well as other useful features

The application structure

One of the most frequently asked questions by newcomers to Express is how to structure an application. There is no definitive answer for this, and we may choose different solutions based on how big our application is or what problem we are trying to tackle. Luckily for us, Express is easy to customize, and we can apply whatever structure we deem necessary.

If the code base is small, we can include everything into a few files or even a single one. This might be the case when exposing a database over HTTP (such as LevelDB and PouchDB) and creating mountable applications (these tend to be small and solve a specific problem) or other small applications.

When dealing with medium and large projects, the best thing to do is to split them into smaller pieces, making them easier to debug and test. If there are parts of the application that can be reused for other projects, the best thing to do is to move them into their separate repository.

Group files by features

An interesting technique to structure an application is to group files by the features they provide instead of grouping them by their function. In MVC, the controllers, models, and views live inside their own folder; however, with this approach, we have folders that group files with the same role. For example, consider the following folders:

- `Signup`: This includes the route handler for the signup process and its view
- `Login`: This is similar to the signup feature
- `Users`: This contains the model for the users so that it can be shared between different features
- `posts-api`: This exposes a RESTful interface for the articles of the site and contains the routes and model of the posts

One could go even further and choose to include things such as tests and static assets that belong to a feature inside its folder.

If there's something that can be reused for multiple features such as the general layout or models, we can group them inside their own folder. Each of these folders can export an Express application with its own view engine, middleware, and other customizations. These folders can reside in a parent `lib` folder, for example. We will then require them in the main `app.js` file like we would any regular middleware. It's a good way to separate concerns, although they are not necessarily complete, independent pieces because they rely on application-specific logic.

An advantage this structure offers is that when we are working on a certain section of an application, all the files that need to be created/edited are in the same location, so there's no need to switch between controllers, models, and views like with MVC.

It's worth mentioning that the creator of Express, TJ Holowaychuk, recommends this approach for larger applications instead of MVC.

Model-View-Controller

The most common technique to structure web applications with Express is MVC. When generating a project using the Express CLI, it almost provides an MVC structure, omitting the `models` folder. The following screenshot lists all the files and folders generated for a sample application using the CLI tool:

```
alexandruvladutu at 192-168-0-100 in ~/www
$ express myapp

   create : myapp
   create : myapp/package.json
   create : myapp/app.js
   create : myapp/public
   create : myapp/public/javascripts
   create : myapp/public/images
   create : myapp/public/stylesheets
   create : myapp/public/stylesheets/style.css
   create : myapp/routes
   create : myapp/routes/index.js
   create : myapp/routes/user.js
   create : myapp/views
   create : myapp/views/layout.jade
   create : myapp/views/index.jade

   install dependencies:
     $ cd myapp && npm install

   run the app:
     $ node app
```

The `package.json` file is automatically populated with the name of the application, the dependencies, the private attribute, and the starting script. This starting script is named `app.js` and loads all the middleware, assigns the route handlers, and starts the server. There are three folders in the root:

- `public`: This folder contains the static assets
- `views`: This folder is populated with Jade templates by default
- `routes`: This folder includes the routes (these are the equivalent controllers)

Apart from these existing folders and the `models` folder, which we need to create ourselves, we might also create folders for tests, logs, or configuration. The best thing about this structure is that it's easy to get started with and is known to most developers.

Developing a real MVC application

Let's apply the theory in practice now and create an MVC file manager application using Express 4.x and Mongoose (an object modeling library for MongoDB). The application should allow users to register and log in and enable them to view, upload, and delete their files.

Bootstrapping a folder structure

We will start by creating the folder structure. First, we'll use the Express CLI tool in the terminal to create the boilerplate. Apart from the `public`, `routes`, and `views` folders, we also need to add folders for `models`, `helpers` (view helpers), `files` (the files uploaded by users will be stored in subfolders here), and `lib` (used for internal app libraries):

```
$ express FileManager
$ cd FileManager
$ mkdir {models,helpers,files,lib}
```

Installing NPM dependencies

By default, the CLI tool will create two dependencies in your `package.json` file—`express` and `jade`—but it won't install them, so we need to manually execute the following `install` command:

```
$ npm install .
```

In addition to these two modules, we also need to install mongoose to interact with MongoDB, async for control flow, pwd to hash and compare passwords, connect-flash to store messages for the user (which are then cleared after being displayed), and connect-multiparty to handle file uploads. We can use the following shortcut to install the packages and have them declared in package.json at the same time if we call NPM with the –save flag:

```
$ npm install –save mongoose async pwd connect-flash connect-multiparty
```

Express 3.x came bundled with the Connect middleware, but that's not the case in the 4.x version, so we need to install them separately using the following command:

```
$ npm install –save morgan cookie-parser cookie-session body-parser
method-override errorhandler
```

> The middleware libraries from Connect were extracted into their separate repos, so starting with Express 4.x, we need to install them separately. Read more about this topic on the Connect GitHub page at https://github.com/senchalabs/connect#middleware.

We can always check what modules are installed by entering the following command in the terminal at the root of our project:

```
$ npm ls
```

That command will output a tree with the dependencies.

> It's worth noting that the versions for the dependencies listed in the package.json file will not be exact when we use the –save flag; instead, they will be using the default npm semver range operator. You can read more from the official npm documentation (https://www.npmjs.org/doc/cli/npm-install.html) and the node-semver page (https://www.npmjs.org/package/semver).

Setting up the configuration file

We can get as inventive as we want with the configuration parameters of a project, like have multiple subfolders based on the environment or hierarchical configuration, but for this simple application, it's enough to have a single config.json file. The configuration variables we need to define in this file are the MongoDB database URL, the application port, the session secret key, and its maximum age so that our file will look like the following code:

```
{
  "mongoUrl": "mongodb://localhost/filestore",
  "port": 3000,
  "sessionSecret": "random chars here",
  "sessionMaxAge": 3600000
}
```

Downloading the example code

You can download the example code files for all Packt books you have purchased from your account at http://www.packtpub.com. If you purchased this book elsewhere, you can visit http://www.packtpub.com/support and register to have the files e-mailed directly to you.

You can also download the example code files for the book from GitHub: https://github.com/alessioalex/mastering_express_code.

The starting script

In the main file of the application, named app.js, we handle the view setup, load the middleware required for the project, connect to the database, and bind the Express application to a port. Later on, we modify this file to set up the route handling as well, but at the moment, the file contains the following code:

```
// Module dependencies
var express = require('express');
var app = express();
var morgan = require('morgan');
var flash = require('connect-flash');
var multiparty = require('connect-multiparty');
var cookieParser = require('cookie-parser');
var cookieSession = require('cookie-session');
var bodyParser = require('body-parser');
var methodOverride = require('method-override');
var errorHandler = require('errorhandler');
var config = require('./config.json');
var routes = require('./routes');
var db = require('./lib/db');

// View setup
app.set('view engine', 'jade');
app.set('views', __dirname + '/views');
app.locals = require('./helpers/index');
```

```
// Loading middleware
app.use(morgan('dev'));
app.use(bodyParser.json());
app.use(bodyParser.urlencoded({ extended: true }));
app.use(methodOverride(function(req, res){
    if (req.body && typeof req.body === 'object' && '_method' in req.
body) {
        // look in url - encoded POST bodies and delete it
        var method = req.body._method;
        delete req.body._method;
        return method;
    }
}));
app.use(cookieParser());
app.use(cookieSession({
    secret: config.sessionSecret,
    cookie: {
        maxAge: config.sessionMaxAge
    }
}));
app.use(flash());

if (app.get('env') === 'development') {
    app.use(errorHandler());
}

// static middleware after the routes
app.use(express.static(__dirname + '/public'));

// Establishing database connection and binding application to
specified port
db.connect();
app.listen(config.port);
console.log('listening on port %s', config.port);
```

The database library

Note that the preceding app.js file contains the code for the database connection. Later on, we will need other database-related functions such as checking for failed data validation, duplicate keys, or other specific errors. We can group this logic into a separate file called db.js inside the lib folder and move the connection functionality there as well, as shown in the following code:

```
var mongoose = require('mongoose');
var config = require('../config.json');

exports.isValidationError = function(err) {
  return ((err.name === 'ValidationError')
         || (err.message.indexOf('ValidationError') !== -1));
};

exports.isDuplicateKeyError = function(err) {
  return (err.message.indexOf('duplicate key') !== -1);
};

exports.connect = /* database connection function extracted from
  app.js should move here */
```

Routes

The `routes` folder will have a file for each controller (`files.js`, `users.js`, and `sessions.js`), another file for the application controller (`main.js`), and an `index.js` file that will export an object with the controllers as properties, so we don't have to require every single route in `app.js`.

The `users.js` file contains two functions: one to display the user registration page and another to create a user and its subfolder inside `/files`, as shown in the following code:

```
var User = require('../models/user');
var File = require('../models/file');
var db = require('../lib/db');

exports.new = function(req, res, next) {
  res.render('users/new', {
    error: req.flash('error')[0]
  });
};

exports.create = function(req, res, next) {
  var user = new User({ username: req.body.username });

  user.saveWithPassword(req.body.password, function(err) {
    if (err) {
      if (db.isValidationError(err)) {
        req.flash('error', 'Invalid username/password');
```

```
        return res.redirect('/users/new');
      } else if (db.isDuplicateKeyError(err)) {
        req.flash('error', 'Username already exists');
        return res.redirect('/users/new');
      } else {
        return next(err);
      }
    }

    File.createFolder(user._id, function(err) {
      if (err) { return next(err); }

      req.flash('info', 'Username created, you can now log in!');
      res.redirect('/sessions/new');
    });
  });
};
```

The `sessions.js` file handles user authentication and sign out as well as renders the login page. When the user logs in successfully, the `username` and `userId` properties are populated on the session object and deleted on sign out:

```
var User = require('../models/user');

exports.new = function(req, res, next) {
  res.render('sessions/new', {
    info: req.flash('info')[0],
    error: req.flash('error')[0]
  });
};

exports.create = function(req, res, next) {
  User.authenticate(req.body.username, req.body.password,
function(err, userData) {
    if (err) { return next(err); }

    if (userData !== false) {
      req.session.username = userData.username;
      req.session.userId = userData._id;
      res.redirect('/');
    } else {
      req.flash('error', 'Bad username/password');
      res.redirect('/sessions/new');
    }
```

```
  });
};

exports.destroy = function(req, res, next) {
  delete req.session.username;
  delete req.session.userId;
  req.flash('info', 'You have successfully logged out');
  res.redirect('/sessions/new');
};
```

The `files.js` controller performs CRUD-type operations; it displays all the files or a specific file for the logged-in user and saves the files or deletes them. We use `res.sendfile` to display individual files because it automatically sets the correct content type and handles the streaming for us. Since the `bodyParser` middleware from Express was deprecated, we replaced it with `connect-multiparty` (a `connect` wrapper around the `multiparty` module), one of the recommended alternatives. Luckily, this module has an API similar to `bodyParser`, so we won't notice any differences. Check out the complete source code of `files.js` as follows:

```
var File = require('../models/file');

exports.index = function(req, res, next) {
  File.getByUserId(req.session.userId, function(err, files) {
    if (err) { return next(err); }

    res.render('files/index', {
      username: req.session.username,
      files: files,
      info: req.flash('info')[0],
      error: req.flash('error')[0]
    });
  });
};

exports.show = function(req, res, next) {
  var file = new File(req.session.userId, req.params.file);

  file.exists(function(exists) {
    if (!exists) { return res.send(404, 'Page Not Found'); }

    res.sendfile(file.path);
  });
};
```

```
exports.destroy = function(req, res, next) {
  var file = new File(req.session.userId, req.params.file);

  file.delete(function(err) {
    if (err) { return next(err); }

    req.flash('info', 'File successfully deleted!');
    res.redirect('/');
  });
};

exports.create = function(req, res, next) {
  if (!req.files.file || (req.files.file.size === 0)) {
    req.flash('error', 'No file selected!');
    return res.redirect('/');
  }

  var file = new File(req.session.userId, req.files.file.
originalFilename);

  file.save(req.files.file.path, function(err) {
    if (err) { return next(err); }

    req.flash('info', 'File successfully uploaded!');
    res.redirect('/');
  });
};
```

The general routes used to require user authentication or other middleware that needs to be reused for different paths can be put inside main.js, as shown in the following code:

```
exports.requireUserAuth = function(req, res, next) {
  // redirect user to login page if they're not logged in
  if (!req.session.username) {
    return res.redirect('/sessions/new');
  }
  // needed in the layout for displaying the logout button
  res.locals.isLoggedIn = true;

  next();
};
```

The `index.js` file is pretty simple; it just exports all the controllers into a single object so they're easier to require in the start script of our application:

```
exports.main = require('./main');
exports.users = require('./users');
exports.sessions = require('./sessions');
exports.files = require('./files');
```

Now that we have seen what the controllers look like, we can add them to our existing `app.js` file:

```
var routes = require('./routes');
// Declaring application routes
app.get('/', routes.main.requireUserAuth, routes.files.index);
app.get('/files/:file', routes.main.requireUserAuth, routes.files.
show);
app.del('/files/:file', routes.main.requireUserAuth, routes.files.
destroy);
app.post('/files', multiparty(), routes.main.requireUserAuth, routes.
files.create);
app.get('/users/new', routes.users.new);
app.post('/users', routes.users.create);
app.get('/sessions/new', routes.sessions.new);
app.post('/sessions', routes.sessions.create);
app.del('/sessions', routes.sessions.destroy);
```

Note that we included the `requireUserAuth` route for all the URLs that need the user to be logged in, and that the `multiparty` middleware is added just for the URL assigned to file uploads (which would just slow the rest of the routes with no reason).

A similarity between all the controllers is that they tend to be slim and delegate the business logic to the models.

Models

The application manages users and files, so we need to create models for both. Since the users will be saved to the database, we will work with Mongoose and create a new schema. The files will be saved to disk, so we will create a file prototype that we can reuse.

The file model

The file model is a *class* that takes the user ID and the filename as parameters in the constructor and sets the file path automatically. Some basic validation is performed before saving the file to ensure that it only contains letters, numbers, or the underscore character. Each file is persisted to disk in a folder named after userId (generated by Mongoose). The methods used to interact with the filesystem use the native Node.js fs module. The first part of the code is as follows:

```
var fs = require('fs');
var async = require('async');
var ROOT = __dirname + '/../files';
var path = require('path');

function File(userId, name) {
  this.userId = userId;
  this.name = name;
  this.path = this._getPath();
}

File.prototype._getPath = function() {
  return path.resolve(File.getUserPath(this.userId) + '/' + this.
name);
};

File.prototype.isValidFileName = function() {
  return /[a-z0-9_]/i.test(this.name);
};

File.prototype.exists = function(callback) {
  if (!this.isValidFileName()) {
    // keep the function async
    return process.nextTick(function() { callback(null, false) });
  }

  fs.exists(this.path, callback);
};

File.prototype.delete = function(callback) {
  this.exists((function(exists) {
    if (!exists) { return callback(); }
    fs.unlink(this.path, callback);
  }).bind(this));
};
```

```
File.prototype.getStats = function(callback) {
  fs.stat(this.path, callback);
};

File.getUserPath = function(userId) {
  return ROOT + '/' + userId;
};

// create a folder if it doesn't exist already
File.createFolder = function(userId, callback) {
  var userPath = File.getUserPath(userId);

  fs.exists(userPath, function(exists) {
    if (!exists) {
      fs.mkdir(userPath, callback);
    }
  });
};
```

The most interesting methods in this model are the ones used to save a file and get all the files that belong to a user. When uploading a file, the `multiparty` module saves it at a temporary location, and we need to move it to the user's folder. We solve this by piping `readStream` into `writeStream` and executing the callback on the `close` event of the latter. The method to save a file should look like the following:

```
File.prototype.save = function(tempPath, callback) {
  if (!this.isValidFileName()) {
    return process.nextTick(function() {
      callback(null, new Error('Invalid filename'))
    });
  }

  var readStream = fs.createReadStream(tempPath);
  var writeStream = fs.createWriteStream(this.path);
  // if an error occurs invoke the callback with an error param
  readStream.on('error', callback);
  writeStream.on('error', callback);
  writeStream.on('close', callback);
  readStream.pipe(writeStream);
};
```

The function that retrieves all the files of a user reads the directory to get the files, then it calls the `getStats` function in parallel for every file to get its stats, and finally, it executes the callback once everything is done. In case there is an error returned because the user's folder does not exist, we call the `File.createFolder()` method to create it:

```
File.getByUserId = function(userId, callback) {
  var getFiles = function(files) {
    if (!files) { return callback(null, []); }

    // get the stats for every file
    async.map(files, function(name, done) {
      var file = new File(userId, name);
      file.getStats(function(err, stats) {
        if (err) { return done(err); }

        done(null, {
          name: name,
          stats: stats
        });
      });
    }, callback);
  };

  fs.readdir(File.getUserPath(userId), function(err, files) {
    if (err && err.code === 'ENOENT') {
      File.createFolder(userId, function(err) {
        if (err) { return callback(err); }

        getFiles(files);
      });
    } else if (!err) {
      getFiles(files);
    } else {
      return callback(err);
    }
  });
};
```

The User model

The only things that we need to store in the database are the users, so the `user.js` file contains the Mongoose schema for the User model, field validation functions, and functions related to hashing and comparing passwords (for authentication). The following code contains the module dependencies along with the validation functions and schema declaration:

```
var mongoose = require('mongoose');
var pass = require('pwd');

var validateUser = function(username) {
  return !!(username && /^[a-z][a-z0-9_-]{3,15}$/i.test(username));
};
var validatePassword = function(pass) {
  return !!(pass && pass.length > 5);
};

var User = new mongoose.Schema({
  username: {
    type: String,
    validate: validateUser,
    unique: true
  },
  salt: String,
  hash: String
}, {
  safe: true
});
```

Since we don't store the password in plain text but use a salt and a hash instead, we cannot add `password` as a field on the schema (in order to enforce its validation rules) nor create a virtual setter for it (because the hashing function is asynchronous). Due to this, we need to create custom functions such as `setPassword`, `saveWithPassword`, and `validateAll` as shown in the following code:

```
User.methods.setPassword = function(password, callback) {
  pass.hash(password, (function(err, salt, hash) {
    if (err) { return callback(err); }
```

```
      this.hash = hash;
      this.salt = salt;

      callback();
    }).bind(this));
  };

  // validate schema properties (username) && password
  User.methods.validateAll = function(props, callback) {
    this.validate((function(err) {
      if (err) { return callback(err); }

      if (!validatePassword(props.password)) {
        return callback(new Error('ValidationError: invalid password'));
      }

      return callback();
    }).bind(this));
  };

  User.methods.saveWithPassword = function(password, callback) {
    this.validateAll({ password: password }, (function(err) {
      if (err) { return callback(err); }

      this.setPassword(password, (function(err) {
        if (err) { return callback(err); }

      this.save(callback);
      }).bind(this));
    }).bind(this));
  };
```

The authentication function is pretty straightforward; it gets the username and then compares the hash stored in the database with the hash generated by the password, which is sent as a parameter:

```
User.statics.authenticate = function(username, password, callback) {
  // no call to database for invalid username/password
  if (!validateUser(username) || !validatePassword(password)) {
    // keep this function async in all situations
    return process.nextTick(function() { callback(null, false) });
  }
```

```
    this.findOne({ username: username }, function(err, user) {
      if (err) { return callback(err); }
      // no such user in the database
      if (!user) { return callback(null, false); }

      pass.hash(password, user.salt, function(err, hash) {
        if (err) { return callback(err); }

        // if the auth was successful return the user details
        return (user.hash === hash) ? callback(null, user) :
callback(null, false);
      });
    });
};

module.exports = mongoose.model('User', User);
```

Views

The first thing to do here is to create a global layout for our application, since we want to reuse the header and footer and only customize the unique part of every web page. We use `jade` as the templating language, so in order to declare the extendable part of the layout, we use the `block` function. The `layout.jade` file will be created inside the `views` folder as follows:

```
!!! 5
html
  head
    title File Store
    link(rel='stylesheet', href='http://fonts.googleapis.com/css?famil
y=IM+Fell+Great+Primer')
    link(rel='stylesheet', href='/stylesheets/normalize.css',
type='text/css')
    link(rel='stylesheet', href='/stylesheets/style.css', type='text/
css')
  body
    header
      h1 File Store
      if isLoggedIn
        div
          form(action='/sessions', method='POST')
            input(type='hidden', name='_method', value='DELETE')
            input(type='submit', class='sign-out', value='Sign out')
```

```
div.container
  block content

script(src='http://code.jquery.com/jquery-1.10.1.min.js')
script(src='/javascripts/file-upload.js')
```

 An interesting detail in the preceding code is that we override the method interpreted on the server side from POST to DELETE by passing a hidden field called _method. This functionality is provided by the methodOverride middleware of Express, which we included in the app.js file.

Sometimes, we need to use functions for date formatting and size formatting or as a link to use some parameters and other similar tasks. This is where view helpers come in handy. In our application, we want to display the size of the files in kilobytes, so we need to create a view helper that will convert the size of a file from bytes to kilobytes. We can replicate the same structure from the routes folder for the helpers as well, which means that we will have an index.js file that will export everything as an object. Besides this, we will only create the helper for the files at the moment, namely files.js, since that's all we need:

```
exports.formatSize = function(sizeInBytes) {
  return (sizeInBytes / 1024).toFixed(2) + ' kb';
};
```

To make the view helpers accessible inside the view, we need to add another piece of code into our app.js main file after the view setup, as shown in the following line of code:

```
app.locals = require('./helpers/index');
```

This will ensure that whatever is assigned to the locals property is globally accessible in every view file.

In the views folder, we create subfolders for files, sessions, and users. The sessions and users folders will contain a new.jade file, each with a form (user login and signup page). The biggest view file from the files subfolder is index.jade since it's the most important page of the application. The page will contain dynamic data such as the logged-in username or the number of files stored and other stuff such as an upload form and a dashboard with a list of files. The code for the index.jade file will look like the following:

```
extends ../layout

block content
  h2 Hello #{username}

  if !files.length
    h3 You don't have any files stored!
  else
    h3 You have #{files.length} files stored!

  if info
    p.notification.info= info

  if error
    p.notification.error= error


  div#upload-form
    form(action='/files', method='POST', enctype="multipart/form-
data")
      div.browse-file
        input(type='text', id='fake-upload-box', placeholder='Upload
new file!')
        input(type='file', name='file')
      button(type='submit') Go!

  if files.length
    table.file-list
      thead
        tr
          th Name
          th Size
          th Delete
      tbody
        each file in files
          tr
            td
              a(href="/files/#{encodeURIComponent(file.name)}")
#{file.name}
            td #{helpers.files.formatSize(file.stats.size)}
            td
              form(action="/files/#{encodeURIComponent(file.name)}",
method='POST')
                input(type='hidden', name="_method", value='DELETE')
                input(type='submit', value='delete')
```

Running the full application

We have not covered the JavaScript static files or stylesheets used by the application, but you can fill in the missing pieces by yourself as an exercise or just copy the example code provided with the book.

To run the application, you need to have Node and NPM installed and MongoDB up and running, and then execute the following commands in the terminal from the project root:

```
$ npm install .
$ npm start
```

The first command will install all the dependencies and the second one will start the application. You can now visit `http://localhost:3000/` and see the live demo!

Summary

In this chapter, we learned about the main features of Express. We compared it to other existing web frameworks and discovered when it is best to use it. We saw how to structure our applications and build a practical, MVC-structured application in the process.

Coming up in the next chapter is learning about middleware in Express. We will create configurable middleware, error-handling middleware, and even our custom implementation of the middleware system, among others, so stay tuned.

2
Component Modularity Using Middleware

In this chapter, we will look at the middleware system used by Express and see how it enables us to create modular web applications. This chapter will cover the following topics:

- How the middleware system works
- Creating configurable middleware
- Differences between the router and the middleware system
- Why loading middleware in order matters
- Handling errors using middleware
- Mounting subapplications with Express
- Creating a middleware system similar to the one used in Express

Connecting middleware

Middleware refers to reusable components that can be plugged into an Express application. Middleware consists of functions that handle HTTP requests, such as the one we would pass to Node's native `http.createServer` function. A middleware component can add features by manipulating the `request` and `response` objects and then send the response to the client or pass control to the following middleware in the stack. There are a lot of middleware libraries that are compatible with Express, the most popular ones being those that were bundled with it but now live in separate modules (`https://github.com/senchalabs/connect#middleware`).

Web applications have to deal with a lot of things, such as managing cookies and sessions, handling file uploads, or serving static files. Middleware libraries can address these problems.

The functionality of middleware

The middleware function takes the following arguments:

- **The request object**: This is a wrapper on top of the request parameter found in Node's `http.createServer` function, with added functionalities

- **The response object**: This is another wrapper that extends the response parameter found in Node's `http.createServer` function

- **A callback**: This is usually named `next`, which might get executed when everything in the current middleware is done so that the following middleware in the stack can be invoked

The following is an example of a middleware that only allows the web application to be accessed by users that are inside the private network, based on their IP address. If a user has access, we will call the `next` function; otherwise, we will display an error message and send the error status code (`403` in this case).

```
function restrictAccess(req, res, next) {
  var ip = req.ip;

  // check if the ip belongs to the server
  // or to a user in the local network
  // meaning his ip starts with 192.168.*
  if (ip === '127.0.0.1' || /^192\.168\./.test(ip)) {
    next();
  } else {
    res.status(403).send('Forbidden!');
  }
}
```

To load a middleware into an Express application, we call the `app.use()` method, so let's integrate the preceding function into a simple application, as shown in the following code:

```
var express = require('express');
var app = express();

app.use(restrictAccess);

app.use(function(req, res, next) {
  res.send('Hello world');
});

app.listen(7777);
```

If we run the application locally and visit `http://localhost:7777/`, then we will see the **Hello world** message, but if we deploy this application elsewhere on a public server and try to access it with our browser, the **Forbidden** message will be displayed.

The `app.use()` method takes an optional path parameter as the first argument, which is useful if we want to mount certain functionalities to an endpoint. When using the path parameter, the middleware will be executed only if the URL matches that path. Practical use cases include serving static assets under the `/public` path or loading special middleware for an admin path, as shown in the following example:

```
var express = require('express');
var app = express();
var logger = require('morgan');

app.use('/public', express.static(__dirname + '/public'));
// each time somebody visits the admin URL
// log the ip address as well as other details
app.use('/admin', logger({ immediate: true }));
app.use('/admin', function auth(req, res, next) {
  // we should authenticate the user somehow but for this demo
  // just set the 'isAdmin' flag directly
  req.isAdmin = true;
});
app.use(function respond(req, res) {
  if (req.isAdmin) {
    res.send('Hello admin!\n');
  } else {
    res.send('Hello user!\n');
  }
});

app.listen(7777);
```

When using a path parameter as the first parameter for `app.use()`, the `req.url` property will be stripped of that path inside the middleware function associated with it, meaning that if we make a request to `/admin/user`, its value will be `/user`. However, we can still access the original URL by using `req.originalUrl` in that middleware. The `req.url` property will remain unaltered for subsequent requests that don't have the path specified (for example, in the preceding function, where we send a "hello" message to the user).

In the preceding example, we are using named functions for our middleware (auth and respond). This is a useful convention for debugging purposes because we will quickly realize that the error came from a function name that is included in the error stack.

Pushing items to an array

As seen in the previous examples, we can add as many middleware functions to an application as needed. Each time middleware is loaded, it's added to a stack internally in Express. A good way to picture this is to think of an array that gets populated with a function each time we load middleware. When a request hits the server, the first function in the array is executed, and then it either sends the response back to the client or calls the next function in the array and so on until the response has ended.

Looking at the execution flow using logs

Express has built-in support for debugging, so it can output logs to the terminal for various actions if the debug flag is enabled. After that, we can see the order in which middleware libraries are loaded initially and then executed with each request.

Let's prepend the following line to our previous example so that it also outputs the ID of the process when booting:

```
console.log('App process id (pid): %s', process.pid);
```

This will be useful because we want to run the node script in the background and then make requests to the server using the cURL command-line tool in the same terminal.

The new router introduced by Express 4.x handles the loading and dispatching of middleware, so we want to enable the debug logs that it outputs. To do that, we have to set the DEBUG environment variable to express:router when running our example:

```
$ DEBUG=express:router node using-middleware.js &
```

Once the application has started, it will output its process ID and the dispatcher logs. The logs will display the middleware loading order and the route parameter used:

```
App process id (pid): 2290
  express:router use / query +0ms
  express:router use / expressInit +1ms
```

```
express:router use /public staticMiddleware +1ms
express:router use /admin logger +3ms
express:router use /admin auth +0ms
express:router use / respond +0ms
```

The first two functions are loaded by Express automatically (`query` and `expressInit`), while the rest of them are specific to our example.

Now, let's make some requests to different URLs in the application and see which middleware executes. We will start by making a request to the main path:

```
$ curl http://localhost:7777/
  express:router dispatching GET / +22s
  express:router trim prefix (/) from url / +3ms
  express:router query / : / +2ms
  express:router trim prefix (/) from url / +1ms
  express:router expressInit / : / +0ms
  express:router trim prefix (/) from url / +1ms
  express:router respond / : / +1ms Hello user!
```

The only function unique to our application (that matches every path) is the `respond` middleware that displays the **hello** message. That's the normal behavior because the rest of the middleware was assigned to other paths: `/public` for `staticMiddleware` and `/admin` for both the `logger` and `auth` functions. Similarly, if we make a request for a static resource, it will invoke the `staticMiddleware` function, but not the middleware associated with the `/admin` path, as shown in the following code:

```
$ curl http://localhost:7777/public/core.js
  express:router dispatching GET /public/core.js +4m
  express:router query  : /public/core.js +3ms
  express:router expressInit  : /public/core.js +0ms
  express:router trim prefix (/public) from url /public/core.js +1
  express:router staticMiddleware /public : /public/core.js +0ms
alert('hello world');
```

The `staticMiddleware` function is the last function in the stack because it sends the response. When requesting the `/admin` URL, both the `logger` and `auth` middleware will be invoked, and since they make a call to `next()`, the `respond` middleware is the function that outputs the response:

```
$ curl http://localhost:7777/admin
  express:router dispatching GET /admin +2m
```

```
express:router query   : /admin +2ms

express:router expressInit  : /admin +1ms

express:router trim prefix (/admin) from url /admin +0ms

express:router logger /admin : /admin +0ms

127.0.0.1 - - [Thu, 03 Jul 2014 10:46:01 GMT] "GET /admin HTTP/1.1" - -
"-" "curl/7.30.0"

express:router trim prefix (/admin) from url /admin +2ms

express:router auth /admin : /admin +0ms

express:router respond  : /admin +0ms Hello admin!
```

 By using & (ampersand) when starting the Node process, we are putting the Node process in the background. In the preceding example, doing this allows us to run other commands in the same terminal. Once we have finished working with the application, we can either close the terminal or manually kill the process (since we know its ID).

Creating configurable middleware

Configurable middleware refers to functions that can be customized, meaning there are variables that are not hardcoded and can be passed as parameters to those functions.

Some of the most widely used configurable components are the `static` and the `session` middleware. For the first one, we can configure the path for the static resources along with some more advanced features, while the session middleware can accept parameters such as `secret`, `key`, and other settings, as shown in the following code:

```
var session = require('express-session');
app.use(express.static('/public'));
app.use(session({
  secret: 'random chars',
  key: 'session_id',
  cookie: {
    secure: true
  }
}));
```

Closures to the rescue

As mentioned earlier in this chapter, the call to `app.use()` expects a function as a parameter in order to work properly. The router (this used to be the dispatcher from the Connect framework) invokes the middleware directly, because it is the only component that knows when to call each function from the stack, so this is the reason we need to return a function for `app.use()`.

When we are passing the result of the static function invoked with our custom values, it returns a second (inner) function that retains access to those values. This is an important concept in JavaScript and is known as a **closure**.

Caching middleware – a practical example

Now that we have learned how things work in theory, it's time to apply that knowledge by creating a practical middleware that we can use for our Express applications. First, we will create a regular middleware component and then we will transform it into a configurable one.

The task is to create a middleware that manipulates the `res.render()` function in a way that makes it return the compiled template directly from the cache (an in-memory object) after the first time it has been executed for a given URL. For instance, if we open the `/hello` URL, it will use the `render` function to compile a template with some variables and display it, but in subsequent visits, it will be faster as the content will be served from the cache.

A first try at the caching middleware

Let's create a sample application that uses **Embedded JavaScript** (**EJS**) templates and displays the current time and the visited URL. For the time being, we will include a single middleware function that renders the template using those two variables. Since we are displaying the time, this means that with each request, the content will be different. The code for the `cache-render.js` file is the following:

```
var express = require('express');
var app = express();

app.set('view engine', 'ejs');

app.use(function respond(req, res, next) {
  res.render('hello', {
```

```
      visited: new Date(),
      url: req.url
    });
});

app.listen(7777);
console.log('Server started: http://localhost:7777/');
```

The application won't work just yet because we don't have the `hello.ejs` template file, so we need to create the `/views` folder (the default location for views) and store it there:

```
<p>Time: <%- visited %></p>
<p>URL: <%- url %></p>
```

At this point, we can start the application and test it out:

```
$ node cache-render.js &
[1] 3190
Server started: http://localhost:7777/
$ curl http://localhost:7777/hello
<p>Time: Thu Jan 09 2014 00:50:36 GMT+0200 (EET)</p>
<p>URL: /hello</p>
$ curl http://localhost:7777/hello
<p>Time: Thu Jan 09 2014 00:50:37 GMT+0200 (EET)</p>
<p>URL: /hello</p>
```

After making the second request, we can see that the time has changed, so everything works fine.

Next, we can start working on the middleware function that manages the cache. We need to create a cache store object so we can assign the key-value pairs to it. The value is the content (the compiled template) and the URL path represents the key, because we want to store the content of specific pages inside the cache. Here's an example of such an object with some entries:

```
{
  '/hello/john': "Hello John!",
  '/hello/alex': "Hello Alex!"
}
```

We will modify the `cache-render.js` script to include a `store` object (as shown in the following line of code) before the middleware is loaded:

```
var store = {};
```

This object cannot be created inside the new middleware because it would be redeclared each time the function is invoked (when a request is made). The next step is to work on the middleware that does the caching and include it before the function that does the rendering. We have to create a callback function that is executed the first time a template is compiled. Since we need to reuse that function in multiple places, we can create a closure that takes two parameters (`res` and `key` to be stored in the cache) and returns the callback:

```
app.use(function cacheRender(req, res, next) {
  var getCacheFunction = function(res, key) {
    // callback expected by res.render()
    return function(err, content) {
      if (err) { throw err; }

      // store the content in cache and serve it to the client
      store[key] = content;
      res.send(content);
    };
  };
```

The final piece of the puzzle is to override `res.render()` with a custom function that checks whether the compiled template exists in the cache and outputs it directly to the client. If it doesn't exist, we need to call the original function with the callback obtained by executing `getCacheFunction()` with the response and path parameters. The `render` function takes three parameters: the name of the template, the variables, and the callback. The last two are optional, so we also need to check the arguments' length in our newly created function. The rest of the code is as follows:

```
var pathname = req.path;

var render = res.render;
// if the compiled template isn't in the cache, then load it
if (!store[pathname]) {
  res.render = function() {
    var args = Array.prototype.slice.call(arguments);
    var cacheIt = getCacheFunction(res, pathname);

    // add the cache function to the arguments array
    if (args.length < 2) {
      args[1] = cacheIt;
    } else {
      if (typeof args[1] === 'function') {
        args[1] = cacheIt;
      } else {
        args[2] = cacheIt;
```

```
        }
      }

      render.apply(res, args);
    };

    next();
  } else {
    // serve the content directly from the cache
    res.send(store[pathname]);
  }
});
```

The application is complete now, so we can go ahead and test it out. For each request we make to the same page, it should output the same date because of the caching mechanism:

```
$ curl http://localhost:7777/sample
<p>Time: Thu Jan 09 2014 18:39:33 GMT+0200 (GTB Standard Time)</p>
<p>URL: /sample</p>
$ curl http://localhost:7777/sample
<p>Time: Thu Jan 09 2014 18:39:33 GMT+0200 (GTB Standard Time)</p>
<p>URL: /sample</p>
```

The timestamp is the same for the second request, meaning everything works as planned.

Measuring the performance benefits of the caching middleware

Now that the middleware function is done, it's time to see how it affects the performance of the application. We will use the same wrk HTTP benchmarking tool used by Express (https://github.com/wg/wrk) to measure how many requests per second the application can handle.

First, we will benchmark the regular application without the middleware, as shown in the following screenshot:

```
 ⊝ ○ ○                        2. bash
alexandruvladutu at 192-168-0-100 in ~
$ wrk 'http://localhost:7777/' -d 3 -c 50 -t 8
Running 3s test @ http://localhost:7777/
  8 threads and 50 connections
  Thread Stats   Avg      Stdev     Max    +/- Stdev
    Latency    13.08ms    1.04ms  20.73ms   86.88%
    Req/Sec     0.00       0.00     0.00   100.00%
  10957 requests in 3.01s, 2.62MB read
Requests/sec:   3644.46
Transfer/sec:      0.87MB
alexandruvladutu at 192-168-0-100 in ~
$ 
```

Let's include the caching middleware we have created and see the difference.

```
 ⊝ ○ ○                        2. bash
$
alexandruvladutu at 192-168-0-100 in ~
$ wrk 'http://localhost:7777/' -d 3 -c 50 -t 8
Running 3s test @ http://localhost:7777/
  8 threads and 50 connections
  Thread Stats   Avg      Stdev     Max    +/- Stdev
    Latency     7.34ms    2.94ms  21.01ms   94.41%
    Req/Sec     0.00       0.00     0.00   100.00%
  20634 requests in 3.00s, 4.90MB read
Requests/sec:   6869.73
Transfer/sec:      1.63MB
alexandruvladutu at 192-168-0-100 in ~
$ 
```

As you might have guessed, the caching function significantly improved the number of requests per second that the application could handle. The big difference between the two scenarios is that the application doesn't have to recompile the template over and over again when using the caching layer.

Making the caching middleware configurable

We can start converting the caching middleware into a configurable middleware. There are two features we will implement: passing a custom cache store object that contains entries (a URL and content pairs), and as the second argument, we will pass an array with URLs that will be cached (defaults to caching everything). We'll create a function called `cacheRender` and insert it before loading the middleware. The function will check whether it needs to assign the default values to the arguments and return the middleware function created in the previous step:

```
var cacheRender = function(store, urlsToCache) {
  var store = store || {};
  var urlsToCache = urlsToCache || [];

  return function(req, res, next) {
    /* middleware code from our previous example */
  };
};
```

The first goal was achieved; now, the store object is passed as an argument, so we can configure it as we'd like. The next thing to do is to check whether `urlsToCache` contains records of URLs, and if it does, make sure the current request is one of them. We will insert the following code right after declaring the `pathname` variable (in the middleware):

```
if ((urlsToCache.length !== 0) && (urlsToCache.indexOf(pathname) ===
-1)) {
  return next();
}
```

In the case the content associated with the URL doesn't need to be cached, we just call `next()` and skip to the following middleware in the stack. The final piece of code loads the new middleware instead of its predecessor:

```
var store = {
  '/index' : 'Hello from the index page\n'
};
var urlsToCache = ['/index', '/test'];
app.use(cacheRender(store, urlsToCache));
```

Using these settings, there are three possible scenarios for our application:

- If the `/index` URL is requested, it will always show the **Hello from the index page** message
- If the `/test` URL is visited, it will render the view and cache it, so all following calls will display the same content
- If any other URL is requested, it will display a new timestamp each time

We will use the cURL tool again to test these scenarios:

```
$ curl http://localhost:7777/index
Hello from the index page
$ curl http://localhost:7777/test
<p>Time: Thu Jan 09 2014 23:24:43 GMT+0200 (EET)</p>
<p>URL: /test</p>
$ curl http://localhost:7777/test
<p>Time: Thu Jan 09 2014 23:24:43 GMT+0200 (EET)</p>
<p>URL: /test</p>
$ curl http://localhost:7777/other
<p>Time: Thu Jan 09 2014 23:24:52 GMT+0200 (EET)</p>
<p>URL: /other</p>
$ curl http://localhost:7777/other
<p>Time: Thu Jan 09 2014 23:24:52 GMT+0200 (EET)</p>
<p>URL: /other</p>
```

This isn't fit for a production-ready application that spawns across multiple processes and servers because the whole cache is loaded into memory. However, with some adjustments such as adding an in-memory database such as Redis or Memcached on top of it and providing more configurable options, it could become fit for real-world applications.

Environment-based loading of middleware

While developing applications locally, we don't need to use components that enable gzip compression or database-backed sessions. Luckily, it's really simple to detect the current application environment.

In Express 3, there was an `app.configure()` function to detect the environment, but that was removed for newer versions. Nevertheless, all we have to do is pass the NODE_ENV environment variable (`process.env.NODE_ENV`) when starting the application; for example, see the following line of code:

```
NODE_ENV=production node env-middleware.js
```

Then, in our application, we can check for that variable and default to the development mode if it doesn't exist. Instead of writing the same `if` logic everywhere, we can create a tiny function to execute a callback if the environment matches the first parameter of the function (which is what `app.configure()` did). In case we want to set the environment in the code, we can create a closure that takes a single argument and returns the configuration function:

```
var configureByEnvironment = function(env) {
  if (!env) { env = process.env.NODE_ENV; }

  // default to development
  env = env || 'development';

  return function(env2, callback) {
    if (env === env2) { callback(); }
  };
};
```

This function acts as a setter for the environment variable and defaults to `process.env.NODE_ENV` if there is no argument sent. The next check detects whether the `env` variable is empty and defaults to `development`. The returned function resembles the `app.configure()` functionality and takes two parameters: the environment and the callback function that gets executed if the first parameter matches the current application mode.

A sample middleware setup can look like the following code:

```
var configure = configureByEnvironment();
var logger = require('morgan');
var compress = require('compression');
var responseTime = require('response-time');
var errorHandler = require('errorhandler');

configure('development', function() {
  app.use(logger('dev'));
  app.use(responseTime());
  app.use(express.static(__dirname + '/public'));
});

configure('production', function() {
  app.use(logger());
  // enable gzip compression for static resources in production
  app.use(compress());
  app.use(express.static(__dirname + '/public'));
});
```

As you might have noticed from the code, there are other things that change in different environments besides the middleware used, such as configuration options. In the production mode, it's better to use a verbose logger that provides more details of the request, while in development, it's enough to display the essential bits.

Express routes

Express makes use of HTTP verbs and path patterns to provide a meaningful API for describing routes:

```
app.verb(path, [callback...], callback)
```

The route handlers take the same arguments (request, response, and next), and the path can be a string (that will be transformed into a regular expression) or a regular expression.

If we were to define a route handler to update an article, then the request method (verb) would be PUT, and the URL could look like /articles/211 (where the number represents the article ID). Here's how to do this with Express:

```
app.put('/articles/:id', function(req, res, next) {
  var id = req.params.id;

  console.log('Updating article ' + id);
  console.log('Attributes: ', req.body);
  // save to database
  // send message or render template
});
```

Specifying the path

The path parameter can be either a string (transformed into a regular expression internally by Express) or a regular expression, in case we need to match very specific patterns (such as an e-mail address or a number). Needless to say, the route handlers only get invoked when the path matches the regular expression.

When using the string version, we can specify placeholders using colons, and they get mapped to the req.params variable. If a question mark is added after a placeholder, it makes it optional.

Let's suppose that we want to create a blog application and we would like to display a post in different formats (HTML, JSON, RSS, or XML) based on the path ending. If the format is missing, the post should still be accessible and the default format would be HTML. The route should catch the following URLs:

- `/blog/routing-with-express.html`
- `/blog/routing-with-express.json`
- `/blog/command-line-node-apps.json`
- `/blog/application-security`

The path always starts with `/blog`, followed by a slug (a URL-friendly version of the post title usually) and an optional format at the end. The slug and format are dynamic, so we need to specify them using placeholders. Additionally, we'll have to add the question mark at the end, since the format is optional, resulting in the following path:

```
/blog/:slug.:format?
```

The dynamic variables (the slug and format, in this case) are accessible from within the route handler, so here's how the route handler should look:

```
app.get('/blog/:slug.:format?', function(req, res, next) {
  var format = req.params.format || 'html';
  var slug = req.params.slug;

  // query the database to find the blog post based on the slug
  database.findBySlug(slug, function(err, post) {
    if (err) { return next(err); }

    switch (format) {
      case 'html':
        /* render html */
        break;
      case 'json':
        res.json(post);
        break;
      default:
        // bad format
        next();
        break;
    }
  });
});
```

The preceding example does not use the res.format() function provided by Express since the format is already included in the URL, and there's no need to perform an extra check for content-negotiation based on the Accept header.

The regular expressions converted from path strings can be inspected either by checking the app._router.stack variable (inside our application) or by creating a small script that uses the NPM module path-to-regexp to output the result.

In the following screenshot, we can see the regexp version of the path variable used in our previous example (for the sake of simplicity, the route handler only sends a basic message):

```
⊙ ○ ○      🔲 <druvladutu/www/mastering_express/chapter_02/middleware-examples) - VIM        ⤢
  1 var express = require('express');
  2 var app = express();
  3
  4 app.get('/blog/:slug.:format', function(req, res, next) {
  5   res.send('Hello world');
  6 });
  7
  8 console.log(app.routes);
  9
 10 app.listen(7777);
~
app-routes.js [+][Git(master)] [unix/JAVASCRIPT][tabs=2]              line:8,col:24  80%
$ node app-routes.js

{ get:
  [ { path: '/blog/:slug.:format',
      method: 'get',
      callbacks: [Object],
      keys: [Object],
      regexp: /^\/blog\/(?:([^\/]+?))(?:\.([^\/\.]+?))\/?$/i } ] }


~
node app-routes.js - 6 [Git(master)] [unix/CONQUE_TERM][tabs=2]   line:9,col:1   90%
── VISUAL ──                                                            24
```

Reusable route handlers

There are a lot of situations where we need to plug in the same middleware for multiple routes to eliminate code duplication, such as requiring user authentication or loading database items based on path placeholders.

Let's think for a moment what routes we would have to make for a web application that publishes articles related to software. There will be two types of users that will interact with the application: guests and admins. The guests will read the articles and the admins will be able to do CRUD actions.

For both types of users, we will need to query the database for the article that's being read or updated, so our first middleware component will populate the `req.article` property with the result returned from the database. In case there's no such article found, the response status will be `404`:

```
// simulate a database using an object
// the keys represent the ids of the articles
var articles = {
  'express-tutorial' : {
    title: 'Practical web apps with Express',
    content: 'Lean how to create web apps with Express'
  },
  'node-videos': {
    title: 'Node.js video tutorials',
    content: 'Practical Node tips!'
  }
};

var loadArticle = function(req, res, next) {
  // we assume that the /:article placeholder
  // is present in the path
  if (!articles[req.params.article]) {
    return res.status(404).send('No such article!');
  }

  req.article = articles[req.params.article];

  next();
};
```

For each route that requires authentication, we need to check whether the user is an admin, so a second middleware comes to life. A user has admin rights in this example if the server is hosted on their local workstation, and if not, the server will respond with a `403 Forbidden` status message:

```
var requireAdmin = function(req, res, next) {
  if (req.ip !== '127.0.0.1') {
    return res.status(403).send('Forbidden');
  }

  next();
};
```

The thing left to do is to create the routes and integrate these two functions in the picture. The first approach is to load the middleware for each separate route, so the code would look like the following:

```
app.get('/articles/:article', loadArticle, function(req, res,
  next) {
  res.send(req.article.content);
});

app.get('/articles/:article/edit', loadArticle, requireAdmin,
  function(req, res, next) {
  res.send('Editing article ' + req.article.title);
});
```

Since the route ordering matters and we want to avoid including the loadArticle middleware for each route, a better way to handle the situation would be to create another route just before the previous two that includes the article-loading component:

```
// this path will match /articles/title as well as
// /articles/title/edit
app.get('/articles/:article/:action?', loadArticle);

app.get('/articles/:article', function(req, res, next) {
  res.send(req.article.content);
});

app.get('/articles/:article/edit', requireAdmin, function(req,
  res, next) {
  res.send('Editing article ' + req.article.title);
});
```

This looks better than our previous example, but we can still make a small adjustment for the future. At the moment, we only have the route for editing articles, which requires admin access, but we will probably have another one for creating new articles, which will look similar to /articles/:article/new. We can create a route that matches them and includes the admin middleware component, and place it at the top, as shown in the following line of code:

```
app.get('/articles/:article/:action', requireAdmin);
```

Although this technique works, it has its caveats. If we add another route, and the article placeholder wouldn't be the second parameter in that path, we would have to modify our code.

A better solution would be to use the native `app.param()` function from Express, which can take two parameters: a placeholder and a route handler. By using it, we wouldn't care anymore if the paths would change, as long as the placeholder still exists. There's only a one-line change to the first route of our sample application:

```
app.param('article', loadArticle);
```

 The `app.param()` function will match all the verbs and not only the GET requests. This means that if we add a PUT route to `/articles/:article` (for updating an existing item), the middleware will be executed for that path as well.

Route wildcards

Apart from the regular HTTP verbs, there is a special method in Express named `all`. It functions in the same way as the other `app.VERB()` methods, but it matches the request no matter what the HTTP `verb` is.

One of the `path` characters (the first argument to the `app.VERB()` method) that has a special meaning is `*`, which is replaced with `(.*)` when creating the regular expression and will thus match everything.

The combination of the method wildcard and the star wildcard is particularly helpful when loading the same middleware for sections of our main application, such as an admin dashboard or an API. Since we would require authentication for every route prefixed with `/api` or `/admin`, we can easily add the following route:

```
app.all('/admin/*', requireAdmin);
```

Ordering of middleware

Express doesn't know what middleware components do internally, so it doesn't reorder them. The framework doesn't try to be overly smart and do complicated things such as checking whether a function depends on another. This means it's our responsibility to make sure we load them in the proper order.

The most popular example to reflect this is the session and cookie middleware. The session handler uses a cookie as an ID to retrieve the session data, so the cookie parsing must take place in advance. The same dependency relation is between the **cross-site request forgery (CSRF)** and session middleware, since the first stores its token on the user's session. An example with the correct inclusion of these three middleware components is as follows:

```
var cookieParser = require('cookie-parser');
var session = require('express-session');
var csrf = require('csurf');

app.use(cookieParser());
app.use(session({
  secret: 'random chars here'
}));
app.use(csrf());
```

There are other reasons for paying attention to the ordering of middleware besides taking care of dependencies, such as the need for authentication. For example, if only certain white-listed IP addresses are allowed to view a certain page, and the component that's doing the authentication is placed after the one that renders that page, then everyone will be able to bypass the authentication. Actually, a better way to say this is that nobody (no request) would ever reach the authentication layer in the first place.

You might be wondering what is the difference between `app.VERB()` and regular middleware loaded with `app.use()`. The fact of the matter is that both methods delegate to the router introduced in Express 4 and behave similarly, with a few exceptions, such as the following:

- The path parameter is stripped and not visible to the middleware function for `app.use()`
- The `app.VERB()` function accepts multiple callbacks instead of just one

Handling errors with middleware

Each time we call the next function inside a middleware or a route handler with an error parameter, it delegates that to the error-handling middleware. Express allows us to plug in a custom error handler, but by default, it just displays the error stack while developing and shows an Internal Server Error message in production.

In the development mode, the error page isn't greatly formatted by default, but we can load the `errorHandler()` middleware that used to be bundled with Express (`https://www.npmjs.org/package/errorhandler`) to sweeten the deal. Let's create a sample application with that handler and include a middleware that calls next with an error argument:

```
var express = require('express');   var app = express();
var errorHandler = require('errorhandler');

app.use(function(req, res, next) {
  next(new Error('custom thrown'));
});

app.use(errorHandler());

app.listen(7777);
```

Now, if we start that application and make any request to the server, the following error page will be displayed:

Express

500 **Error: custom thrown**

```
at Object.handle (/Users/alexandruvladutu/www/mastering_express/chapter_02/middleware-examples/generating-errors.js:5:8)
at next (/Users/alexandruvladutu/www/mastering_express/chapter_02/middleware-examples/node_modules/express/node_modules/connect/lib/proto.js:193:15)
at Object.expressInit [as handle] (/Users/alexandruvladutu/www/mastering_express/chapter_02/middleware-examples/node_modules/express/lib/middleware.js:30:5)
at next (/Users/alexandruvladutu/www/mastering_express/chapter_02/middleware-examples/node_modules/express/node_modules/connect/lib/proto.js:193:15)
at Object.query [as handle] (/Users/alexandruvladutu/www/mastering_express/chapter_02/middleware-
examples/node_modules/express/node_modules/connect/lib/middleware/query.js:45:5)
at next (/Users/alexandruvladutu/www/mastering_express/chapter_02/middleware-examples/node_modules/express/node_modules/connect/lib/proto.js:193:15)
at Function.app.handle (/Users/alexandruvladutu/www/mastering_express/chapter_02/middleware-examples/node_modules/express/node_modules/connect/lib/proto.js:201:3)
at Server.app (/Users/alexandruvladutu/www/mastering_express/chapter_02/middleware-examples/node_modules/express/node_modules/connect/lib/connect.js:65:37)
at Server.EventEmitter.emit (events.js:98:17)
at HTTPParser.parser.onIncoming (http.js:2108:12)
```

This looks good in development and provides useful information for developers, but showing stack traces in production is not the way to go. For live applications, we can use the error handler as the unified place to deal with errors and display messages based on different conditions, such as the following:

- The status code that we want to send back to the user
- The content type
- The type of the request, whether the current request is an Ajax request or not

Let's begin with a tiny application and then create the error handler for it:

```
var express = require('express');
var app = express();
var logger = require('morgan');
var fs = require('fs');

app.use(logger('dev'));

app.get('/', function(req, res, next) {
  res.send('Hello world');
});
app.get('/error', function(req, res, next) {
  next(new Error('manually triggered error'));
});

app.listen(7777);
```

We have only defined two routes for this application, but what happens if the clients try to access different URLs? When the router doesn't find any route that matches the request, the next middleware in the stack is called, and if there's no custom middleware, it will simply display the message **Cannot GET /visited-url**.

This isn't extremely helpful, not to mention a bit scary for the end user because the style of the website is gone, so we need to customize this page by creating our own 404 - Page Not Found handler. Since the middleware is executed in order, all we have to do is place our function as the last one in the stack, so it will catch everything that is not picked up by its predecessors. We have mentioned before that we want to handle all the errors inside the error handler, and we can do that with this one. We will create a middleware that passes a 404 error to the error handling middleware, as seen in the following code:

```
app.use(function(req, res, next) {
  var err = new Error('Page Not Found');
  err.statusCode = 404;

  // pass the error to the error handler
  next(err);
});
```

In the preceding code, we have created a custom error with the statusCode property of 404. The reason for doing this is that it will allow us to treat this error differently because we know its code.

So far, we have two possible error scenarios: an internal error thrown inside the application and another error thrown if the URL does not exist on the server. We will create two files named 404.html and 500.html and display them on the frontend when those errors occur.

Finally, we will work on the custom error handler, which will log the errors, display the right content, and send the status code based on the type of the error. Instead of requiring the content of the two files each time the handler is called, we will grab that content only once when the application has started:

```
// not to be placed inside the error handler
var notFoundPage = fs.readFileSync(__dirname +
    '/404.html').toString('utf8');
var internalErrorPage = fs.readFileSync(__dirname +
    '/500.html').toString('utf8');
```

 Normally, synchronous calls aren't recommended in Node applications because they block the event loop, but since we are doing the initial configuration before booting the server, and it's not supposed to start without loading these files, it's an acceptable evil.

The error handler will contain a switch statement based on the status code of the error object, and it will display one of the two newly-created error pages or a simple error message in case the code differs from 404 and 500. The difference between the error handler and the rest of the middleware functions is that it takes four arguments instead of three, and the first one is an error object. The following code must be placed after the last middleware in the application:

```
// custom error handler where we handle errors
// passed by other middleware
app.use(function(err, req, res, next) {
  // if not specified, the statusCode defaults to 500
  // meaning it's an internal error
  err.statusCode = err.statusCode || 500;

  switch(err.statusCode) {
    case 500:
      res.status(err.statusCode).send(internalErrorPage);
      // log the error to stderr
      console.error(err.stack);
      break;
    case 404:
      res.status(err.statusCode).send(notFoundPage);
```

```
      break;
    default:
      console.error('Unhandled code', err.statusCode, err.stack);
      res.status(err.statusCode).send('An error happened');
  }
});
```

Now, if we visit http://localhost:7777/error, the contents of the file 500.html will be displayed, and the same goes for unknown pages and the 404.html file. Additionally, for internal server errors and other codes except 404, the error stack is logged to the terminal.

We can further improve the handler to have more fine-grained control over the errors, such as checking for Ajax requests or doing content negotiation. An example for internal errors (code 500) is as follows:

```
case 500:
  if (req.xhr) {
    return res.status(err.statusCode).send({
      error: '500 - Internal Server Error'
    });
  }

  res.format({
    text: function() {
      res.status(500).send('500 - Internal Server Error');
    },
    html: function() {
      res.status(err.statusCode).send(internalErrorPage);
    },
    json: function() {
      res.status(err.statusCode).send({
        error: '500 - Internal Server Error'
      });
    }
  });
  // log the error to stderr
  console.error(err.stack);
  break;
```

When dealing with Ajax requests in this application, we send back a JSON response, because we operate under the assumption that all Ajax requests will work with JSON and they won't have the content type header properly set. This might not be the case for all applications, but it's good to know about this technique.

Most client-side JavaScript frameworks send the `X-Requested-With` header to identify Ajax requests (such as jQuery), but this is not mandatory.

We can simulate sending an Ajax request using cURL with a custom `X-Requested-With` header set to `xmlhttprequest` to see if the handler works:

```
$ curl -H "X-Requested-With:xmlhttprequest" http://localhost:7777/error
{
  "error": "500 - Internal Server Error"
}
```

The response, if JSON, means that it worked as expected. The content negotiation part is done using the native `res.format()` function from Express, which allows us to send a message that is understandable to the client (based on the content type). We can use the same cURL tool for testing, but this time, we'll send a custom `Accept` header for each of the three content types:

```
$ curl -H "Accept:application/json" http://localhost:7777/error
{
  "error": "500 - Internal Server Error"
}
$ curl -H "Accept:text/plain" http://localhost:7777/error
500 - Internal Server Error
$ curl -H "Accept:text/html" http://localhost:7777/error
<!DOCTYPE HTML>
<html lang="en">
<head>
  <meta charset="UTF-8">
  <title>500 - Internal Server Error</title>
</head>
<body>
  500 - Internal Server Error
</body>
</html>
```

Mounting subapplications

Each Express application is a middleware on its own, so it can be mounted into another application. This feature makes it easy to plug subapplications into a parent one. Possible use cases include the following points:

- Creating applications in a modular way, where each subapplication is totally independent of the others and possibly developed by other team members
- Adding a blogging platform or a forum to an endpoint
- Integrating third-party tools such as a monitoring dashboard or an FTP client along with a text editor

There are two possible approaches we can take when working with mountable applications: either the main application deals with crosscutting concerns such as logging and error handling, or the subapplications handle these things on their own. If we require third-party applications, we might not be able to control some of these aspects, but if we are creating a modular web application from scratch, then it's our choice to begin with.

Next, we will create an example application on how to mount a subapplication and discuss what the advantages are and the problems we might bump into.

We will create three files in the same folder: an index.js file for the main application and two other files, blog.js and admin.js, for the subapplications (let's assume we are plugging in an admin dashboard and a blog system). The main application will be light and it will only load the other two:

```
var express = require('express');
var app = express();

var blog = require('./blog');
var admin = require('./admin');

app.use('/blog', blog);
app.use('/admin', admin);

app.listen(7777);
```

Generally, when mounting applications, we specify a path for each application, as is the case in the preceding example. The blog and admin applications are small, since we are focusing here on the mounting feature instead of creating complex applications. The following sample code is for the blog subapplication (the admin one is similar):

```
var express = require('express');
var app = express();

app.get('/', function(req, res, next) {
  res.send('Blog app says hello');
});

app.get('/error', function(req, res, next) {
  return next(new Error('err'));
});

app.use(function(err, req, res, next) {
  console.error(err.stack);
  res.send('BLOG: an error occured');
});

module.exports = app;
```

 With the new Express 4 router, we can use express.Router() instead of express() to create a mountable application.

As you might have noticed, these two applications don't bind to a port because that's the job of the master application. Also, they are decoupled from the main application and can use their own rendering engine, settings, and other features.

By using a simple comment or an if statement, we can disable or enable their inclusion, making it easy to use this system for feature flags. Instead of creating these modular applications, if we would have made a big monolith, it would have been harder to switch off the /blog or /admin endpoints.

There are some things we need to take into consideration with mountable applications, which are as follows:

- Avoid code duplication; for example, if we intend to use a logging solution for all the endpoints, it would be better to include it in the parent application
- If we want to redirect to an absolute path, then the argument must start with a forward slash (/); otherwise, for a relative path, we should omit it

- If the applications need to share sessions, then the master application should load them

- When creating general-purpose applications, it's a good thing to move them into their separate repositories and publish them to the NPM registry; other people and projects may need them

 The middleware that used to come bundled with Express are self-aware, meaning they are not loaded twice. Each of them makes a check to see whether the function has been called previously (using some kind of flag), similar to what the session middleware does:

```
// self-awareness
if (req.session) return next();
```

This means that if a middleware function has been loaded in the master application, it won't do the same work in the subapplications.

Replicating the middleware system

So far, we have learned a lot of things about the middleware system used in Express. Now, we will refresh that knowledge and create a practical application. We will create a middleware framework of our own that partly resembles the one found in Express.

All the files will be placed inside an `app` folder, and the main entry point of the application will be named `index.js`.

The main file

This file will contain an `App` class similar to the one found in Express, with its constructor and the `use` and `handleRequest` methods.

 JavaScript doesn't have classes in the language yet, but we can simulate them by using a function as the constructor and adding other functions (methods) to the prototype.

The constructor will initialize the stack variable (that holds the middleware) to an empty array, and it will bind the `handleRequest` function to the App scope, as shown in the following code:

```
function App() {
  // allows us to call App() without using the `new` keyword
  if (!(this instanceof App)) {
    return new App();
  }

  this.stack = [];
  this.handleRequest = this.handleRequest.bind(this);
}
```

The original Express constructor does a bit of magic so it can return the app function that handles the requests and contains the use function. For example, consider the following code:

```
var http = require('http');
var express = require('express');
var app = express();

app.use(middlewareFn);

http.createServer(app).listen(7777);
```

Our application will be simpler (internally), but we will have to use app. handleRequest instead of passing app to the http connection handler, as shown in the following example:

```
var http = require('http');
var express = require('./app');
var app = express();

app.use(middlewareFn);

http.createServer(app.handleRequest).listen(7777);
```

This is why we need to bind the `handleRequest` function to the App context; otherwise, this will refer to the context of the server handler.

The use() function will take the same two parameters as in Express: the route and the middleware handler. The optional route argument defaults to /. Besides the regular trailing slash check performed on the route, the thing that is pending to be done is the most important: we have to push the middleware to the stack in case the handler doesn't take four parameters, and if it does, then we assign the handler to the customErrorHandler property. The following is the complete code for this method:

```
App.prototype.use = function(route, fn) {
  if (typeof route !== 'string') {
    fn = route;
    route = '/';
  }

  // strip trailing slash
  if (route !== '/' && route[route.length - 1] === '/' ) {
    route = route.slice(0, -1);
  }

  if (fn.length !== 4) {
    this.stack.push({
      handle: fn,
      route: route
    });
  } else {
    this.customErrorHandler = fn;
  }
};
```

We can assume that the handleRequest method takes only two arguments (a request and a response), since the next callback could be used internally when executing each middleware in the stack. This assumption is wrong because in the case we mount the current application into another Express application, there would be another next parameter coming from the master application, as shown in the following example:

```
app.use(subApplication.handleRequest);
app.use(notFoundHandler);
```

In case the handleRequest method uses two parameters and the third one is ignored, then in the preceding example, the notFoundHandler middleware would never be called, since the subapplication will end the response itself. Now that we have concluded that the handleRequest function takes three parameters (like any Express middleware does), we can go on and think about how to finish it.

Every time a request comes in, we must initialize an internal index that points to the current element in the middleware stack that needs to be executed next. Then, the first middleware is run, which might end the response or call the `next` callback function. When the `next` function is executed, the index is incremented and a check is performed to determine whether the first (and single) argument is an error or not; if it is, then the error handler is called, and if it's not, the process is repeated with the following middleware in the stack.

Since there is a lot of stuff to do with handling requests and we need an internal variable (the index) each time a request is made, it's a good idea to separate this logic into another class. We will create a new instance of that class in the `handleRequest` function with the following arguments: the stack, the custom error handler, and a not found handler:

```
// we need to create the request handler, but for
// the moment let's include it to finish this file
var RequestHandler = require('./requestHandler');
var util = require('util');

App.prototype.handleRequest = function(req, res, _next) {
  var next;

  if (_next) {
    next = function(err) {
      if (util.isError(err)) {
        _next(err);
      } else {
        _next();
      }
    };
  }

  new RequestHandler(this.stack, this.customErrorHandler,
    next).next(req, res);
};

module.exports = App;
```

The `_next` function argument is not empty in case the current application is mounted into another parent one. This callback is relevant because we pass it onto the request handler as the custom not found handler (the very last function that ends the response in case its predecessors didn't do so). In case the `_next` function exists, we must override it and make sure it's called with the error argument, or with no arguments at all, because inside our request handler code, we will invoke the regular middleware functions with the request and response objects as arguments.

As you have seen in the previous code, we not only initialize the request handler instance, but we also call its `next` method, so it knows that it must start handling the request.

Handling requests

We know that the request handler constructor takes three arguments:

- The middleware (array) stack
- The custom error-handling function
- The custom not found function

The last two will default to something simple, like we have seen in Express during development. The only thing left to do in the constructor is to initialize the index, because we need that for each instance of the class (the handler will start at 0 and increment after a middleware function call). The code for the constructor is as follows:

```
function RequestHandler(stack, errorHandler, notFoundHandler) {
  this.index = 0;
  this.stack = stack;
  this.errorHandler = errorHandler || function(err, req, res) {
    res.writeHead(500, { 'Content-Type': 'text/html' });
    res.end('<h1>Internal Server Error</h1><pre>' + err.stack +
      '</pre>');
  };
  this.notFoundHandler = notFoundHandler || function(req, res) {
    res.writeHead(404, { 'Content-Type': 'text/html' });
    res.end("Cannot " + req.method.toUpperCase() + " " + req.url);
  };
}
```

The other missing part is the `next` function, which will execute each middleware handler until one of the following things happen:

- A function sends the response to the client (and does not call the `next` function again)
- The `next` function is called with an error argument, and in that case, the error handler is invoked
- There is no middleware handler left in the stack, so the `notFoundHandler` function is executed

The next function also needs to perform the following actions:

- Check whether the index exceeds the stack length, so it knows whether it has to call the notFoundHandler function
- Call the errorHandler function in case the first argument is an error
- Wrap the middleware function in a try-catch block like Express does
- Check whether the route was set up for the current middleware (if it is different than /) and whether the URL matches the route
- Remove the custom route part from the URL in case it's set up (because it shouldn't be exposed to the middleware)

With the preceding goals in mind, here is the remaining code:

```
RequestHandler.prototype.next = function(req, res) {
  if (this.index < this.stack.length) {
    var _next = (function(err) {
      if (!err) {
        this.next(req, res);
      } else {
        this.errorHandler(err, req, res);
      }
    }).bind(this);

    try {
      var middleware = this.stack[this.index++];

      if (middleware.route !== '/') {
        var regexp = new RegExp('^\/' + middleware.route.substring(1)
 + '\/?$');
        // custom route, so we need to alter `req.url`
        // and remove the 'root'
        if (regexp.test(getPathname(req.url))) {
          req.originalUrl = req.url;
          req.url = req.url.replace(middleware.route, '/');
        } else {
          // the route isn't matched, so we call `_next()`
          return _next();
        }
      }

      middleware.handle(req, res, _next);
    }
```

```
    catch(err) {
      this.errorHandler(err, req, res);
    }
  } else {
    this.notFoundHandler(req, res);
  }
};
```

For the custom route matching, we are using a function called `getPathname` that returns the pathname from the URL, so we need to include that too:

```
var url = require('url');

function getPathname(str) {
  return url.parse(str).pathname;
}
```

Last but not least, we need to export the `RequestHandler` function, as shown in the following line of code:

```
module.exports = RequestHandler;
```

Demonstrating the application

We have written around 100 lines of code so far, and we hope to have a working implementation of a middleware system that's similar to the one used by Express, so it's time to test all its features.

Let's create an application so that we can test the basic functionality of our framework: loading middleware and calling `next` and special pages (the not found page and internal server error):

```
var http = require('http');
var express = require('./app');
var app = express();

app.use(function(req, res, next) {
  if (req.url === '/') {
    res.writeHead(200, { 'Content-Type': 'text/html' });
    return res.end('Hello world!');
  }
  next();
});
```

```
app.use('/404', function(req, res, next) {
  res.writeHead(404, { 'Content-Type': 'text/html' });
  return res.end('No such page');
});

app.use('/500', function(req, res, next) {
  return next(new Error('something bad happened'));
});

http.createServer(app.handleRequest).listen(7777);
```

Instead of loading the `express` module, we have required our custom Express-like solution, and at the very end, we have passed `app.handleRequest` to the `http` server function instead of simply passing `app` (as we would have done with an Express application). Also, we are not using functions such as `res.send` or `res.status` to manage the response because they are provided by Express (and do not exist in our framework).

There are four possible responses shown by the sample application:

- A **Hello world** message for the main page
- A **No such page** message if we visit the /404 URL
- Error content for the /500 route
- A **Cannot GET** message for other (GET) requests

You can now run the example and see how the application behaves in each case. If everything is set up correctly (the sample application is in the root folder and the framework in the `app` folder), it should work each time.

We can add new code to the sample application to test other stuff, such as mounting subapplications and assigning a custom error handler:

```
var app2 = express();
app2.use('/app2', function(req, res, next) {
  res.writeHead(200, { 'Content-Type': 'text/html' });
  return res.end('Response from the second app.');
});

app.use(app2.handleRequest);

app.use(function(err, req, res, next) {
  res.writeHead(500, { 'Content-Type': 'text/html' });
  res.end('<h1>500 Internal Server Error</h1>');
});
```

If we rerun the example and make a request to the /app2 URL, we should see the message **Response from the second app**. Also, the /500 URL should now display **500 Internal Server Error** as the heading, without the error stack this time.

Adding the routes handler

Now that we have the middleware framework done, how hard would it be to add support for routes just like Express does with app.VERB()?

We have learned the following things about routes in Express:

- The app.use() method is used to define the route handlers
- Multiple handlers can be added to a route
- The path parameter for app.VERB() accepts either a string (that is translated into a regular expression) or a regular expression
- The named route parameters are automatically mapped to the params property of the request object
- The app.all() method behaves like every other verb but matches all the request methods
- The path parameter (*) acts as a wildcard for routes

The conclusion is that we can add the routes functionality on top of the existing middleware system by extending it. All the added functionality will live in the app.VERB() methods.

We will create a file called router.js and place it in the app folder (along with the files index.js and requestHandler.js). Besides the index module dependency, we will also need to include the native Node util module (used for inheritance) and the custom path-to-regexp module (to transform path strings to regular expressions, like Express does), which will need to be installed:

```
npm install path-to-regexp
```

Let's create the router constructor and make it inherit from the custom-built middleware system:

```
var util = require('util');
var pathToRegexp = require('path-to-regexp');
var App = require('./index');

function Router() {
  if (!(this instanceof Router)) {
```

```
      return new Router();
  }

  // call the 'super' constructor
  App.call(this);
}

util.inherits(Router, App);
```

 This system is similar to the one used in Express 4, but in our case, the router only handles the routes and not the other middleware defined with the app.use() function.

Like in the index.js file, we will have to use the getPathname function later on, so we should add it to our code:

```
var url = require('url');

function getPathname(str) {
  return url.parse(str).pathname;
}
```

Since we are using the same code in two different modules, an optimization would be to extract this function into its own file, but consider this a home exercise.

We are done with the easy part. Next, we need to concentrate on adding the verb methods and their features. We will set an array of verbs, then iterate through each, and attach the same function that does all the checks:

```
var VERBS = ['all', 'get', 'post', 'put', 'delete', 'head',
  'options'];

VERBS.map(function(verb) {
  Router.prototype[verb] = function(path, fn) {
    var _this = this;
    var keys = [];
    var regex = (path.constructor.name === 'RegExp') ? path :
      pathToRegexp(path, keys);

    var args = Array.prototype.slice.call(arguments);
    // multiple handlers (functions) can be specified
    // for a given path
    var handlers = args.slice(1);
```

In case the path parameter is not a regular expression, we use the `path-to-regexp` module to transform it. Then, we extract all the route handlers from the arguments by slicing every item from the array after the first element, since that one holds the path parameter.

Next, for each `verb`, we will attach a function that calls `app.use()`, check whether the `verb` method matches the request method or if it is equal to `all`, and check whether the route matches the URL and extracts the parameters into the `req.params` property:

```
handlers.forEach(function(fn) {
  _this.use(function(req, res, next) {
    // app.all behaves like a regular verb
    // but it matches all HTTP verbs
    if ((verb !== 'all') && (req.method !==
      verb.toUpperCase())) { return next(); }
    // '*' matches all routes
    if ((path !== '*') && !regex.test(getPathname(req.url))) {
      return next(); }

    var params = regex.exec(getPathname(req.url)).slice(1);

    if (keys.length) {
      req.params = {};
      keys.forEach(function(key, i) {
        if (params[i]) {
          req.params[key.name] = params[i];
        }
      });
    } else {
      req.params = {};
    }

    fn(req, res, next);
  });
});
```

Now that we have finished the router, it's time to test it out with another sample application that covers most of its functionality, using the following code:

```
var http = require('http');
var express = require('./app/router');
var app = express();
```

```
app.get('/', function(req, res, next) {
  req.message = 'Hello';
  next();
}, function(req, res, next) {
  req.message += ' World!';
  next();
}, function(req, res, next) {
  res.end(req.message);
});

app.get('/app2', function(req, res, next) {
  res.writeHead(200, { 'Content-Type': 'text/html' });
  res.end('app2');
});

app.get('/users/:user/:name?', function(req, res, next) {
  res.writeHead(200, { 'Content-Type': 'text/html' });
  res.end(JSON.stringify(req.params));
});

app.all('*', function(req, res, next) {
  res.writeHead(404, { 'Content-Type': 'text/html' });
  res.end('404 - Page Not Found');
});

http.createServer(app.handleRequest).listen(7777);
```

If we make a request to `http://localhost:7777/`, the **Hello World!** message will be displayed, that is, the three route handlers assigned to the home page have been loaded in order.

To test the `req.params` functionality, we need to visit the page `http://localhost:7777/users/the_wizzard/alex`, which should output the following JSON response:

```
{ user: "the_wizzard", name: "alex" }
```

For every other URL we visit, the **404 - Page Not Found** message will be shown, so we know that the route wildcard did its job.

Summary

This chapter has provided us with a great deal of information about middleware. We can now create middleware components and even our custom framework that replicates Express up to a certain point. We have discussed the similarities between the router and the middleware system. We have seen the advantages of error-handling middleware and also learned how to set up the 404 page. An important insight we got was the fact that each Express application is a middleware of its own, so we can mount the subapplication into a master one.

Now that we know how to use middleware to our advantage, it is time to create a RESTful application with Express.

3
Creating RESTful APIs

This chapter will guide you through building a RESTful API from scratch using Express and Mongoose. We will use a test-driven approach in the process, which means we will first create the tests and then implement the functionality. Not only will we write functional tests for the API endpoints, but we will also write unit tests for the models. In this chapter, we will cover the following topics:

- Best practices for designing RESTful APIs
- Writing unit tests for the models
- Writing functional tests with Supertest
- Versioning APIs
- Implementing rate limiting

An overview of REST

Representational State Transfer (**REST**) is an architecture style for designing network applications. REST is all about resources, so when creating an API, we need to separate it into logical resources. Resources represent information, and they need to be nouns, not verbs.

To manipulate resources, we use HTTP requests where the methods/verbs are meaningful: GET, POST, PUT, PATCH, and DELETE.

HTTP methods (verbs)

HTTP methods are used to specify the action that should be performed on a resource. The most popular methods are GET and POST, but there are others that are defined as well: CONNECT, DELETE, HEAD, OPTIONS, PUT, PATCH, and TRACE.

Some HTTP methods do not generate any side effects, so they are called safe methods. GET, HEAD, OPTIONS, and TRACE are considered safe, while other methods such as POST, PUT, PATCH, and DELETE are unsafe because they are normally used to change the state of a resource on the server.

Another property of methods is idempotence. A method is idempotent if multiple invocations of it have the same result as a single one. For example, calling DELETE twice won't remove the same resource two times because after the first call it will have already been deleted.

It's really important to correctly implement the safeness and idempotence properties for HTTP clients to do their job. For example, you may have noticed that the browser asks for confirmation when trying to reperform a POST request. This happens because it needs to make sure that you understand the implications of that request, such as creating the same item multiple times.

Now, let's have a quick look at the most common HTTP methods. We are going to use these methods in RESTful applications:

- GET: This method is used to retrieve information for the requested resource.
- HEAD: This method is similar to GET, but should not contain the message body in the response. It is useful to check the validity, accessibility, and modification of resources.
- POST: This method sends a new subordinate of the resource to the server. If a new resource has been created, the server should respond with the 201 Created status code; however, if the action did not result in an identifiable resource, it should respond with 200 OK or 204 No Content.
- PUT: This method requests that the entity sent is stored at the requested URI. It can be used to update a resource or create a new one if the URI does not point to an existing one.
- DELETE: This method is used to remove the entity stored at the requested URI; it should respond with 200 OK, 204 No Content, or 202 Accepted (which means the deletion has not occurred yet, but it will).

For a more detailed description of these methods, you can read the *Method Definitions* section of *Hypertext Transfer Protocol -- HTTP/1.1* at `http://www.w3.org/Protocols/rfc2616/rfc2616-sec9.html`.

Aside from the HTTP methods described previously, there is another method called `PATCH` that is being adopted more and more. `PATCH` is similar to `PUT` since it is used to modify the resource identified by the requested URI or create a new one in case it does not exist. However, the big difference between the two is that `PATCH` performs a partial update on a resource, so it will not send the whole updated resource, but instead just send the pieces that have been modified. In addition, as opposed to `PUT`, the protocol (`https://tools.ietf.org/html/rfc5789`) states that the entity sent by `PATCH` should contain instructions on how the resource needs to be modified:

> *"The PATCH method requests that a set of changes described in the request entity be applied to the resource identified by the Request- URI. The set of changes is represented in a format called "patch document" identified by a media type."*

This means that it is not quite correct to send only a partial JSON representation of the resource without describing how the changes should be applied, as shown in the following command:

```
PATCH /api/users/john HTTP/1.1
   Host: www.example.com
   Content-Type: application/json


   {
     "age": 32,
     "website": "johndoe.domain"
   }
```

In the preceding example, there is no description of the changes needed to modify the existing user called John. Fortunately, there is a proposed draft called **JSON Patch** that aims to solve the problem. The draft specifies how to use JSON objects to describe the operations that need to be applied when updating the resource, `http://tools.ietf.org/html/rfc6902`. Let's rewrite the example and see how it should work according to this standard:

```
PATCH /api/users/john HTTP/1.1
   Host: www.example.com
   Content-Type: application/json-patch+json
```

```
[{
    "op": "replace",
    "path": "/age",
    "value": 32
}, {
    "op": "replace",
    "path": "/website",
    "value": "johndoe.domain"
}]
```

The JSON body has now become more verbose, but it's standards-compliant according to the JSON Patch draft. This specification allows us to perform more complex operations, such as adding an element to an array property without sending the whole value of the array (and the same goes for an object property).

HTTP status codes

Status codes represent three-digit integers sent by the server to the client that describe the result of the action performed. The first digit of the code is an indication of the class of the response, which can be one of the following:

- 1xx – informational
- 2xx – success
- 3xx – redirection
- 4xx – client error
- 5xx – server error

 You can read more about HTTP status codes from the official RFC page at http://www.w3.org/Protocols/rfc2616/rfc2616-sec10.html.

There are some applications that only use the 200 OK and 500 Internal Server Error status codes, but that is not the way to do it. Since we are creating RESTful applications, we should embrace the HTTP status codes to make our lives easier and not duplicate existing functionality.

For example, you might have seen the following response when trying to retrieve information on a resource without being logged in or sending the proper authentication data:

```
HTTP/1.1 200 OK
Content-Type: application/json


{"error":"unauthorized"}
```

Instead of using the correct status code, `401 Unauthorized`, the server responded with `200 OK` and an unauthorized error message in the message body.

Next, we are going to have a look at some of the most-used status codes and their meaning.

Successful 2xx

The following Successful 2xx class of status codes tell us that the request has been received, understood, and accepted by the server:

- `200 OK`: This status code indicates that the request has succeeded

- `201 Created`: This status code indicates that the request has succeeded and a new resource has been created

- `202 Accepted`: This status code does not say anything about the actual result; it only states that the request has been accepted and that it is being processed asynchronously

- `204 No Content`: This status code indicates that the request has succeeded, but it does not include a message body

Redirection 3xx

The following Redirection 3xx status codes are all about sending the client somewhere else for the actual resource:

- `301 Moved Permanently`: This status code indicates that the resource has a new permanent URI, provided by the `Location` response header

- `302 Found`: This status code indicates that the resource is temporarily located at another URI, provided by the `Location` field

- `304 Not Modified`: This status code should be used when the client makes a conditional `GET` request but the document has not been modified

Client error 4xx

The following Client error 4xx group of status codes are intended for situations related to a client error, and the server should indicate whether it is a temporary or permanent error:

- `400 Bad Request`: This indicates that the syntax of the request is malformed and could not be understood by the server.

- `401 Unauthorized`: This indicates that the client is not authenticated and thus cannot access the resource.

- `403 Forbidden`: This indicates that the client does not have access to the resource, and authorization will not help. The server might not want to let the user know that the resource exists at this URI and could respond with `404 Not Found` (for example, because of privacy or security reasons).

- `404 Not Found`: This indicates that the server could not find anything at the requested URI.

- `409 Conflict`: This indicates that the request was not completed because of a conflict with the current state of the resource.

- `429 Too Many Requests`: This status code is defined in the proposed standard for *Additional HTTP Status Codes* (http://tools.ietf.org/search/rfc6585#section-4), and it indicates that the client has exceeded the imposed rate limit (the client has sent too many requests) and they should only retry after a certain period (defined by the `Retry-After` header).

- `422 Unprocessable Entity`: This status code has been defined in the proposed standard for *HTTP Extensions for Web Distributed Authoring and Versioning (WebDAV)* (https://tools.ietf.org/html/rfc4918#section-11.2), and it indicates that the content type is understood and the syntax is not malformed, but it was not able to process the request.

Server error 5xx

The following Server error 5xx group of HTTP status codes indicate a problem on the server, which can be temporary or permanent:

- `500 Internal Server Error`: This indicates that the server could not fulfill the request due to an unexpected error

- `501 Not Implemented`: This is used when the server does not recognize the request method

- `503 Service Unavailable`: This indicates that the server was unable to handle the request at the time due to a temporary overload or maintenance

The status codes presented so far are the ones we will most likely use, but if we want to check out their detailed definition or read about the other status codes available, the following links will help:

- `http://www.w3.org/Protocols/rfc2616/rfc2616-sec10.html` (*Status Code Definitions*)

- `https://tools.ietf.org/html/rfc4918` (*HTTP Extensions for Web Distributed Authoring and Versioning (WebDAV)*)

- `http://tools.ietf.org/search/rfc6585` (*Additional HTTP Status Codes*)

SmartNotes application requirements

In the remaining part of this chapter, we will create a RESTful API for a sample application called **SmartNotes**. This application will have two types of users: guests and registered users. Guests represent unauthenticated users that can perform the following actions:

- Create a new username so they can manage their notes

- Get the public details of a username

- Retrieve a list of public (shared) notes that belong to a username

- Get a specific public note of a username

Registered users will be authorized to use the HTTP basic authentication scheme, and they will be able to perform the following activities:

- Edit their details

- Perform CRUD operations on notes

- Perform all actions that guests have access to

The model for the registered users will contain the attributes `username`, `name`, and `email`. Both the `username` and the `email` fields are mandatory fields as well as being unique in the database. Additionally, the username needs to be alphanumeric and have a maximum length of 255 characters.

Apart from these three attributes, the `passport-local-mongoose` module takes care of generating and comparing passwords as well as adding the hash and salt attributes to the user document. The `Note` model contains more attributes in order to allow users to generate more complex queries, as follows:

- `title`: This is a required field (a string) that represents the title of the note

- `description`: This is a required field (a string) that keeps the note description

- `userId`: This is a required field that holds the `_id` of the user (MongoDB `ObjectId` by default) who created the note
- `rating`: This is an integer between `0` and `10`; it defaults to `0` (unrated)
- `category`: This is an optional string that represents the note category
- `public`: This is a Boolean to know whether the note is publically shared or not (only its creator can get its details); it defaults to `false`
- `createdAt` and `updatedAt`: These timestamps are used to determine the creation time as well as when the last update to the note was made

Both the models contain an `_id` field and are added by Mongoose automatically.

Creating RESTful URLs of the application

Now that we know what the application requirements are, we can move on to designing its API.

An important principle when creating RESTful URLs is to avoid using verbs in the URLs. Instead of having URLs such as `/notes/getAll` or `/notes/deleteNote`, we need to leverage existing HTTP methods such as `GET` or `DELETE`.

The thing to remember here is that we need to use nouns for resources and operate on them using HTTP methods. Let's apply this theory in practice and see how our endpoints will look; refer to the following table:

URL	HTTP Method	Action
`/users/<username>`	`GET`	This is used to get the public details of a specific user
`/users`	`POST`	This is used to create a new user
`/users/<username>`	`PATCH`	This is used to partially update the authenticated user
`/users/<username>/notes`	`GET`	This is used to retrieve the list of public notes shared by a specific user

URL	HTTP Method	Action
/users/<username>/notes/<note_id>	GET	This is used to get a certain publicly shared note of a user
/notes	GET	This is used to retrieve the list of notes for the authenticated user (which can be filtered using different options)
/notes	POST	This is used to add a new note
/notes/<note_id>	GET	This is used to retrieve a specific note
/notes/<note_id>	PATCH	This is used to partially update a specific note
/notes/<note_id>	DELETE	This is used to delete a specific note

Just as we used HTTP methods to avoid repetition and keep our URLs clean, in the same spirit, we will use existing HTTP status codes to express the results of these actions when we implement them.

 To read more about the things to avoid when creating RESTful APIs, visit http://www.lornajane.net/posts/2013/five-clues-that-your-api-isnt-restful.

Implementing the SmartNotes application

Next, we start by bootstrapping the application. We then create a validation library so we can reuse it in our models. Once this is done, we create the routes and integrate them into the current application.

For each part that requires writing code, we first create tests, run them to see them fail, and only then continue with the actual implementation. This has multiple benefits, one of the most important being that we will have a better understanding of what we are going to create.

The bootstrapping phase

Let's take a look at how the structure of our application will look after we have finished it:

```
.
├── ./config.json
├── ./lib
│   ├── ./lib/db.js
│   └── ./lib/validator.js
├── ./models
│   ├── ./models/note.js
│   └── ./models/user.js
├── ./package.json
├── ./routes
│   ├── ./routes/index.js
│   ├── ./routes/notes.js
│   └── ./routes/users.js
├── ./server.js
└── ./test
    ├── ./test/fixtures
    │   ├── ./test/fixtures/notes.json
    │   └── ./test/fixtures/users.json
    ├── ./test/functional
    │   ├── ./test/functional/notes.js
    │   └── ./test/functional/users.js
    ├── ./test/unit
    │   ├── ./test/unit/note.js
    │   ├── ./test/unit/user.js
    │   └── ./test/unit/validator.js
    └── ./test/utils
        ├── ./test/utils/db.js
        └── ./test/utils/helpers.js
```

In the root folder of the application, we create the following folders:

- `lib`: This folder is used for custom functionality

- `models`: This folder contains Mongoose models for users and notes

- `routes`: Instead of putting all the routes in the `server.js` file, we put them in this folder and require them in the main file

- `test`: This folder contains all the tests for the application

 It's worth noting that there are other ways of structuring projects (such as the feature-based way), but in this project, we use the MVC style.

The fastest way to create the `package.json` file is to use the `npm init` command inside the root folder of the application, after which NPM will guide us step-by-step through creating the properties.

Using the following code, we create a basic `config.json` file that contains an environment-based configuration with the database URL and the port required by the application:

```
{
  "development": {
    "mongoUrl": "mongodb://localhost/smartnotes-dev",
    "port": 3000
  },
  "test": {
    "mongoUrl": "mongodb://localhost/smartnotes-test",
    "port": 3000
  },
  "production": {
    "mongoUrl": "mongodb://localhost/smartnotes",
    "port": 3000
  }
}
```

The `lib` folder will contain the following `db.js` file with basic functions to connect to the database and check the error type:

```
var mongoose = require('mongoose');

exports.isValidationError = function(err) {
  return (err && err.message && /ValidationError/i.test(err.message));
};

exports.isDuplicateKeyError = function(err) {
  return (err && err.message && /duplicate
    key/i.test(err.message));
};

exports.connect = function(url, cb) {
  cb = cb || function(err) {
    if (err) {
      console.error('database connection failure: \n' +
        err.stack);
      process.exit(1);
    }
  };

  mongoose.connect(url, { safe: true }, cb);
};
```

The next logical step is to install the dependencies and include them automatically into the `dependencies` and `devDependencies` array properties inside `package.json`. Fortunately, we can do this very easily using NPM as well, as we will see in a moment.

For this project, we use MongoDB as the database as it also speaks JavaScript like Node and understands JSON documents. We use `Mongoose` to interact with the database; `mongoose-timestamp` to automatically manage the `createdAt` and `updatedAt` fields; `passport-local-mongoose` for user authentication; the `validator` module to perform all sorts of validations on our data; the `async` module for control flow; `lodash` for general utility functions; and Express, of course. So, let's install them as follows:

```
npm i express mongoose mongoose-timestamp passport-local-mongoose
validator async lodash --save
```

NPM supports shortcuts, so we can just use `i` instead of writing `install`. The `--save` flag is used so that the dependencies will automatically be added to the `package.json` file.

Now that we have finished with the production dependencies, it's time to think of the development dependencies used by the project. We will test the application using the `Mocha` test framework along with `should.js`; we will use `sinon` for spies, stubs, and mocks; and finally, we will use `proxyquire` so we can mock the required dependencies for a file. We will install them in the same way as before; only this time, we will use the `--save-dev` flag instead of `--save` (to make sure they will be added to the `devDependencies` property in the `package.json` file):

```
npm i mocha should.js sinon proxyquire --save-dev
```

There are two types of tests that we are going to write for this application: unit tests and functional tests. The convention for running the tests of a Node application is to include a `test` property under the `scripts` property in `package.json` and call `npm test` to execute these tests. Since we are using Mocha for testing, the property will look like the following code:

```
"scripts": {
  "test": "NODE_ENV=test node node_modules/.bin/mocha --reporter
    spec test/unit/ test/functional/",
  "start": "node server.js"
},
```

We called the local `mocha` executable instead of just calling `mocha` globally because neither can we be sure that the module is installed globally nor can we control its version. We could have called the script directly without prepending `node`, but this way, we make sure it runs properly on Windows as well.

When one-liners tend to be too long, we can put these tasks into separate files and call them with Node or with a tool such as Grunt/Gulp. This gives us flexibility when dealing with complex environments.

Another convention seen previously is the `start` script, which lets us call `npm start` to boot the server instead of remembering which file is our main one and manually starting it with Node.

Last but not least, let's add a basic skeleton for the `server.js` main file of the application. If the file is required by another module, we will export the application and not boot up the server, but if `server.js` is the master file, we will start the server. The code for the file is shown as follows:

```
var express = require('express');
var app = express();
var db = require('./lib/db');
var config = require('./config.json')[app.get('env')];

var methodOverride = require('method-override');
var bodyParser = require('body-parser');

db.connect(config.mongoUrl);

app.use(bodyParser.urlencoded({ extended: true }));
app.use(bodyParser.json());
app.use(methodOverride(function(req, res) {
  if (req.body && typeof req.body === 'object' && '_method' in
    req.body) {
    // look in urlencoded POST bodies and delete it
    var method = req.body._method;
    delete req.body._method;
    return method;
  }
}));

module.exports = app;

if (!module.parent) {
  app.listen(config.port);
  console.log('(%s) app listening on port %s', app.get('env'),
    config.port);
}
```

The `module.parent` check, used in the preceding code, is to determine whether the module was run directly or loaded via `require()`. If it's the latter, it means that we are most likely in a test environment and don't want the server to listen on a port. In this case, exporting the application would suffice.

Dealing with validation

Mongoose has some built-in validations, but sometimes, we need more complex validations, such as checking for a valid IP address or a URL.

At the time of writing, there is a module called `mongoose-validator` that provides an easy way to specify Mongoose-compatible validation functions using the `validator` module. However, the module bundles a really old version of the `validator` module, so it's not ideal.

Whenever you want to quickly check out the page of a certain module on the NPM website, just type `http://npm.im/<MODULE_NAME>`, and it will redirect you there.

Creating a custom validation module

Luckily, the `validator` module has a simple API that allows us to make our own wrapper on top of it. Once we are finished with this wrapper, we can use it in the `Mongoose` models as the `validate` method of an attribute.

We will extend the `validator` module with another method (a closure) that proxies the validation function to the intended validation function (on the same `validator` object). We have to do that because we cannot specify the value ahead of time (when declaring the Mongoose schema). The function signature for it will be the following:

```
validator.validate(nameOfTheMethod, value, ...arguments)
```

This `validate` function will actually make a call to the method that was passed as the first parameter, as shown in the following line of code:

```
validator[nameOfTheMethod](value, ...arguments)
```

Now that we know how the `validate` function should look, let's go write some tests! We will create a file called `validator.js` inside `/test/unit/` and start with our first test. The following code will check whether an error is thrown if the method does not exist on the `validator` object:

```
var should = require('should');
var validator = require('../../lib/validator');

describe('validator', function() {
  describe('validate', function() {
    it("should throw an error if the delegated method doesn't
      exist", function() {
      delete validator.unknownMethod;
      (function() {
        validator.validate('unknownMethod');
      }).should.throw(/validator method does not exist/i);
    });
  });
});
```

If we run the tests, we will get an error since the validator file we required does not exist yet:

```
$ npm test


> SmartNotes@0.0.0 test /Users/alexandruvladutu/www/SmartNotes

> node node_modules/.bin/mocha --reporter spec test/unit/ test/functional



module.js:340

    throw err;

         ^

Error: Cannot find module '../../lib/validator'
```

Good, now let's create the `validator` file, assign an empty function to the `validate` method, and rerun the test afterwards.

Note that since we want to extend the `validator` object (returned by the `validator` module) and not modify it directly, we will need to copy all its properties to a newly created object and return that one instead. We could do that ourselves, but luckily, we can use the `extend` function from `lodash` instead:

```
npm i lodash --save
```

The code for the `validator` file will be the following:

```
var validator = require('validator');
var extend = require('lodash').extend;

var customValidator = extend({}, validator);

customValidator.validate = function() {};

module.exports = customValidator;
```

Running the tests will generate the following output:

```
validator
  validate
    1) should throw an error if the delegated method doesn't exist


  0 passing (7ms)
  1 failing

  1) validator validate should throw an error if the delegated method
doesn't exist:
     AssertionError: expected [Function] to throw exception
```

The next step is to add the existence check to the function and throw an error if the method is not available:

```
customValidator.validate = function(method) {
  if (!customValidator[method]) {
    throw new Error('validator method does not exist');
  }
};
```

Now, when we run the tests, everything will work as expected:

```
validator
  validate
    ✓ should throw an error if the delegated method doesn't exist


  1 passing (7ms)
```

Next, we write a test to make sure `validate` returns a function:

```
it("should return a function", function() {
  validator.noop = function(){};
  validator.validate('noop').should.be.a.Function;
});
```

When running the tests again, we see these tests fail, as they should. We include the bare minimum needed to make these tests pass, which means that we return `function(){};` at the end of the `validate` function. Now, both tests will pass:

validator

  validate

    ✓ **should throw an error if the delegated method doesn't exist**

    ✓ **should return a function**

After that, we add a test that checks whether the inner function returned the `validator` function with the correct arguments when using it. We use the `sinon.spy` function to check the arguments being called on the delegated method:

```
describe("inner function", function() {
  it("should call the delegated method with the arguments in
      order", function() {
    var method = sinon.spy();

    validator.myCustomValidationMethod = method;
    validator.validate('myCustomValidationMethod', 1, 2,
      3)('str');

    method.calledWith('str', 1, 2, 3).should.be.true;
  });
});
```

So, let's do a short recap: the `validate` function returns another function (the inner function) that, when called, invokes the method named by the first argument on the `validator` object.

We need to first run the tests as usual, ensure that the newly created one fails, and move on to the implementation. We add the following bits to the `validate` function (instead of returning an empty function):

```
// get an array of the arguments except the first one (the
  method name)
var args = Array.prototype.slice.call(arguments, 1);
```

```
  return function(value) {
    return customValidator[method].apply(customValidator,
      Array.prototype.concat(value, args));
  };
```

Now, if we run the tests, everything is nice and green, which means that all the tests are being passed.

Improving performance with memoization

Note that each time we call the `validate` function with the same parameters, it returns a new (different) function. We can use the `memoizejs` module to memoize the result of the `validate` function called with some specific arguments so that the next time the function is called with the exact same arguments, it returns the result from the cache. Don't forget to install the module:

npm i memoizejs --save

We include the `proxyquire` module in our test file because we want to use it instead of the custom `require` function. We use it to replace the `memoizejs` dependency from our `validator` module in order to test that it's being called, and the result is assigned to the `validate` function.

 A common mistake people make here is to test whether the `validate` function is being memoized. This functionality is not our responsibility; the third-party module itself tests it. All we need to do is ensure that the `memoizejs` function is called once and the result is stored in the `validate` function.

We use the `proxyquire` module instead of the native Node `require` function when requesting the `validator` module (in our test file) because we need to override the result returned by the `memoizejs` dependency. The test will look like the following:

```
it("should be memoized", function() {
  var noop = sinon.stub();
  var memoize = sinon.spy(function(fn) { return noop; });
  var validator = proxyquire('../../lib/validator', {
    'memoizejs': memoize
  });

  memoize.calledOnce.should.be.true;
  validator.validate.should.eql(noop);
});
```

The test will fail since we haven't implemented this feature yet, so after that, we update our `validator` module accordingly to include the following lines (before exporting the module):

```
var memoize = require('memoizejs');
customValidator.validate = memoize(customValidator.validate);
```

Now, let's run the tests again and make sure they pass:

```
validator
  validate
    ✓ should throw an error if the delegated method doesn't exist
    ✓ should return a function
    ✓ should be memoized
    inner function
      ✓ should call the delegated method with the arguments in order


4 passing (10ms)
```

Implementing the models

There are two Mongoose models we need to create: the User model and the `Note` model. For each model, we first write their tests and then create the Mongoose schema with the appropriate attributes.

Test helpers

Before writing the tests, we implement some handy helpers that will definitely make our lives easier when we test the models. For Mongoose models, we have to test reusable features, such as the following:

- Making sure that an attribute has been set to `required`
- Ensuring that the attribute has the correct type
- Making sure that the proper validation rules have been defined for an attribute
- Testing whether a plugin has been loaded
- Testing whether the schema has been registered with Mongoose

Instead of using the real `mongoose` module, we stub it using `sinon` and then check whether `mongoose.Schema` has been called with the right arguments. The same approach will work to test whether a plugin has been loaded in the schema or whether the schema has been registered with `mongoose.model`.

Let's create a file called `helpers.js` inside `test/utils/`; this will contain the helpers:

```
var sinon = require('sinon');
var should = require('should');
var validator = require('../../lib/validator');

exports.getMongooseStub = function() {
  var mongoose = {};

  mongoose.Schema = sinon.stub();
  mongoose.Schema.ObjectId = 'ObjectId';
  mongoose.Schema.prototype.plugin = sinon.stub();
  mongoose.model = sinon.stub();

  return mongoose;
};
```

An important function is `shouldDefineSchemaProperty`, which checks whether an object property (schema attribute) has been called with a certain value. The following helpers that assert the type of the schema attribute, its default value, or its presence are actually delegating the work to this function:

```
exports.shouldDefineSchemaProperty = function(Schema, property) {
  sinon.assert.called(Schema.withArgs(sinon.match(property)));
};

exports.shouldBeRequired = function(Schema, property) {
  var obj = {};
  obj[property] = {
    required: true
  };
  exports.shouldDefineSchemaProperty(Schema, obj);
};

exports.shouldBeUnique = function(Schema, property) {
  var obj = {};
  obj[property] = {
    unique: true
  };
```

```
  exports.shouldDefineSchemaProperty(Schema, obj);
};


// checks the type of the property
exports.shouldBeA = function(Schema, property, type) {
  var obj = {};
  obj[property] = {
    type: type
  };
  exports.shouldDefineSchemaProperty(Schema, obj);
};

exports.shouldDefaultTo = function(Schema, property, defaultValue) {
  var obj = {};
  obj[property] = {
    default: defaultValue
  };
  exports.shouldDefineSchemaProperty(Schema, obj);
};

exports.shouldBeBetween = function(Schema, property, opts) {
  var obj = {};
  obj[property] = {
    min: opts.min,
    max: opts.max
  };
  exports.shouldDefineSchemaProperty(Schema, obj);
};
```

We also need to check whether the validation function for an attribute has been called with the correct parameters. We can do this by checking whether the value of the `validate` property on the object is equal to the function returned by `validator. validate`, which is called with the exact parameters. Since the function uses `memoizejs` to cache the result, it will return the same value when called multiple times with the same parameters, as shown in the following code:

```
exports.shouldValidateThat = function(Schema, property) {
  var args = Array.prototype.slice.call(arguments, 2);
  var obj = {};
  obj[property] = {
    validate: validator.validate.apply(validator, args)
  };
```

```
    exports.shouldDefineSchemaProperty(Schema, obj);
  };

  // when using an array of validation functions
  exports.shouldValidateMany = function(Schema, property,
    validation1, validation2) {
    var obj = {};
    obj[property] = {
      validate: [{
        validator: validator.validate.apply(validator,
          validation1.args),
        msg: validation1.msg
      }, {
        validator: validator.validate.apply(validator,
          validation2.args),
        msg: validation2.msg
      }]
    };
    exports.shouldDefineSchemaProperty(Schema, obj);
  };
```

The helpers left to be created are the ones that check whether a plugin has been loaded on the schema and whether the schema itself has been registered. The two functions will look like the following:

```
  exports.shouldRegisterSchema = function(Model, Schema, name) {
    Model.calledWith(name).should.be.true;
    Model.args[0][1].should.be.an.instanceOf(Schema);
  };

  exports.shouldLoadPlugin = function(Schema, plugin) {
    sinon.assert.called(Schema.prototype.plugin.withArgs(plugin));
  };
```

The Note model

This model file will define the schema and load the `mongoose-timestamp` plugin. Before we start writing tests and implementing code for the model, we need to think of how to shape our documents by defining a schema with proper attributes. In order to do this, let's have a short recap of the attributes needed for notes:

* `title`: This is a (required) string of 3-255 chars
* `description`: This is a (required) string of 10-255 chars

- `userId`: This is a MongoDB `ObjectId` that points to the User model; it is a required field
- `rating`: This is a number between `0` and `10` that defaults to `0` (unrated)
- `category`: This is a string that defaults to `general`
- `public`: This is a Boolean that defaults to `false`

Besides setting the attributes, we will load the `mongoose-timestamp` plugin (which will automatically take care of the `createdAt` and `updatedAt` attributes) and register the schema. We will use the `proxyquire` module to stub both the plugin as well as the `mongoose` module.

Let's create a file called `note.js` inside `/test/unit` and complete the initial preparation: we define the dependencies and bind `mongoose.Schema` to the helper functions (so that we won't have to pass it as an argument each time we use it):

```
var should = require('should');
var sinon = require('sinon');
var proxyquire = require('proxyquire');
var helpers = require('../utils/helpers');
var mongoose = helpers.getMongooseStub();

var shouldDefineSchemaProperty =
  helpers.shouldDefineSchemaProperty.bind(null, mongoose.Schema);
var shouldRegisterSchema = helpers.shouldRegisterSchema.bind(null,
  mongoose.model, mongoose.Schema);
var shouldBeRequired = helpers.shouldBeRequired.bind(null,
  mongoose.Schema);
var shouldBeA = helpers.shouldBeA.bind(null, mongoose.Schema);
var shouldDefaultTo = helpers.shouldDefaultTo.bind(null,
  mongoose.Schema);
var shouldBeBetween = helpers.shouldBeBetween.bind(null,
  mongoose.Schema);
var shouldValidateThat = helpers.shouldValidateThat.bind(null,
  mongoose.Schema);
var shouldLoadPlugin = helpers.shouldLoadPlugin.bind(null,
  mongoose.Schema);
```

Now, there is one thing left to do before writing the tests, and that is to use `proxyquire` to stub the `mongoose-timestamp` module when requiring the `Note` model:

```
describe('Note', function() {
  var Note, mongooseTimestamp;
```

```
    before(function() {
      mongooseTimestamp = sinon.stub();
      Note = proxyquire('../../models/note', {
        'mongoose-timestamp': mongooseTimestamp,
        'mongoose': mongoose
      });
    });

    // the tests will be included here
  });
```

We need to write a test, see it fail, and then implement the functionality on the model. For the sake of brevity, this time we will see all the model tests and then we will check out the model implementation. The following are the global tests (the plugin check and registration of the model) and the tests for the title attribute; the rest will be left as an exercise for you since they are similar:

```
  it('should register the Mongoose model', function() {
    shouldRegisterSchema('Note');
  });

  it('should load the timestamps plugin', function() {
    shouldLoadPlugin(mongooseTimestamp);
  });

  describe('title', function() {
    it('should be required', function() {
      shouldBeRequired('title');
    });

    it('should be a string', function() {
      shouldBeA('title', String);
    });

    it('should have a length of 3-255 chars', function() {
      shouldValidateThat('title', 'isLength', 3, 255);
    });
  });
```

The tests look really clean and expressive, as intended. The `Note` model is really light; it only declares the schema (its attributes), loads the `mongoose-timestamp` plugin, and registers the model, as shown in the following code:

```
var validator = require('../lib/validator');
var timestamps = require('mongoose-timestamp');
var mongoose = require('mongoose');

var Schema = mongoose.Schema;
var ObjectId = Schema.ObjectId;

var Note = new Schema({
  title: {
    type: String,
    required: true,
    validate: validator.validate('isLength', 3, 255)
  },
  description: {
    type: String,
    required: true,
    validate: validator.validate('isLength', 10, 255)
  },
  userId: {
    type: ObjectId,
    required: true,
    ref: 'User'
  },
  rating: {
    type: Number,
    default: 0,
    min: 0,
    max: 10
  },
  category: {
    type: String,
    default: 'general'
  },
  public: {
    type: Boolean,
    default: false
  }
});

Note.plugin(timestamps);

module.exports = mongoose.model('Note', Note);
```

The User model

There are two main things we need to cover in the User model: the schema definition and managing passwords (by simply loading the `passport-local-mongoose` plugin). The user schema will contain the following attributes:

- `username`: This is a unique, alphanumeric string (required) with 4-255 chars
- `email`: This is a unique, valid e-mail string (required)
- `name`: This string is optional

We will not handle the `password` field by ourselves, but instead, we will use the `passport-local-mongoose` module to take care of authentication, hashing, and storing the proper attributes in the database (`salt` and `hash`).

Since the tests are similar to the `Note` model, they will also be left as a home exercise (feel free to check out the attached source code of this chapter). The code for the User model is as follows:

```
var validator = require('../lib/validator');
var passportLocalMongoose = require('passport-local-mongoose');

var mongoose = require('mongoose');
var Schema = mongoose.Schema;
var ObjectId = Schema.ObjectId;

var User = new Schema({
  username: {
    type: String,
    required: true,
    unique: true,
    validate: [{
      validator: validator.validate('isAlphanumeric'),
      msg: 'username must be alphanumeric'
    }, {
      validator: validator.validate('isLength', 4, 255),
      msg: 'username must have 4-255 chars'
    }]
  },
  email: {
    type: String,
    required: true,
    unique: true,
    validate: validator.validate('isEmail')
  },
```

```
  name: {
    type: String
  }
});

User.plugin(passportLocalMongoose);

module.exports = mongoose.model('User', User);
```

Functional tests and route implementation

Now that we have finished with the code for the models, we can concentrate on writing functional tests for the API endpoints and implementing the associated Express routes.

We will use the `supertest` module to write functional tests for the application, so let's install it as follows:

npm i supertest --save-dev

Before creating the functional tests, we need to take care of one aspect: we have to empty the database each time we run the tests and populate it again with fixtures so that we can test certain routes.

For this, we create a file called `db.js` inside `test/utils/`. This file will contain functions that take care of the following: connecting to the database, emptying the database, and populating it with fixtures. There will also be a master function that calls the previous three so that we can easily set up the test database. The code is as follows:

```
var config = require('../../config.json');
var db = require('../../lib/db');
var async = require('async');
var Note = require('../../models/note');
var User = require('../../models/user');
var userFixtures = require('../fixtures/users.json');
var notesFixtures = require('../fixtures/notes.json');

exports.connect = function(callback) {
  db.connect(config.test.mongoUrl, callback);
};
```

```
// empty the database
exports.reset = function(callback) {
  async.parallel([
    function emptyNotesCollection(cb) {
      Note.remove({}, cb);
    },
    function emptyUsersCollection(cb) {
      User.remove({}, cb);
    }
  ], callback);
};

// populate the database with fixtures
exports.populate = function(callback) {
  async.each(userFixtures, function(data, next) {
    User.register(new User({
      username: data.username,
      email: data.email,
      name: data.name
    }), data.password, next)
  }, function(err) {
    if (err) { return callback(err); }

    User.findOne({ username: 'johndoe' }, function(err, user) {
      if (err) { return callback(err); }

      async.each(notesFixtures, function(data, next) {
        var note = new Note(data);
        note.userId = user._id;
        note.save(next);
      }, callback);
    });
  });
};

// connect to, reset and populate database with fixtures
exports.setupDatabase = function(callback) {
  exports.connect(function(err) {
    if (err) { return callback(err); }

    exports.reset(function(err) {
      if (err) { return callback(err); }
```

```
    exports.populate(callback);
  });
 });
};
```

Apart from that, we need to create two JSON files with Note and User fixtures inside `/test/fixtures/`. Here is the `users.json` sample:

```
[
  {
    "username": "johndoe",
    "password": "johns_password",
    "email": "johndoe@example.com",
    "name": "John Doe"
  }
]
```

User endpoints

Now, we can start writing the functional tests for the users' API endpoints (`/test/functional/users.js`). We will test that we can retrieve a user's public information as well as the ability to create and edit users. The full code for achieving this should look like the following:

```
var request = require('supertest');
var should = require('should');
var app = require('../../server');
var db = require('../utils/db');

var user = require('../fixtures/users.json')[0];

describe('User-Routes', function(done) {
  before(function(done) {
    db.setupDatabase(done);
  });

  after(function(done) {
    db.reset(done);
  });

  it('should return the user details', function(done) {
    request(app)
      .get('/users/' + user.username)
      .expect(200)
```

```
      .expect('Content-Type', /json/)
      .end(function(err, res) {
        if (err) { throw err; }

        res.body.should.have.properties('username', 'email',
          'name');

        done();
      });
  });

  it('should create a new user', function(done) {
    request(app)
      .post('/users')
      .send({
        username: 'newuser',
        password: 'newuser_password',
        email: 'newuser@example.com',
        name: 'doe'
      })
      .expect(201)
      .expect('Content-Type', /json/)
      .expect('Location', '/users/newuser')
      .expect({
        username: 'newuser',
        email: 'newuser@example.com',
        name: 'doe'
      }, done);
  });

  it('should update the current user', function(done) {
    request(app)
      .patch('/users/' + user.username)
      .set('Authorization', 'Basic ' + new Buffer(user.username +
        ':' + user.password).toString('base64'))
      .send([{
        op: 'replace',
        path: '/email',
        value: 'johndoe_the_third@example.com'
      }, {
        op: 'replace',
        path: '/name',
        value: 'John Doe The Third'
      }])
```

```
      .expect(204, done);
  });

});
```

At the beginning of our tests, we clean the database and populate it with the fixtures, and at the end, we clean it up again. Another interesting fact is that we are using HTTP basic authentication to check for access.

We are not testing every possible use case because it's beyond the scope of this chapter, but for production applications, it's highly recommended that you cover as much code as possible with tests.

If we run the tests, they should all fail at this point, so next, we will implement the user routes. We will start by assigning the models on the request object and defining the routes in the `server.js` code:

```
// put these along with the other dependencies
var mongoose = require('mongoose');
var User = require('./models/user');
var Note = require('./models/note');
var routes = require('./routes');

// ...

// these go after the middleware is declared
app.use(function(req, res, next) {
  req.User = User;
  req.Note = Note;
  next();
});

app.get('/users/:username', routes.users.show);
app.post('/users', routes.users.create);
app.patch('/users/:username', routes.users.authenticate,
  routes.users.update);
```

The `index.js` file inside `/routes` just exports the `users` and `notes` routes. We will create the `users` routes next (`/routes/users.js`), starting with the authentication route. The authentication function is fairly simple; we use the `express.basicAuth()` middleware along with the `passport-local-mongoose` functionality to populate the `req.user` variable if the user successfully authenticates, and if not, `basicAuth` will return `401 Unauthorized`:

```
var _ = require('lodash');
var db = require('../lib/db');
```

```
var publicAttributes = ['username', 'email', 'name'];
var basicAuth = require('basic-auth-connect');

exports.authenticate = function(req, res, next) {
. basicAuth(function(user, pass, fn) {
    // function from passport-local-mongoose
    req.User.authenticate()(user, pass, function(err, userData) {
      // no need to store salt and hash
      fn(err, _.pick(userData, ['_id', 'username', 'email',
        'name']));
    });
  })(req, res, next);
};
```

The show function returns the user's public details (excluding hash and salt, for example), and if there is no such user, it responds with 404 Not Found:

```
var publicAttributes = ['username', 'email', 'name'];

exports.show = function(req, res, next) {
  req.User.findOne({ username: req.params.username },
    function(err, userData) {
    if (err) { return next(err); }

    if (!userData) {
      return res.status(404).send({ errors: ['user not found'] });
    }

    res.send(_.pick(userData, publicAttributes));
  });
};
```

The create function does what we would expect; it checks for validation errors and returns 201 Created with the user details if the operation succeeded, otherwise it returns 422 Unprocessable Entity along with the error:

```
exports.create = function(req, res, next) {
  var newUser = new req.User(_.pick(req.body, publicAttributes));

  req.User.register(newUser, req.body.password, function(err,
    userData) {
    if (err) {
      if (db.isValidationError(err)) {
        res.status(422).send({ errors: ['invalid data'] });
      } else if (db.isDuplicateKeyError) {
```

```
        res.status(422).send({ errors: ['username/email already
          exists'] });
      } else {
        next(err);
      }
    } else {
      res
        .status(201)
        .set('Location', '/users/' + userData.username)
        .send(_.pick(userData, publicAttributes));
    }
  });
};
```

Next is the most complicated part regarding updating users, where we will have to verify a lot of conditions, such as making sure that the user is not trying to update other users and checking for validation or if the user is not found:

```
// using the JSON Patch protocol http://tools.ietf.org/html/rfc6902
exports.update = function(req, res, next) {
  function saveAndRespond(user) {
    user.save(function(err, userData) {
      if (err) {
        if (db.isValidationError(err)) {
          res.status(422).send({ errors: ['invalid data'] });
        } else if (db.isDuplicateKeyError) {
          res.status(422).send({ errors: ['email already exists']
            });
        } else {
          next(err);
        }
      } else {
        res.status(204).send();
      }
    });
  };

  if (req.params.username !== req.user.username) {
    return res.status(403).send({ errors: ['cannot update other
      users'] });
  } else {
    if (!Array.isArray(req.body)) {
      return res.status(400).send({ errors: ['use JSON Patch'] });
    } else {
```

```
    if (req.body.some(function(item) { return item.op !==
      'replace'; })) {
      return res.status(422).send({ errors: ['only replace is
        supported atm'] });
    } else {
      req.User.findOne({ username: req.user.username },
        function(err, user) {
        if (err) { return next(err); }

        if (!user) {
          return res.status(404).send({ errors: ['no such user']
            });
        }

        req.body.forEach(function(item) {
          // shouldn't be able to change username
          if (item.path !== '/username') {
            user[item.path.replace(/^\//, '')] = item.value;
          }
        });

        // handling special password case
        if (user.password) {
          var password = user.password;
          delete user.password;

          // function from passport-local-mongoose
          user.setPassword(password, function(err) {
            if (err) { return next(err); }

            saveAndRespond(user);
          });
        } else {
          saveAndRespond(user);
        }
      });
    }
  }
};
```

Now, if we run the tests, everything should be green once more.

Notes endpoints

The functional tests for notes are similar to the ones for users; we check the content type header, the status code, and the body:

```
before(function(done) {
  db.setupDatabase(done);
});

after(function(done) {
  db.reset(done);
});

it("should return the user's notes", function(done) {
  request(app)
    .get('/notes')
    .set('Authorization', 'Basic ' + new Buffer(user.username +
      ':' + user.password).toString('base64'))
    .expect(200)
    .expect('Content-Type', /json/)
    .end(function(err, res) {
      if (err) { throw err; }

      res.body.should.be.an.Array;

      done();
    });
});

it("should retrieve a particular note", function(done) {
  request(app)
    .get('/notes/' + note._id)
    .set('Authorization', 'Basic ' + new Buffer(user.username +
      ':' + user.password).toString('base64'))
    .expect(200)
    .expect('Content-Type', /json/)
    .end(function(err, res) {
      if (err) { throw err; }

      res.body.should.have.properties('createdAt', 'updatedAt',
        '_id', 'userId', 'title', 'description');
```

```
        done();
      });
  });

  it("should create a note", function(done) {
    request(app)
      .post('/notes')
      .set('Authorization', 'Basic ' + new Buffer(user.username +
        ':' + user.password).toString('base64'))
      .send({
        title: 'my random note',
        description: 'random description here'
      })
      .expect(201)
      .expect('Location', /\/notes\/[0-9a-f]{24}/)
      .expect('Content-Type', /json/)
      .end(function(err, res) {
        if (err) { throw err; }

        res.body.should.have.properties('createdAt', 'updatedAt',
          '_id', 'userId', 'title', 'description');

        done();
      });
  });

  it("should return the user's public notes", function(done) {
    request(app)
      .get('/users/' + user.username + '/notes')
      .expect(200)
      .expect('Content-Type', /json/)
      .end(function(err, res) {
        if (err) { throw err; }

        res.body.should.be.an.Array;
        res.body.forEach(function(note) {
          note.public.should.be.true;
        });

        done();
      });
  });
```

As you might have guessed, we will need to update the `server.js` main file to include the notes routes before we implement them, so here is the full code for all the routes:

```
app.get('/users/:username', routes.users.show);
app.post('/users', routes.users.create);
app.get('/users/:username/notes', routes.notes.showPublic);
app.patch('/users/:username', routes.users.authenticate,
  routes.users.update);
app.get('/notes', routes.users.authenticate, routes.notes.index);
app.post('/notes', routes.users.authenticate,
  routes.notes.create);
app.get('/notes/:id', routes.users.authenticate,
  routes.notes.show);
```

The notes route functions are straightforward; as in the `users.js` file, we execute the queries on the model and perform validation where it's needed (when creating and updating notes). Not every function related to the `notes` endpoints is included in the following code since they are similar to what we have created before, but you can finish the rest of the API as a home exercise using the following code:

```
exports.index = function(req, res, next) {
  req.Note.find({ userId: req.user._id }, function(err, notes) {
    if (err) { return next(err); }

    res.send(notes);
  });
};

exports.show = function(req, res, next) {
  req.Note.findOne({ _id: req.params.id, userId: req.user._id },
    function(err, note) {
    if (err) { return next(err); }

    res.send(note);
  });
};

exports.create = function(req, res, next) {
  var note = new req.Note(_.pick(req.body, ['title',
    'description', 'rating', 'category', 'public']));
  note.userId = req.user._id;
```

```
note.save(function(err, noteData) {
  if (err) {
    if (db.isValidationError(err)) {
      res.status(422).send({ errors: ['invalid data'] });
    } else {
      next(err);
    }
  } else {
    res
      .status(201)
      .set('Location', '/notes/' + noteData._id)
      .send(noteData);
  }
});
};

exports.showPublic = function(req, res, next) {
  req.User.findOne({ username: req.params.username },
    function(err, user) {
    if (err) { return next(err); }

    if (!user) { return res.status(404).send({ errors: ['no such
      user'] })};

    req.Note.find({ userId: user._id, public: true },
      function(err, notes) {
      if (err) { return next(err); }

      res.send(notes);
    });
  });
};
```

Now, after we run all the tests, everything should work as expected again, as shown in the following screenshot:

```
  ✓ should be unique
  ✓ should be alphanumeric and have 4-255 chars
email
  ✓ should be required
  ✓ should be a string
  ✓ should be unique
  ✓ should be a valid email
name
  ✓ should be a string

validator
  validate
    ✓ should throw an error if the delegated method doesn't exist
    ✓ should return a function
    ✓ should be memoized
    inner function
      ✓ should call the delegated method with the arguments in order

Notes-Routes
  ✓ should return the user's notes (1245ms)
  ✓ should retrieve a particular note (1229ms)
  ✓ should create a note (1175ms)
  ✓ should return the user's public notes

User-Routes
  ✓ should return the user details
  ✓ should create a new user (1148ms)
  ✓ should update the current user (1203ms)

40 passing (8s)
```

API versioning

At this time, the URLs of the SmartNotes application are not prefixed with anything, so it will be hard to add a new version of our API.

Normally, we should always have in mind that APIs deprecate over time and new versions are released. Fortunately, since Express applications can be mounted onto others, we can achieve this by modifying a code segment in `server.js`. All we have to do is replace `app.listen(config.port)` with the following code:

```
var masterApp = express();
masterApp.use('/api/v1/', app);
masterApp.listen(config.port);
```

Now, instead of making a GET HTTP request to /users/johndoe, for retrieving user information (for example), the API clients will make a request to /api/v1/users/johndoe. This means that when a new version of the API is available, we can make it available using the /api/v2/ prefix, so it's mission accomplished!

Remember to update the functional tests after doing this; otherwise, they will fail because they will be sending requests to the old URLs.

API rate limiting

Sometimes, we may want to rate limit our API to prevent abuse or because the system can handle a limited amount of requests per second. There are several ways to rate limit our API, such as by limiting the number of requests by IP address or username. If we choose to implement rate limiting based on the username, we can create a middleware that can be reused for all the routes that require authentication.

There is an excellent module by TJ Holowaychuk (the creator of Express) called node-ratelimiter (https://github.com/visionmedia/node-ratelimiter) that will basically do all the heavy lifting for us.

We create a configurable middleware that takes three arguments: the database connection to Redis (the in-memory database needed by the rate limiter), the maximum number of requests allowed in the time frame specified, and the duration of the limit. Here's how our middleware will look:

```
var Limiter = require('ratelimiter');
var ms = require('ms');

module.exports = function(db, maxRequests, duration) {
  return function limitNumberOfRequests(req, res, next) {
    var id = req.user._id;
    var limit = new Limiter({
      id: id,
      db: db,
      max: maxRequests,
      duration: duration
    });

    limit.get(function(err, limit){
      if (err) return next(err);

      res.set('X-RateLimit-Limit', limit.total);
      res.set('X-RateLimit-Remaining', limit.remaining);
      res.set('X-RateLimit-Reset', limit.reset);
```

```
      // all good
      if (limit.remaining) return next();

      // not good
      var delta = (limit.reset * 1000) - Date.now() | 0;
      var after = limit.reset - (Date.now() / 1000) | 0;
      res.set('Retry-After', after);
      res.send(429, 'Rate limit exceeded, retry in ' + ms(delta, {
        long: true }));
    });
  }
};
```

 You can read more about bitwise operators at `https://`
`developer.mozilla.org/en/docs/Web/JavaScript/`
`Reference/Operators/Bitwise_Operators#Bitwise_OR`.

Note that we are using the ms module to convert milliseconds into a human-readable duration. Now, here's how we can plug this middleware into our existing code from server.js:

```
var redis = require('redis')
var db = redis.createClient();
// 5000 requests, duration 1 day
var limiter = require('./lib/rate-limiter')(db, 5000, 60 * 60 *
  24);

// using the limiter for this route
app.get('/notes/:id', limiter, routes.users.authenticate,
  routes.notes.show);
```

Throttling

Besides setting a maximum request limit, there may be situations where we would like to slow down response such that it sends a chunk every x milliseconds. This can be useful when testing slow connections.

Usually, you will want to limit file uploads because it wouldn't be relevant to throttle a JSON response of 20 KB.

There are several NPM modules that do throttling, such as `slow-stream` and `throttle`. Let's say we have a file attached to a note and want to send a 64-byte chunk at a time, each 100 milliseconds, using `slow-stream`, as follows:

```
streamFromDatabaseOrFileSystem('note-attachment-asdAsd21j3o8uad',
    { bufferSize: 64 })
.pipe(new SlowStream({ maxWriteInterval: 400 }))
.pipe(res);
```

Both the modules mentioned work with streams, as you can see from the preceding example. The `slow-stream` module can also handle back pressure, so if we're dealing with a proper implemented stream, we won't have memory leaks.

Facilitating caching

Caching is frequently used for static resources and taken care of by a file-serving module or web server. However, there's nothing stopping us from implementing caching with dynamic resources as well.

The ETag is a cache mechanism for HTTP requests, which allows the client to make conditional requests.

> You can read more about the ETag mechanism and its usefulness at https://developer.yahoo.com/blogs/ydnfiveblog/ high-performance-sites-rule-13-configure- etags-7211.html.

There are several NPM modules that handle ETag generation and conditional requests, but we can implement our own Express middleware to do this in a few lines of code. We need to set the ETag and check whether the current request matches that ETag. If it does, we will send `304 Not Modified`, and if it doesn't, we will send the whole body. The specification says that we shouldn't include content headers when sending `304 Not Modified`, so we will remove them if they exist. The full code for this middleware is as follows:

```
var crypto = require('crypto');
var cacheAndServe = function(req, res, next) {
  res.cachable = function(content) {
    var stringContent = JSON.stringify(content);

    var hash = crypto.createHash('md5');
    hash.update(stringContent);
    res.set({ 'ETag': hash.digest('hex') });
```

```
// 304 Not Modified
if (req.fresh) {
  // remove content headers
  if (res._headers) {
    Object.keys(res._headers).forEach(function(header) {
      if (header.indexOf('content') === 0) {
        res.removeHeader(header);
      }
    });
  }

  res.statusCode = 304;
  return res.end();
} else {
  res.setHeader('Content-Type', 'application/json');
  res.end(stringContent);
}
};

next();
};
```

Note that we only handle JSON objects here since the SmartNotes application only uses that format.

In our application, we need to include this middleware and change the res.send() function to res.cachable():

```
// in server.js
app.get('/notes/:id', routes.users.authenticate, cacheAndServe,
  routes.notes.show);
// in the show function (/routes/notes.js)
res.cachable(note);
```

Content negotiation

Content negotiation is a mechanism that allows us to serve the best representation for a given response when several are available.

 You can read more about content negotiation on MDN at https://developer.mozilla.org/en-US/docs/Web/HTTP/Content_negotiation.

There are two ways in which we can perform content negotiation with Express: by appending the format to the URL or by checking for the `Accept` header field.

The first option requires us to change the URL path and add a `format` placeholder at the end; for example, consider the following line of code:

```
app.get('/notes/:id.:format', ...)
```

Then, in the route handlers, we can use a `switch` statement to serve the different content types, as follows:

```
switch (req.params.format) {
  case 'json':
    res.send(note);
    break;
  case 'xml':
    res.set('Content-Type', 'application/xml');
    res.end(convertToXml(note));
    break;
  default:
    res.status(400).send({ 'error': 'unknown format' });
}
```

The other approach would be to use the `res.format()` function from Express that checks the `Accept` header to get the content type; for example, consider the following code:

```
res.format({
  'application/json': {
    res.send(note);
  },
  'application/xml': {
    res.set('Content-Type', 'text/xml');
    res.end(convertToXml(note));
  }
});
```

Summary

In this chapter, we learned how to create a RESTful API from the ground up using Express. We also studied how to reuse HTTP as much as possible by leveraging HTTP methods and status codes.

By writing the tests first and the application code afterwards, not only did we validate the correctness of our code, but we also drove its design from the start.

Last but not least, we tackled different issues when creating APIs, such as versioning, caching, and rate limiting, and we saw how the framework helps us solve them easily.

There was no point in using templates while creating this RESTful API since it always returns JSON, but we will remedy this in the next chapter when we explore Express templating in depth.

Leveraging the Power of Template Engines

Node has a rich ecosystem of template engines available, and they can be used with Express, either out of the box or by writing a custom adapter.

In this chapter, we will cover the following topics:

- The different types of template engines
- View helpers and application-level data
- Reusing code with layouts and partials
- Updating cacheable templates in production
- Integrating a template engine with Express

The different types of template engines

Template engines are tools that help us separate the application logic from the presentation layer. They usually combine multiple templates with a data model, thus improving the maintenance and flexibility of our web applications.

There are a lot of template engines that we can install with NPM and use in Express and perhaps in the browser too. They can be split into the following categories:

- **Logic-less template engines**: Their goals are to have no explicit control-flow statements and to make it impossible to embed application logic

- **Template engines with logic**: These engines allow us to use JavaScript or DSL code and evaluate it within the templates

- **Programmatic template engines**: These are engines that build HTML from scratch or augment it using data

Next, we are going to talk about each category and see what solutions are available for them in the NPM registry.

Logic-less template engines

A big advantage of this type of template engine is that it forces you to think in terms of separation of concerns. The templates will become uncluttered because the logic will move elsewhere.

Mustache is one of the most popular logic-less web template systems with implementations in a lot of languages besides JavaScript. It uses section tags instead of conditionals or loops.

Mustache.js (https://github.com/janl/mustache.js/) is an implementation of the Mustache template system in JavaScript. We can use it in Express with the consolidate.js library (https://github.com/visionmedia/consolidate.js), as shown in the following code:

```
// server.js
var express = require('express');
var cons = require('consolidate');
var app = express();

// assign the mustache engine to .html files
app.engine('html', cons.mustache);

// set .html as the default extension
app.set('view engine', 'html');
app.set('views', __dirname + '/views');
```

 The view folder defaults to the views folder in the root of the project, but for the sake of clarity, we have explicitly set it.

Now, let's try something simple such as displaying a different salutation based on the user's gender, along with the full name. The index.html file would look like the following:

```
{{#user}}
  {{salutation}} {{name}}
{{/user}}
```

There are no if-else conditions and no native JavaScript loops, just tags. Next, we will need to create the functions for getting the salutation and the full name of a user (inside the server.js file), knowing that the properties available are firstName, lastName, and gender:

```
var getSalutation = function() {
  return (this.gender === 'male') ? 'Hello sir' : 'Hello madam';
};
var getFullName = function() {
  return this.firstName + ' ' + this.lastName;
};
```

The last part of our example consists of setting up a dummy users array, creating the route handler, assigning a path to the route, as well as binding the application to a port:

```
var users = [{
  firstName: 'John',
  lastName: 'Doe',
  gender: 'male'
}, {
  firstName: 'Jane',
  lastName: 'Doe',
  gender: 'female'
}];

app.get('/users/:index', function(req, res){
  res.render('index', {
    user: users[parseInt(req.params.index) || 0],
    salutation: getSalutation,
    name: getFullName
  });
});

app.listen(7777);
```

Now, if we visit `http://localhost:7777/users/0`, the page will display the message **Hello sir John Doe**, and for `http://localhost:7777/users/1`, it will display **Hello madam Jane Doe**. Other popular template engines that fall into this category include `Dust.js` or `Hogan.js`.

 There is an active fork of `Dust.js` actively maintained by LinkedIn at `https://github.com/linkedin/dustjs`.

Template engines with logic

Embedded JavaScript is simple to understand when you know ERB (Ruby), PHP, or JSP (Java). It allows us to use JavaScript code inside HTML templates. Such engines may also include other goodies such as partials or filters.

A popular implementation is EJS (`https://github.com/visionmedia/ejs/`), which was implemented by the creator of Express, TJ Holowaychuk. Considering the previous example of rendering users, our `index.html` file would be transformed into the following:

```
<% if (user) { %>
  <% if (user.gender === 'male') { %>
    Hello sir
  <% } else { %>
    Hello madam
  <% } %>
  <%- (user.firstName + ' ' + user.lastName) %>
<% } %>
```

This example looks a bit messier, but we can use functions and just call them inside our templates instead of writing a lot of logic there.

Jade is another popular template engine that allows us to insert JavaScript code. It is inspired by HAML (Ruby) and has whitespace-sensitive syntax for writing HTML. To achieve the same end result as you did with the previous template engines for the user example, the code will be as follows:

```
doctype html
html(lang="en")
  body
    if user
      if user.gender === 'male'
        |Hello sir
      else
        |Hello madam
      =user.firstName + ' ' + user.lastName
```

This is a bit far-fetched because instead of building the full name each time, we could create a function and call it from the template. However, the point here is Jade allows us to do this in the templates.

Some template engines such as EJS or Haml.js (`https://github.com/visionmedia/haml.js`) not only provide custom filters, but also allow us to define our own filters. Let's pretend for a second that there is no filter to convert a string to uppercase, and we need to add it to EJS. First, we would need to add the filter to the EJS `filters` object and then use it in the template:

```
// server file
require('ejs').filters.toUpper = function(str) { return
  str.toUpperCase(); }

// view template
<%-: (user.firstName + ' ' + user.lastName) | toUpper %>
```

Programmatic template engines

The previous engines that we presented either have their own syntax that compile to HTML or they add custom syntax to HTML.

This category of template engines builds HTML from scratch or augments it with dynamic data. Some engines such as `hyperglue` (`https://www.npmjs.org/package/hyperglue`) use CSS style selectors to bind attributes, text, and hypertext to HTML elements. Others create HTML code out of JSON objects, such as `transparency` (`https://www.npmjs.org/package/transparency`) or `json2html` (`https://www.npmjs.org/package/node-json2html`). Let's see how we can update our example to use `json2html` instead. First, we will need to install and require the module using the following line of code:

```
var json2html = require('node-json2html').transform;
```

This module takes a JSON object that represents dynamic data, and another JSON object for the transformation (tags and attributes). Our route handler becomes the following:

```
app.get('/users/:index', function(req, res){
  var data = {
    tag: "p",
    html: function() {
      var str = '';

      if (this) {
        if (this.gender === 'male') {
```

```
            str += 'Hello sir ';
          } else {
            str += 'Hello madam ';
          }

          str +=  this.firstName + ' ' + this.lastName;
          return str;
        }
      }
    };

    res.send(json2html(users[parseInt(req.params.index) || 0],
      data));
});
```

View helpers and application-level data

Things tend to get messy when including a lot of control-flow statements into our templates, such as `if` statements. You might have even noticed this from some of the previous examples.

The first step to clean this up would be to extract the logic from the templates into functions (view helpers). They can reside either in the route handler or, better yet, in a separate folder. An example of such a function would be the one used to construct the full name of a user:

```
function getFullName(firstName, lastName) {
  return firstName + ' ' + lastName;
}
```

Now, we can pass this function as a local variable to the template and invoke it from there, as shown in the following snippet:

```
// route handler
res.render('index', {
  user: users[parseInt(req.params.index) || 0],
  getFullName: getFullName
});
// ejs template
<%= getFullName(user.firstName, user.lastName) %>
```

It's a bit better now since we removed that inline logic, and we can reuse this function for multiple views. However, this can be kind of tedious because we would have to pass the same function over and over again each time `render` gets called.

An even better way to do this is to make this function globally accessible for all the templates, without having to pass it as a parameter to the `render` function. We can do this by assigning it as a property on the `app.locals` object provided by Express:

```
app.locals.getFullName = getFullName;
```

Besides the view helpers, we can assign other application-level variables such as the application title or contact e-mail for the admin.

Express only exposes one application level, variable by default, which is called `settings`. Every time we set a property using `app.set()`, which will be automatically visible in the templates using the settings variable, we don't need to manually include it again by using `app.locals`. The code for `settings` might look like the following snippet:

```
{ 'x-powered-by': true,
  etag: true,
  env: 'development',
  'subdomain offset': 2,
  view: [Function: View],
  views: '/Users/alexandruvladutu/www/mastering_express/chapter_04/ ',
  'jsonp callback name': 'callback',
  'json spaces': 2,
  'view engine': 'html' }
```

It's worth mentioning that other template engines such as Handlebars.js allow us to register custom helpers on the engine object itself. For more information, you can visit `https://github.com/wycats/handlebars.js/#registering-helpers`.

 Handlebars.js is a superset of Mustache that supports compiling and has other additional features such as the one mentioned previously. It is generally better suited than Mustache for larger projects.

Sharing code between templates with partial views

Partial views (more commonly known as partials) allow us to define commonly shared parts of a web page (for example, the header and the footer) that can be reused in multiple views.

Partials have been removed from Express since Version 3, and they are now template-specific, meaning it's the decision of the template engine to provide them or not.

Let's consider a sample application that has multiple pages but each one shares the header and the footer. For starters, we are going to create this application using EJS and then achieve the same with Jade.

The `server-ejs.js` file will initialize everything and render `index.html` as the main page of the application, as shown in the following code:

```
var express = require('express');
var ejs = require('ejs');
var app = express();

// assign the ejs engine to .html files
app.engine('html', ejs.renderFile);

// set .html as the default extension
app.set('view engine', 'html');
app.set('views', __dirname + '/views');

app.get('/', function(req, res, next) {
  res.render('index');
});

app.listen(7777);
```

> It's not necessary to create a view template with the `.html` extension, but some editors might not recognize the `.ejs` format, and this will make sure that at least the HTML syntax will be properly highlighted.

Next, we will just create the `index.html` template inside `/views` that contains some basic information:

```
<!DOCTYPE HTML>
<html lang="en">
<head>
  <meta charset="UTF-8">
  <title>Hello app</title>
</head>
<body>
  <header>
    <h1>Hello app!</h1>
  </header>
```

```
  Welcome from the main page!

  <footer>
    Mastering Express
  </footer>
</body>
</html>
```

When creating a new page each time, we will want to reuse the header and footer code, so let's extract it into `/views/header.html` and `/views/footer.html`. The `index.html` page should only contain the bits that are original to that page and include the partials:

```
<%- include header.html %>
  Welcome from the main page!
<%- include footer.html %>
```

 In the preceding code, we use `<%- content %>` to output unescaped content. To escape the HTML, we should use `<%= content %>` instead.

Now, if, for example, we want to create a search page, we will have to include the two partial views as well as the original content for that specific page:

```
<%- include header.html %>

<form action="/search" method="POST">
  <input type="text" name="term" />
  <input type="submit" value="search site" />
</form>

<%- include footer.html %>
```

EJS is not the only template engine that provides the partial view functionality; many others do so as well (such as Jade or Handlebars). Usually, this is achieved by using the `include` keyword.

DRY templates with layouts

Being able to reuse code using partials is a good thing, but it's still not ideal to copy all the include statements with the same partial views over and over again. When more than one page needs the same partial views, and they are located in different sections of the page (such as the header at the top and the footer at the bottom), it's not possible to make another partial that includes them and defines a placeholder for the content. That's where layouts come in handy.

With layouts, we can establish an inheritance-like system, where the subviews not only inherit code from a master view but also extend parts of it (usually called blocks).

Just like partial views, layouts are template-engine-specific, so they might be available or not (depending on which engine we use).

Jade supports layouts with the use of its extends and block citizens. A template can extend a layout and also fill in a certain gap/placeholder by using the block functionality.

As usual, we will create a simple server.js file at first, which does the initial setup and adds a route for the home page:

```
var express = require('express');
var jade = require('jade');
var app = express();

app.set('views', __dirname + '/views');

app.get('/', function(req, res, next) {
  res.render('index.jade');
});

app.listen(7777);
```

Next, we will create the layout.jade file inside /views, which will contain two placeholders: one for content inside the head section and another one for the main content of the website:

```
doctype html
html
  head
    block head
  body
    #container
      block content
```

Now, in the `index.jade` file, we will need to reference the `layout.jade` file (let the engine know we are extending it) and define the content for the two blocks:

```
extends layout

block head
  title App homepage

block content
  h1 Hello && welcome to the homepage!
```

Template engine consolidation with consolidate.js

Not all template engines have out-of-the-box support for Express, nor do they have the same API.

Consolidate.js (`https://github.com/visionmedia/consolidate.js`) is meant to help with that and provides the same function signature for the various template engines it supports. Another benefit of this module is that it makes it easy to switch from one engine to another with minimal effort. The signature it supports is the same as the one used in Express: `(path[, locals], callback)`.

To use a certain template engine, we still have to install it with NPM, but the rest is just a few lines of code in our server setup:

```
var cons = require('consolidate');
app.engine(jade', cons.jade);
```

From this point on, we can just use `response.render()` as we have done before.

View caching in production

During development, it's useful to be able to make changes to the templates, refresh the browser, and see the new changes without having to reload the server.

However, when the application enters production, you would not want the template files to be read over and over again with each page load, because that would decrease throughput considerably.

The view cache setting and its effect

Express automatically enables the `view cache` setting when run in production mode, as shown in the following source code snippet:

```
if (env === 'production') {
  this.enable('view cache');
}
```

We can enable that flag by ourselves using `app.enable('view cache')`. This might be useful at times when we want to stress test our application, for example, but run it in a different environment mode (other than production).

Let's make a sample application using Jade that displays a list of users. We will check its throughput with the `view cache` setting disabled first and then with it enabled.

We will create a JSON file called `users.json` with dummy user records, so here's an example of some items from the array:

```
[{
    "id": 0,
    "employed": false,
    "age": 33,
    "name": "Daniels Richmond",
    "gender": "male",
    "company": "Dogtown",
    "email": "danielsrichmond@dogtown.com",
    "friends": [
        {
            "id": 0,
            "name": "Harding Terrell"
        },
        {
            "id": 1,
            "name": "Nichols Carey"
        },
        {
            "id": 2,
            "name": "Mai Bradley"
        }
    ]
},
    {
        "id": 1,
        "employed": false,
        "age": 21,
```

```
                "name": "Molly Fields",
                "gender": "female",
                "company": "Xleen",
                "email": "mollyfields@xleen.com",
                "friends": [
                    {
                        "id": 0,
                        "name": "Tameka Sears"
                    },
                    {
                        "id": 1,
                        "name": "Bean Hebert"
                    },
                    {
                        "id": 2,
                        "name": "Antonia Williamson"
                    }
                ]
            }
        ]
```

The `server.js` file is straightforward; it requires the users, does the initial setup, and assigns the route handler to the `/users` path:

```
var express = require('express');
var jade = require('jade');
var app = express();

app.engine('jade', jade.renderFile);
app.set('views', __dirname + '/views');

var users = require('./users.json');

app.get('/users', function(req, res, next) {
  res.render('users.jade', { users: users });
});

app.listen(7777);
```

Now, for the last piece of the puzzle, we will create the view file that renders the users:

```
doctype html
html(lang="en")
  head
    title Sample page that lists users details
```

```
body
  h1 Sample page that lists users details
  ul
    each user in users
      li
        p(class="user-item")
          strong Name:
          | #{user.name}
        p(class="user-item")
          strong Age:
          | #{user.age}
        p(class="user-item")
          strong Gender:
          | #{user.gender}
        p(class="user-item")
          strong Friends:
          ul
            each friend in user.friends
              li=friend.name
```

All that we do in this template is iterate through the list of users, and for each user, display some properties such as name, gender, age, or friends.

If we start the server and visit the /users URL in the browser, we should see the following page:

Sample page that lists users details

- **Name:** Daniels Richmond

  Age: 33

  Gender: male

  Friends:

    - Harding Terrell
    - Nichols Carey
    - Mai Bradley

- **Name:** Molly Fields

  Age: 21

  Gender: female

  Friends:

    - Tameka Sears
    - Bean Hebert
    - Antonia Williamson

- **Name:** Burnett Riddle

  Age: 25

  Gender: male

Now that we have our server running in development mode, it's time to see how many requests per second the /users page can handle with view caching disabled. We will use the ab (Apache Benchmark) tool:

```
$ ab -n 300 -c 10 http://127.0.0.1:7777/users
```

 There are other HTTP benchmarking tools out there, such as wrk (https://github.com/wg/wrk), siege (http://www.joedog.org/siege-home/), and httperf (http://www.hpl.hp.com/research/linux/httperf/).

The output will include the number of requests per second:

```
Requests per second:    46.53 [#/sec] (mean)
```

We found out that it can support 46 requests per second; that's not great at all. The next step is to run the application in production mode (with view caching enabled) and see how it behaves:

```
$ NODE_ENV=production node server.js
$ ab -n 300 -c 10 http://127.0.0.1:7777/users
```

The result is as follows:

```
Requests per second:    1036.98 [#/sec] (mean)
```

That's more than 20 times the number of requests it can handle without view caching enabled, which is really impressive.

However, what happens exactly to justify this enormous difference between development and production (view caching disabled and then enabled)? Without caching enabled, Jade has to perform the following steps:

- Read the file from the disk
- Parse the input and compile it into a JavaScript function
- Run the compiled JavaScript function with the locals (dynamic data)

When caching is enabled, Jade will only perform these three steps once for a specific filename and then store the compiled function into the cache. For all subsequent requests that use the same filename, Jade will only run the compiled function with the data, because it already has it in the cache. This means instead of performing three steps, Jade will skip to the final step and basically run a function using locals as the argument.

These operations aren't exclusive to Jade; most template engines act in the same way, so be sure to run your application in production mode (`NODE_ENV=production`) or manually enable `view cache` when it matters (in production mode or while performing load testing, for example).

Clearing the cache without a restart

The performance improvements with the cache enabled are significant, but there is a problem that we often need to tackle, that is, how to cache the views while simultaneously allowing them to be updated without restarting the server.

We could simply spin up new processes that use the updated templates and get rid of the old processes one by one (known as zero downtime redeploys). That feels like overkill since we only want to update the views code, like we did during development, and not the rest of the application.

There is a way to benefit from view caching as well as from being able to clear the cache at some point in time for most template engines. These template engines either have a `cache` object that can be manipulated or can provide a function that can be used for clearing the cache.

Next, we will look at how to clear the cache when using EJS, Jade, Handlebars (more specifically, the `express-hbs` module), and Swig.

First, we will create the `server.js` file that renders a view with each of these templates:

```
var express = require('express');
var app = express();

var ejs = require('ejs');
var jade = require('jade');
var hbs = require('express-hbs');
var swig = require('swig');

app.set('views', __dirname + '/views');

app.engine('hbs', hbs.express3({
  partialsDir: [__dirname + '/views']
}));

app.engine('swig', swig.renderFile);
```

```
app.get('/', function(req, res, next) {
  res.render('example.ejs');
});

app.get('/jade', function(req, res, next) {
  res.render('example.jade');
});

app.get('/hbs', function(req, res, next) {
  res.render('example.hbs');
});

app.get('/swig', function(req, res, next) {
  res.render('example.swig');
});

app.listen(7777);
```

The example.<template extension> files will only contain static data, as we are only testing the feature. If we read the source code of these template engines, we will discover that Jade and Handlebars (express-hbs) have a cache object, while Swig and EJS both have functions for cache invalidation. The easiest way to integrate this cache-clearing feature is to create a GET route that triggers it:

```
app.get('/clean-cache', function(req, res, next) {
  swig.invalidateCache();
  ejs.clearCache();
  jade.cache = {};
  hbs.cache = {};

  res.end('Cache cleared');
});
```

To test the clearing functionality, we need to run the application in production mode and visit the relevant URLs in the browser (or just use cURL) so that the cache is built:

```
$ NODE_ENV=production node server.js
```

After modifying the sources for the views, we need to visit /clean-cache to clear the cache (the whole cache for the views), and voila; if we visit /swig or /ejs for example, the content will be updated.

This works but requires an extra step besides modifying the view files, so it's not ideal. There are several ways in which we can improve this in production:

- Watch the `views` folder and clear the cache when changing a file (this works well if we don't have the application running on multiple servers but on a single server)

- Create a post-commit hook that checks whether the view files have changed and triggers the cache invalidation (by making a request or sending a message using a message queue)

- If the application needs to scale across multiple processes, then a good option would be to use a shared cache and have a separate job to take are of the update

We'll explore the first option to watch the `views` folder for file changes using the `watch` module from NPM, and invalidate the cache once such a change occurs. To achieve this, we only need to add a few lines of code to our existing example:

```
var watch = require('watch');
watch.createMonitor(__dirname + '/views', function(monitor) {
  monitor.on("changed", function(file) {
    swig.invalidateCache();
    ejs.clearCache();
    jade.cache = {};
    hbs.cache = {};
  });
});
```

 Another module we could have used instead of `watch` for watching a file is `chokidar` (https://www.npmjs.org/package/chokidar).

Integrating a template engine with Express

In the remaining part of the chapter, we are going to integrate a template engine with Express, specifically the `template` function from the `lodash` module (this can be applied for other template engines too).

But what do we have to do exactly? We are going to tackle the following issues:

- How the template engine's rendering function gets called (what arguments are called)
- What the function should return
- Caching and cache invalidation
- Partials and layouts

The rendering function from Express calls the template engine function with the following arguments:

- The path of the template file
- The locals passed to the `response.render` function when called (as the second argument)
- A callback function that should be called with the (`error` and `content`) arguments

Let's make a small sample application and an empty view file and see exactly what gets logged to the console:

```
app.set('views', __dirname + '/views');
app.engine('html', function() {
  console.log(arguments);
});

app.get('/', function(req, res, next) {
  res.render('home', {
    firstLocal: 1,
    secondLocal: 2
  });
});
```

If we start the application and visit the home page, we should get the following output:

```
alexandruvladutu at MBP in ~/www/mastering_express_code/chapter04/integrating
-template-engine on master*
$ node simple.js
{ '0': '/Users/alexandruvladutu/www/mastering_express_code/chapter04/integrat
ing-template-engine/views/home.html',
  '1':
   { settings:
      { 'x-powered-by': true,
        etag: true,
        env: 'development',
        'subdomain offset': 2,
        view: [Function: View],
        views: '/Users/alexandruvladutu/www/mastering_express_code/chapter04/
integrating-template-engine/views',
        'jsonp callback name': 'callback',
        'json spaces': 2,
        'view engine': 'html' },
     APP_NAME: 'Sample Express App',
     firstLocal: 1,
     secondLocal: 2,
     _locals: [Function: locals],
     cache: false },
  '2': [Function] }
```

Express exposed the application's settings variable to the templates, but we also see a cache Boolean variable as well. When the view caching setting is enabled, the cache variable will be set to true.

Let's create a sample project and start working on the template engine's integration in the engine.js file. First, we will include the module dependencies and initialize the cache:

```
var fs = require('fs');
var path = require('path');
var _ = require('lodash');

exports.cache = {};
```

In the following code, we will create the main `renderFile` function that will call the `render` function using the file path, cache, and data parameters:

```
exports.renderFile = function(filePath, data, callback) {
  var isCacheEnabled = !!data.settings['view cache'];

  try {
    var tmpl = exports.render(filePath, isCacheEnabled, data);
    return setImmediate(callback.bind(null, null, tmpl));
  }
  catch(err) {
    return setImmediate(callback.bind(null, err));
  }
};
```

The main function, `render`, does the following things:

- If the cache is set and the compiled template exists, send the evaluated result
- If the cache is not set, then read the file, compile the template, store it in the cache, and send the evaluated result back
- While compiling the template, check whether there is `<% extend layoutPath %>` somewhere, replace it with the content from `layoutPath` (that will be the way of defining layouts), and place the current content in the layout within the `<% body %>` placeholder

The code for this function will therefore be as follows:

```
exports.render = function(filePath, isCacheEnabled, data) {
  var layoutPath, compiledFn;

  if (!isCacheEnabled || (isCacheEnabled &&
    !exports.cache[filePath])) {
    content = fs.readFileSync(filePath, 'utf8').replace(/<%
      extends (.*) %>/, function(arg1, p) {
      layoutPath = path.resolve(data.settings.views, p);
      return '';
    });

    if (layoutPath) {
      content = fs.readFileSync(layoutPath, 'utf8').replace('<%
        body %>', content);
    }
```

```
      // compile template
      content = exports.compileTemplate(content,
        data.settings.views);
      compiledFn = content;

      // cache the compiled template if caching enabled
      if (isCacheEnabled && !exports.cache[filePath]) {
        exports.cache[filePath] = content;
      }
    } else {
      // compiled function can be found in cache
      compiledFn = exports.cache[filePath];
    }

    // evaluate the compiled function
    return compiledFn(data || {});
  };
```

 In the previous code, we are making synchronous calls while reading the content of the template, which we shouldn't normally do. Because the content is cached after the first read, the `readFileSync()` function will be called only once per template. This makes for an acceptable use case for the synchronous function.

There are two pieces left to complete this template engine puzzle: compiling the template and making sure partials are supported.

The code for including partials will be similar to the code used for including the layout, but with the difference that we will have to perform a recursive check in each partial view to see whether it includes another view. This wasn't the case for layouts as only a single layout is supported. Here is the implementation for the remaining two methods:

```
exports.getPartials = function(template, currentPath) {
  return template.replace(/<% include (.*) %>/g, function(arg1,
    filePath) {
    var fullPath = path.resolve(currentPath, filePath);
    var content = fs.readFileSync(fullPath, 'utf8');

    if (/<% include (.*) %>/.test(content)) {
      return exports.getPartials(content, path.dirname(fullPath));
    }
```

```
      return content;
    });
};

exports.compileTemplate = function(template, viewsPath) {
    template = exports.getPartials(template, viewsPath);

    return _.template(template);
};
```

This concludes the work for our template engine integration; it's now time to take it for a spin. As always, we'll write the code for `server.js` first and then create the templates:

```
var express = require('express');
var app = express();

var tmpl = require('./engine');

app.locals.APP_NAME = 'Sample Express App';

app.set('views', __dirname + '/views');
app.set('view engine', 'html');
app.engine('html', tmpl.renderFile);

app.get('/', function(req, res, next) {
    res.render('home', { pageTitle: 'home' });
});

app.get('/now', function(req, res, next) {
    res.render('now', { pageTitle: 'now' });
});

var watch = require('watch')
watch.createMonitor(__dirname + '/views', function(monitor) {
    monitor.on("changed", function(file) {
        tmpl.cache = {};
    });
});

app.listen(7777);
```

There is nothing special about this file; we make the initial setup, declare the routes, and clear the view cache on file changes.

Next, let's create the `layout.html` file inside `/views` so that we can test both the layout and the partial functionality:

```
<% include header.html %>
<% body %>
<% include footer.html %>
```

Here, we actually include two partial files and specify the location for the main content (using `<% body %>`). The header and footer files are pretty basic; the only thing to note is that the header will include two variables, as shown in the following code:

```
// header.html file follows:
<!DOCTYPE HTML>
<html lang="en">
<head>
  <meta charset="UTF-8">
  <title><%= APP_NAME %></title>
</head>
<body>

  <h1><%= pageTitle %></h1>


// footer.html file follows:
  <hr />
  Copyright might be here.

</body>
</html>
```

The remaining view files are `home.html` and `now.html`; both of them extend the layout. The `now.html` file also displays the current timestamp. You can see the code for both of them as follows:

```
// home.html
<% extends layout.html %>

<p>Welcome to the homepage!</p>


// now.html
<% extends layout.html %>

<h2>Current time: </h2>
```

```
<p>
    <%= new Date() %>
</p>
```

The project is complete, so let's boot up the server in production mode using the following command line:

```
$ NODE_ENV=production node server.js
```

If we visit the main page, we should see the following page:

The (dynamic) page title was successfully displayed. The layout was extended, and we know that the partials system worked as well as the layout file used it.

We can also verify the clearing of the cache when a view file gets modified. In our code, we have watched the file changes using watch (https://www.npmjs.org/package/watch) and reset the cache once that happened. Let's modify the welcome message in the home page to **This is the homepage** and see whether the page gets updated:

The page indeed got updated, so that means the cache invalidation worked.

The last thing we need to take care of now is stress testing. We know that the cache invalidation functions correctly, but the easiest way to check whether the caching system itself is working (besides outputting debugging messages to the console) is to make some load tests for development and then production. For the sake of diversity, we will use the **wrk** (https://github.com/wg/wrk) tool this time with the same settings as the ones used to benchmark Express (https://github.com/visionmedia/express/blob/master/benchmarks/run). After running it, you should see an output similar to the following screenshot:

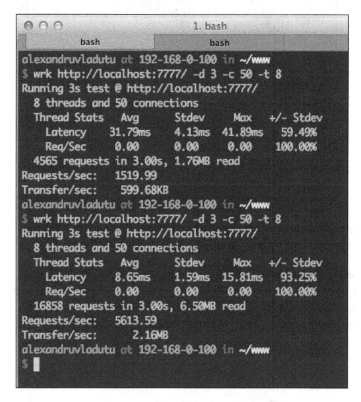

We run the first test with caching disabled (development mode) and can handle 1519 requests per second (because we don't have anything too complicated in the template). We run the second test with caching enabled (production mode) and it can handle approximately three times more requests per second.

We shouldn't interpret these results as being conclusive for what the server can handle in production because the views aren't too complicated (no conditionals, no loops, and little content). The scope of these tests, however, is to check two things:

- The server can handle a decent amount of requests per second with caching enabled.

- The difference between the two environments should be considerable (unless caching is enabled for all environments). This is a clear indicator that the application is not trying to read the views from the disk and compile them each time.

> These tests aren't a replacement for unit tests, but they are complementary. You should always create unit tests for the code you are writing.
>
> This template engine integration can be extracted into a separate module with its own repository that can be published to NPM. You can read more on tiny reusable modules at `https://gist.github.com/substack/5075355`.

Choosing a template engine

It's not easy to choose a template engine considering that there are so many of them available with different features. Instead of choosing a clear winner, we should focus on what criteria we should have in mind when selecting them:

- Do you plan on using it both with Express and the browser? A few examples include EJS, Handlebars.js, and Jade.

- Should it have logic or not? Some of them support regular JavaScript (such as EJS), others just have the basics, while the rest disallow logic inside templates.

- Is it widely used and maintained? To see a list of the most depended-on modules, check out the NPM registry (`https://www.npmjs.org/browse/depended`).

- Should it be the best performing? It would be good to run benchmarks with potential use cases and see how they perform. However, if you are using a caching mechanism to store the whole responses, you might not need to touch the template engine more than a few times.

- Does it precompile templates or not?

- Should it support streaming?

These are just a couple of questions you should be asking yourself before choosing a template engine. In the end, it's a subjective choice, and therefore, there's no clear winner.

[You can find a tool to help you choose a template engine at
`http://garann.github.io/template-chooser/`.]

Summary

In this chapter, we learned how to differentiate template engines and what the characteristics of each category are. We then studied how to extract complex logic from templates to view helpers and how to make globally-accessed variables (for all the views).

By using layouts and partial views, we managed to eliminate repetition and keep our code base DRY.

Next, we tackled the importance of view caching and how to clear the cache without restarting the server once the templates have been updated.

In the final part of the chapter, we integrated a template engine with Express by providing the correct function signature needed by the framework as well as other advanced features such as partials, layouts, and caching.

In the next chapter, we will look at other modules and techniques that help us keep our code base DRY. We will discover ways of handling control flow with tiny modules, elegant error checking, creating custom errors, and making sure callbacks are executed only once.

5
Reusable Patterns for
a DRY Code Base

When creating web applications with Express or Node in general, there are situations that keep repeating, and we handle them by writing the same code over and over again. In this chapter, we will create a sample application and then refactor it to eliminate the duplicated logic using the existing NPM modules.

In this chapter, we will cover the following topics:

- Eliminating the `if (err) {}` pieces of code spread throughout our application
- Using control-flow modules instead of counters and avoiding a tree-like code structure
- Ensuring that the callback method execution only happens once
- Extending objects in a reusable way with properties
- Creating custom errors without having to manually define them and their properties each time

The repetitive code portions found in our sample application are common to most Express applications. They are not something specifically catered for the purpose of this chapter alone.

Creating the MovieApp sample application

Throughout this chapter, we will create a sample movie application using **The Movie Database API** provided at `http://www.themoviedb.org/`. This application will allow users to search for movies by name, browse the results, and view a page containing the details of a specific movie (such as the cast, release date, trailer, and so on).

In the first version of our code, we are not going to use any NPM modules besides the one used for communicating with the API. This means that we will use raw Node for things such as control-flow, error handling, extending objects, or to ensure that the callbacks get executed once.

After that, we will eliminate code repetition step by step for each of these topics and introduce the NPM modules that will do most of the work for us.

Before we begin writing the code, we will need to register and create an API key on the site and check out the documentation available at `http://docs.themoviedb.apiary.io`.

Application structure and required modules

To have a better picture of the files and folders used by the project in a tree-view-like form, there is a really handy command-line tool named `tree`.

 The `tree` tool might not be installed by default for some operating systems, such as Windows or Mac. To install it on Mac, you can use homebrew (`brew install tree`), while for Windows, you can download it from `http://gnuwin32.sourceforge.net/packages/tree.htm`.

We don't want to see the files stored inside the `node_modules` folder, so we will be using the `-I` flag. In the root of the project, we need to execute the following command in the terminal:

```
$ tree -I node_modules
```

The result will be similar to the following screenshot:

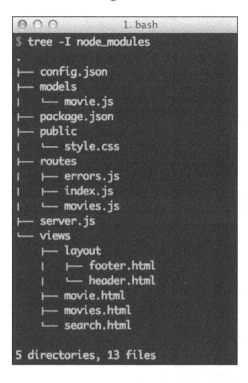

As you can see in the screenshot, we will have the following files and folders:

- The `server.js` file will contain the `express` startup code
- The `config.json` file will hold our API key to access `http://www.themoviedb.org/`
- The basic CSS style sheet for the application will be put inside the `public` folder
- The `movie.js` file under the `models` folder will contain the functions needed to communicate with the external API and process the results
- The `routes` folder will have two files: one for the movie-related routes and another for handling the errors
- The `views` application will reside inside the `views` folder
- The `package.json` file will define the dependencies, as always

Besides the `express` module, we will use the `ejs` module for templates, `body-parser` to populate `req.body` with the parsed request bodies, and the `moviedb` module to communicate with the external REST API.

Let's create the `package.json` file next using the NPM wizard, and then install the following modules:

```
$ npm init
$ npm i express ejs body-parser moviedb -save
```

 Instead of typing npm `install` each time, we will install a new module and use the shorthand version instead, namely npm `i`.

Creating the server.js file

To get started with the application, we will create its main entry point, named `server.js`. This file will contain the initialization of the Express application, set up the view logic, load the middleware and the routes, as well as create the movie model.

This API key will be used to initialize the model object inside `server.js` and is loaded as an environment variable. This object will be stored as the `movie` property on the request, so we can easily access it from the route handlers.

The complete code for the file is as follows:

```
var bodyParser = require('body-parser');
var express = require('express');
var app = express();
var config = require('./config');

app.set('view engine', 'html');
app.set('views', __dirname + '/views');
app.engine('html', require('ejs').renderFile);

app.use(bodyParser());
app.use(express.static(__dirname + '/public'));

var Movie = require('./models/movie');
var movie = new Movie(process.env.API_KEY);

app.use(function(req, res, next) {
  req.movie = movie;
  next();
});
```

```
var routes = require('./routes');
app.get('/', routes.movies.search);
app.get('/movies', routes.movies.index);
app.get('/movies/:id', routes.movies.show);
app.all('*', routes.errors.handleNotFound);

app.use(routes.errors.handleInternalError);

app.listen(7777);
```

> Here, we are extending the request object with the movie model,
> making it available throughout our route handlers. Another
> approach would be to add the object creation functionality in its own
> file and export it as a singleton. These two approaches are similar, but
> the first one is more convenient because we don't need to have the
> movie object inside each route.

Creating the route handlers

We will create two route files for this application (index.js will just export these files into a single object): one for movies (movies.js), and another one for handling different errors generated by the application (errors.js).

The movie route handlers will take care of the following cases:

- If there is a parameter required, check its validity and pass an error to the next() function
- Retrieve the dynamic data using model functions
- Render the view with the dynamic data (except for the search page)

The complete code for the movies.js file is as follows:

```
exports.search = function(req, res, next) {
  res.render('search', {
    pageTitle: 'Search for movies'
  });
};

exports.index = function(req, res, next) {
  if (!req.query.title) {
```

```
      var err = new Error('Missing search param');
      err.code = 422;
      return next(err);
  }

  req.movie.search(req.query.title, function(err, movies) {
    if (err) { return next(err); }

    res.render('movies', {
      pageTitle: 'Search results for ' + req.query.title,
      movies: movies
    });
  });
};

exports.show = function(req, res, next) {
  if (!/^\d+$/.test(req.params.id)) {
    var err = new Error('Bad movie id');
    err.code = 422;
    return next(err);
  }

  req.movie.getMovie(req.params.id, function(err, movie) {
    if (err) { return next(err); }

    res.render('movie', {
      pageTitle: movie.title,
      movie: movie
    });
  });
};
```

The errors.js file is a lot slimmer, having two functions that handle the display of different errors (by looking at their status code) and not of the found pages:

```
var STATUS_CODES = require('http').STATUS_CODES;

// 500 - Internal Server Error
exports.handleInternalError = function(err, req, res, next) {
  var html = '';

  if (err.code === 404 || /not found/.test(err.message)) {
    return exports.handleNotFound(req, res, next);
```

```
    } else if (err.code && STATUS_CODES[err.code]) {
      html = '<h1>' + err.code + ' - ' + STATUS_CODES[err.code] +
        '</h1>';
      html += '<p>' + err.message + '</p>';

      res.send(err.code, html);
    } else {
      console.error(err.stack);
      res.send(500, '<h1>500 - Internal Server Error</h1>');
    }
};

exports.handleNotFound = function(req, res, next) {
  res.send(404, '<h1>404 - Page Not Found</h1>');
};
```

Doing the heavy lifting inside the model

After defining the constructor of our model class, we will create a function
to get the configuration (the images' base path and poster sizes interest us):

```
var mdb = require('moviedb');

function Movie(API_KEY) {
  if (!API_KEY) { throw new Error('API_KEY is required'); }

  this.client = mdb(API_KEY);
  this.imagesPath = '';
  this.posterSizes = '';
}

Movie.prototype.getConfiguration = function(callback) {
  var that = this;

  if (!this.imagesPath) {
    this.client.configuration(function(err, config) {
      if (err) { return callback(err); }

      that.imagesPath = config.images.base_url;
      that.posterSizes = config.images.poster_sizes;

      callback();
    });
```

```
    } else {
      process.nextTick(callback);
    }
  };
```

The `getFullImagePath` method takes the relative path of an image as the first parameter and retrieves the full image path. The second parameter of the function that is taken into consideration is the size, which is included in the generated path and is a string (the possible values returned by the configuration API call at the moment are `'w92'`, `'w154'`, `'w185'`, `'w342'`, `'w500'`, `'w780'`, and `'original'`):

```
Movie.prototype.getFullImagePath = function(relativePath, size) {
    if (!relativePath) { return ''; }

    if (!size) {
      // Default to the smallest size
      size = this.posterSizes[0];
    } else {
      var index = this.posterSizes.indexOf(size);
      size = this.posterSizes[index];

      if (!size) {
        throw new Error('unknown image size');
      }
    }

    return this.imagesPath + size + relativePath;
  };
```

The `search` method is fairly simple; it retrieves the movies that match a certain string and converts the relative images' paths to full URLs:

```
Movie.prototype.search = function(title, callback) {
    var that = this;

    this.getConfiguration(function(err) {
      if (err) { return callback(err); }

      that.client.searchMovie({ query: title }, function(err, movies) {
        if (err) { return callback(err); }

        // Convert relative to full path
        movies.results.forEach(function(movie) {
```

```
            movie.poster_path =
                that.getFullImagePath(movie.poster_path);
        });

        callback(null, movies);
      });
    });
};
```

The majority of the code is located within the `getMovie` method, which does a lot of things in the following order:

1. Retrieves the movie details based on its ID.

2. After this, it makes two parallel requests to get the trailer and the cast.

3. For each cast member, it then retrieves that person's details, again using parallel requests.

4. Once the two previous actions are finished, it returns the aggregated results in a single movie object.

A thing to note in the code for this method is that we are not using any control-flow library; instead, for parallel requests, we are using a counter that decreases until it reaches 0 and then executes the `callback` function. The first control-flow function looks like the following code:

```
var doneCalled = false;
var tasksCount = 2;
var done = function(err) {
  if (doneCalled) { return; }

  if (err) {
    doneCalled = true;
    return callback(err);
  };

  tasksCount--;

  if (tasksCount === 0) {
    movieInfo.trailers = trailers;
    movieInfo.cast = cast;

    callback(null, movieInfo);
  }
};
```

Both of the two main functions inside the `getMovie` method will call the `done` function, which in turn will know when to call the main `callback` function.

We will apply the same logic to retrieve the details of the cast members. This time, the counter will be set to the number of existing members:

```
var cb = function(err) {
  if (called) { return; }

  if (err) {
    called = true;
    return done(err);
  };

  count--;

  if (count === 0) {
    that.getConfiguration(function(err) {
      if (err) { return done(err); }

      movieInfo.poster_path =
        that.getFullImagePath(movieInfo.poster_path, 'w185');

      done();
    });
  }
};
```

The complete code for this method is available in the code bundle provided with the book.

Wrapping it up

The remaining files of the application are the templates and the CSS style sheet, which we won't show here since they are simple and beyond the scope of this chapter. You can find them in the source code accompanying the book.

Basically, there are three pages in this application; the first page shows a basic search form, the second page displays the results, and the final page shows the details of a movie. Here's how the movie details page should look once you have installed the required modules, started the application, and followed the steps previously described:

Error checks and callback functions

A well-established pattern with the Node programs is to have an error argument as the first parameter of the `callback` function, since we cannot use try-catch for asynchronous code and we also don't want our programs to break each time an error occurs.

The most common line found in our sample application is the one that checks for an error and returns early by executing the `callback` function with the error parameter:

```
if (err) { return callback(err); }
// or:
if (err) { return next(err); }
```

If there is no error, the rest of the code that follows will execute.

Luckily for us, there are some modules that can help us avoid having to write this boilerplate code each time we need to delegate the error to the `callback` function. These modules are available at the following URLs:

- `https://www.npmjs.org/package/errto`
- `https://www.npmjs.org/package/okay`
- `https://www.npmjs.org/package/err-handler`

Each of these modules provides a function that takes two parameters and should be used as the `callback` argument to the asynchronous function. The two parameters are as follows:

- The function that should be executed early if there's an error (we can call it the error handler)
- The function that should be executed if there was no error; the success handler will be called with the rest of the parameters passed to the `callback` function (other than the error)

The `errTo` module consists of just a couple of lines of code to achieve this:

```
var slice = Array.prototype.slice;

module.exports = function(errorHandler, successHandler) {
  var called = false;
  function errTo(err) {
    if (called) return; // Ignore all calls after the first one.
    called = true;

    if (err) {
      if (errorHandler && !errorHandler._errToCalled) {
        errorHandler._errToCalled = true; // Prevent calling
          error handler several times.
        errorHandler.apply(this, slice.call(arguments, 0));
      }
    } else {
      if (successHandler) {
        successHandler.apply(this, slice.call(arguments, 1)); //
          Give all arguments except err.
      }
    }
  };
```

```
    errTo.errorHandler = errorHandler;
    errTo.successHandler = successHandler;
    return errTo;
};
```

As you can see from its source code, the errTo module does a simple check to see whether the first parameter of the function is the error and calls the error handler if it is. For the success use case, it calls the other handler with the rest of the arguments except the error (which should be null or undefined).

Now, it's time to see how we can actually improve parts of our code by integrating the errTo module. An example would be the following code inside the show function (routes/movies.js):

```
req.movie.getMovie(req.params.id, function(err, movie) {
    if (err) { return next(err); }

    res.render('movie', {
        pageTitle: movie.title,
        movie: movie
    });
});
```

After we update the callback of the getMovie function to use the errTo module, it will look like the following:

```
req.movie.getMovie(req.params.id, errTo(next, function(movie) {
    res.render('movie', {
        pageTitle: movie.title,
        movie: movie
    });
}));
```

Besides the route handlers (where we constantly delegate the error to next()), the model has a lot of places that can benefit by using this approach.

Tiny modules for better control flow

In the getMovie() function from the movie.js model file, there are two places where we are performing parallel tasks. In both scenarios, we are creating counters and decrementing them in a custom callback function (called done or cb) that is executed when each asynchronous task finishes (the counters reach 0), and in the end, the main callback function is run.

Another thing we have taken care of in the custom `callback` function is whether or not the main `callback` function has been invoked (because passing an error argument at least once to the custom `callback` function will trigger this).

To get a better picture of the custom `callback` code, check out the following snippet:

```
var doneCalled = false;
var tasksCount = 2;
var done = function(err) {
  if (doneCalled) { return; }

  if (err) {
    doneCalled = true;
    return callback(err);
  };

  tasksCount--;

  if (tasksCount === 0) {
    movieInfo.trailers = trailers;
    movieInfo.cast = cast;

    callback(null, movieInfo);
  }
};
```

Fortunately, there is a module that can help us out with these kinds of situations, so we don't have to manually define custom callbacks that get executed each time a task is completed. This module is called `after` (https://www.npmjs.org/package/after), and its signature is straightforward. It takes two parameters: a number (related to the number of concurrent tasks) and a `callback` function to be executed when the tasks are completed. Here's a small example:

```
var next = after(number, callback);
```

We first have to call the module function with the two parameters. The result is another function that we invoke each time a task is completed.

We can, therefore, rewrite the preceding custom `callback` function as follows:

```
var done = after(2, errTo(callback, function() {
  movieInfo.trailers = trailers;
  movieInfo.cast = cast;

  callback(null, movieInfo);
}));
```

This version is lighter and focuses on the things that are indeed unique to the done function: extending the `movieInfo` object and invoking the main `callback` function.

We can refactor the other custom `callback` function that retrieves the cast's details concurrently as well:

```
var next = after(credits.cast.length, errTo(done, function(err) {
  that.getConfiguration(errTo(done, function() {
    movieInfo.poster_path =
      that.getFullImagePath(movieInfo.poster_path, 3);

    done();
  }));
}));
```

In the model code, there aren't many levels of indentation, but without using a control-flow library in some complex situations, the source code can resemble a tree and become harder to read.

The `async-series` (`https://www.npmjs.org/package/async-series`) module can make our lives easier because it allows us to run a series of asynchronous functions in a sequence. We have to pass them as the first argument representing an array, while the other parameter consists of a `callback` function that gets executed when all of them have finished.

Although the `search` function inside the model is pretty small, we can still update it to use the `async-series` module so that it's more clear which actions execute in which order. The original code for the function is (after applying the `errTo` update) as follows:

```
Movie.prototype.search = function(title, callback) {
  var that = this;

  this.getConfiguration(errTo(callback, function() {
    that.client.searchMovie({ query: title }, errTo(callback,
      function(movies) {
      // Convert relative to full path.
      movies.results.forEach(function(movie) {
        movie.poster_path =
          that.getFullImagePath(movie.poster_path);
      });

      callback(null, movies);
    }));
  }));
};
```

Now, after we have applied the changes, it will become the following code:

```
Movie.prototype.search = function(title, callback) {
  var that = this;
  var movies = {};

  series([
    function(next) {
      that.getConfiguration(next);
    },
    function(next) {
      that.client.searchMovie({ query: title }, errTo(next,
        function(mov) {
        // Convert relative to full path.
        mov.results.forEach(function(movie) {
          movie.poster_path =
            that.getFullImagePath(movie.poster_path);
        });

        movies = mov;

        next();
      }));
    }
  ], errTo(callback, function() {
    callback(null, movies);
  }));
};
```

This isn't a dramatic change since we don't have a lot of nested indentation levels, but this makes it clearer that the functions are executed sequentially. The same changes can be applied to the `getMovie()` function, but consider that homework.

There are a ton of control-flow modules out there. And in the end, it comes down to personal preference, but the point of this exercise is to show you that lightweight and simple alternatives are available and that they can be easily integrated in our projects to improve the existing code base.

Ensuring a single callback execution

We have used the `after` module to handle the parallel task, and this module does internal checks to ensure that the `callback` function has not already been executed. This check usually needs to be done because a function could be called with an error argument, triggering the callback function to be executed early. If the callback function has been run with an error parameter, we don't care about sending the final result after all the tasks have finished, because we expect the callback function to be executed only once.

Let's take a moment to reflect on the `done` callback function before using the `after` module to modify it:

```
var doneCalled = false;
var tasksCount = 2;
var done = function(err) {
  if (doneCalled) { return; }

  if (err) {
    doneCalled = true;
    return callback(err);
  };

  tasksCount--;

  if (tasksCount === 0) {
    movieInfo.trailers = trailers;
    movieInfo.cast = cast;

    callback(null, movieInfo);
  }
};
```

There is a `doneCalled` Boolean variable that is set to `true` after the `callback` function has been invoked, so all the subsequent calls to the `done` function will not re-execute it.

Using a flag for this type of a check is a common thing (as we could see from the errTo source code as well); so, there is an NPM module that can help us out in this situation called once (https://www.npmjs.org/package/once). Instead of checking for a doneCalled variable each time, we can simply redefine the callback function using once without performing checks anymore, making our code look like the following code:

```
var tasksCount = 2;
callback = once(callback);
var done = function(err) {
  if (err) {
    return callback(err);
  };

  tasksCount--;

  if (tasksCount === 0) {
    movieInfo.trailers = trailers;
    movieInfo.cast = cast;

    callback(null, movieInfo);
  }
};
```

Extending objects in a reusable way

We have probably been confronted with situations where we have to assign multiple properties to the same object, as shown in the following example:

```
person.name = values[0];
person.age = values[1];
person.job = values[2];
```

In the preceding example, there are only three properties, but when we have more, it becomes kind of tedious to write object.property = value each time. There is a better way to do this: by using the xtend module (https://www.npmjs.org/package/xtend):

```
var xtend = require('xtend');
person = xtend(person, {
  name: values[0],
  age: values[1],
  job: values[2]
});
```

The preceding code looks much cleaner, doesn't it?

These properties from an object (the source) are merged into another object (the target). This approach enables us to use mixins efficiently and in an elegant manner.

> **Mixins** allow objects to reuse existing properties or functions (from other objects) without having to redefine them. This pattern facilitates the inheritance of a functionality from different sources, which makes it really valuable.

Taking a look back at our application, we can apply this to the following code:

```
movieInfo.trailers = trailers;
movieInfo.cast = cast;
```

The updated version will look as follows:

```
movieInfo = xtend(movieInfo, {
  trailers: trailers,
  cast: cast
});
```

Another use case for the xtend module (which is probably the most popular one) is to have some default settings that get merged with the settings manually specified as a parameter to the parent function.

A simple way to create custom errors

Sometimes, we need to create errors with additional properties so that we can treat them differently in our error handlers or simply to provide more information for logging and monitoring purposes.

Here are some practical examples extracted from our sample movie application (/routes/movies.js):

```
// First example.
if (!req.query.title) {
  var err = new Error('Missing search param');
  err.code = 422;
  return next(err);
}

// Second example.
if (!/^\d+$/.test(req.params.id)) {
  var err = new Error('Bad movie id');
  err.code = 422;
  return next(err);
}
```

Instead of directly calling `next()` using the error object, we need another two lines to create and extend it with the custom properties.

Fortunately, there are some modules that help us with this:

- `https://www.npmjs.org/package/custom-err`
- `https://www.npmjs.org/package/createerror`
- `https://www.npmjs.org/package/error-create`

The `custom-err` module accepts two parameters: the first parameter is the error message, and the second is a properties object. With this in mind, our two examples transform into the following code:

```
// At the top of the file.
var Err = require('custom-err');

// First example updated.
if (!req.query.title) {
  return next(Err('Missing search param', { code: 422 }));
}

// Second example updated.
if (!/^\d+$/.test(req.params.id)) {
  return next(Err('Bad movie id', { code: 422 }));
}
```

Now, instead of writing the same code snippet over and over again, we simply pass the newly-created error to the `callback` function.

Summary

In this chapter, we created a sample movie application that we have later refactored step by step to use the available NPM modules for keeping the code base DRY.

There are many tiny reusable modules that allow us to make the most out of code reuse. We have only tackled some of them in this chapter, but the NPM registry contains a lot more of these modules that await our attention.

In the next chapter, we are going to learn how to handle errors in our Express applications. We will be covering topics such as how to create a custom error handler, the different types of errors that can occur and how to handle them, enabling longer stack traces, and handling uncaught exceptions.

6
Error Handling

In this chapter, we will learn how to handle errors in the Express applications. More specifically, the following topics will be covered:

- Error categories — runtime and programmer errors
- Synchronous, asynchronous, and eventful errors
- Writing a custom Express error handler
- Return errors, not strings
- Handling uncaught exceptions
- Longer stack traces

Most of these topics not only apply to the Express applications but also to the Node applications in general, so try not to skim through this chapter. To make it more interesting, we will be creating a Wall microblogging application (from scratch), where people can publish posts and be notified in real time about the updates.

Runtime (operational) errors and human errors

There are two big categories of errors: those that happen at runtime (also called **operational** errors) and bugs caused by programmers.

Some examples of the runtime errors include:

- System out of memory
- Failure to look up domains
- Database connection time out
- Failure to proxy requests because the server is down

These types of errors do not occur because our programs were badly written, but because a server is down, the network is unreliable, or some other problem that is not caused by an error in the code.

On the other hand, human errors are bugs and can be avoided, for instance:

- Trying to read a property of an object that may be undefined
- Calling a function with the wrong parameters
- Specifying a bad path when requiring a Node module

Operational errors are unavoidable and can happen in any program, so they must be dealt with. Programmer errors, on the other hand, cannot be dealt with reliably. In these situations, we should log the error and let the server crash.

Ways of delivering errors in the Node applications

Due to the asynchronous nature of Node, there are two additional ways to deliver errors while writing applications, besides the synchronous style: using callbacks that have the error as the first parameter and for the more complicated cases (streams, for example), emitting error events.

Throwing errors in the synchronous style

A common situation to throw errors synchronously is when we call a function with the wrong parameters, as shown in the following example:

```
function startServer(port) {
  if (typeof port !== 'number') {
    throw new Error('port should be a number');
  }

  // Do stuff.
}

startServer('8888');
```

The preceding program will throw an error (which can be caught using `try` and `catch`) because the parameter has a wrong type. There is a more elegant way to achieve the same result using the native `assert` module:

```
var assert = require('assert');

function startServer(port) {
  assert.equal(typeof (port), 'number', 'port should be a
    number');
  // Do stuff.
}

startServer('8888');
```

We can use `try` and `catch` to capture these synchronous errors thrown, as shown in the following example:

```
try {
  JSON.parse(input);
}
catch(err) {
  // Could not parse the input.
}
```

The error-first callback pattern

Since `try` and `catch` will not help us trap the errors for asynchronous operations, the `callback` function takes an error as the first argument usually, as shown in the following code:

```
var fs = require('fs');

fs.readFile('/i-dont-exist', function(err, content) {
  if (err) { /* handle the error here */ }

  // Success case.
});
```

When creating our own function, we should respect this pattern and have the error as the first argument of the callback function. It's important not to throw an error synchronously inside the asynchronous function since there is no clean way to catch it; this will blow up our program:

```
// word-count.js
var fs = require('fs');

function getWordCount(callback) {
  fs.readFile(__filename, 'utf-8', function(err, content) {
    // Bad, don't do this.
    // if (err) { throw err; }

    // The proper way.
    if (err) { return callback(err); }

    return callback(null, content.split(' ').length);
  });
}
```

The EventEmitter errors

In more complex situations, when there are objects that inherit the EventEmitter publish-subscribe functionality (such as streams), we cannot return a callback function with the error since there is no callback function to begin with. Instead, we can emit an error event when an error occurs, as shown in the following example:

```
// eventemitter-errors.js
var EventEmitter = require('events').EventEmitter;
var util = require('util');

function WalkyTalky() {
  setTimeout(function() {
    this.emit('error', new Error('sample error'));
  }.bind(this), 2000);
}

util.inherits(WalkyTalky, EventEmitter);

new WalkyTalky();
```

In the `getWordCount` example, we had a callback function with the error as the first argument (and we could potentially ignore it—not recommended at all). Now, if we forget to bind a handler to the `error` event, the program will crash, as shown in the preceding example (just as if we would have used `throw` directly).

A more concrete example is when dealing with streams and piping the output to a stream:

```
// stream-error.js
var fs = require('fs');

fs.createReadStream('/i-dont-exist')
  .on('error', function(err) {
    // Log the error and exit.
    console.error('Something bad happened with the stream: ' +
      err.message);
    process.exit(1);
  })
  .pipe(process.stdout);
```

Note that in the preceding example, we have handled the `error` event and chose to exit the program ourselves. However, there are situations when you can simply log the error and move on (when there are no reasons to crash the application).

Strings instead of errors as an antipattern

One of the worst things you can do is to throw or return a string instead of an error. However, why is that? Let's describe a few features that the error objects have:

- The stack property is fundamental, and it lets you know where the error originated from

- Different types that allow us to treat errors distinctly (using `instanceof` for example)

- Since an error is an object, we can assign custom properties on it

All of these functionalities are gone in an instant when you use strings instead of errors. However, let's take a look at a practical example:

```
// err-vs-string.js
var fs = require('fs');

function getWordCount(filename, callback) {
  fs.readFile(filename, 'utf-8', function(err, content) {
    if (err) { return callback(err); }

    return callback(null, content.split(' ').length);
  });
}

getWordCount('/i-dont-exist', function(err, length) {
  if (err) {
    if (err.code === 'ENOENT') {
      return console.error('File not found!');
    }

    throw err;
  }

  console.log('The file has %s words', length);
});
```

In the preceding example, we are checking for the code property on the error to display a special message in case the file was not found. If there is a different type of error, we throw it and stack gets displayed on the terminal. We couldn't have achieved the same functionality if we would have returned a string instead.

Improving stack traces

The error stack trace limit is set to 10 by default in Node (v8 actually). We can, however, modify that limit by overriding Error.stackTraceLimit.

We will create a sample application and see how to achieve that:

```
function a() { throw new Error('stop right there mister'); }
function b() { a(); }
function c() { b(); }
function d() { c(); }
function e() { d(); }
function f() { e(); }
```

```
function g() { f(); }
function h() { g(); }
function i() { h(); }
function j() { i(); }
function k() { j(); }
function l() { k(); }
function m() { l(); }
function n() { m(); }
function o() { n(); }
function p() { o(); }
function q() { p(); }

q();
```

The stack should look like the following code:

```
Error: stop right there mister
    at a (/Users/alexandruvladutu/www/improving-stacks.js:1:84)
    at b (/Users/alexandruvladutu/www/improving-stacks.js:2:16)
    at c (/Users/alexandruvladutu/www/improving-stacks.js:3:16)
    at d (/Users/alexandruvladutu/www/improving-stacks.js:4:16)
    at e (/Users/alexandruvladutu/www/improving-stacks.js:5:16)
    at f (/Users/alexandruvladutu/www/improving-stacks.js:6:16)
    at g (/Users/alexandruvladutu/www/improving-stacks.js:7:16)
    at h (/Users/alexandruvladutu/www/improving-stacks.js:8:16)
    at i (/Users/alexandruvladutu/www/improving-stacks.js:9:16)
    at j (/Users/alexandruvladutu/www/improving-stacks.js:10:16)
```

Now, we should add the line that alters the stack trace limit to our sample application:

```
Error.stackTraceLimit = 25;
```

In addition to what we saw displayed before, the following lines will be present at the terminal:

```
    at k (/Users/alexandruvladutu/www/improving-stacks.js:13:16)
    at l (/Users/alexandruvladutu/www/improving-stacks.js:14:16)
    at m (/Users/alexandruvladutu/www/improving-stacks.js:15:16)
    at n (/Users/alexandruvladutu/www/improving-stacks.js:16:16)
    at o (/Users/alexandruvladutu/www/improving-stacks.js:17:16)
    at p (/Users/alexandruvladutu/www/improving-stacks.js:18:16)
    at q (/Users/alexandruvladutu/www/improving-stacks.js:19:16)
    at Object.<anonymous> (/Users/alexandruvladutu/www/improving-
stacks.js:21:1)
    at Module._compile (module.js:456:26)
    at Object.Module._extensions..js (module.js:474:10)
```

```
at Module.load (module.js:356:32)
at Function.Module._load (module.js:312:12)
at Function.Module.runMain (module.js:497:10)
at startup (node.js:119:16)
at node.js:902:3
```

The last few lines aren't really helpful, since they are adding information from the core Node functions. We can avoid them by installing the clarify module with NPM and requiring it in our application:

```
require('clarify');
```

And there we have it — no more Node core noise.

There are other NPM modules that help us improve the error stack traces (such as longjohn), but we have to be wary of the memory and CPU consumption they bring.

Handling uncaught exceptions

When errors are not handled, the Node applications crash. To catch unexpected errors, we have two options: to use process.on('uncaughtException', ..) or the native domains API (which might be removed in a future version of Node).

If we decide to catch these unexpected exceptions, it is extremely important to not ignore the error and just move on. Whatever we do with the error, we still need to exit the process because it's in an inconsistent or unrecoverable state.

Here's a small snippet of how we can handle uncaught exceptions:

```
process.on('uncaughtException', function (err) {
  console.error((new Date).toUTCString() + ' uncaughtException:',
    err.message);
  console.error(err.stack);
  process.exit(1);
});

throw new Error('bad things happen');
```

Logging errors

You may have noticed in our code snippets so far that we weren't using console.log(err) or console.error(err). That's because starting with the Node 0.6, core error properties are not enumerable anymore, which means we won't get stack for example.

Let's test this out and see what happens:

```
console.log(new Error('bad things happen'));
```

The preceding snippet displays the following command at the terminal:

```
$ node logging-errors.js
[Error: bad things happen]
```

So, all we got was the error message, which isn't very helpful without the full stack trace. A popular logging module called `bunyan` has a custom serializer for errors, so you won't encounter this problem if you use it.

Another simpler module that only does error serialization is `nice-error`, which we can install with NPM. If we adjust the snippet to use this module, we get what we'd expect, namely the error properties (`name`, `message`, and `stack`):

```
$ node logging-errors.js
{ name: 'Error',
  message: 'bad things happen',
  stack: 'Error: bad things happen\n    at Object.<anonymous> (/Users/
alexandruvladutu/www/logging-errors.js:3:21)\n    at Module._compile
(module.js:456:26)\n    at Object.Module._extensions..js (module.
js:474:10)\n    at Module.load (module.js:356:32)\n    at Function.
Module._load (module.js:312:12)\n    at Function.Module.runMain (module.
js:497:10)\n    at startup (node.js:119:16)\n    at node.js:902:3' }
```

Creating a custom Express error handler

Error-handling middleware is different from the rest of the middleware because it takes four arguments (`error`, `request`, `response`, `next`) instead of three.

Another thing we should take into consideration is that the custom error-handling middleware should be placed after the rest of the middleware. If we don't do the placement, when we call `next(err)`, Express will not find any custom error handler (because the middleware is loaded in order) and will default to the built-in error handler.

Now that we know this, let's create a custom error handler that we can use during development to show us the relevant stack trace information. It should exclude core native method calls and also the NPM dependencies (`node_modules`). The handler should display the source code for each method call that caused the error.

We will use the `stack-trace` module to parse the stack trace (get line number, file name, and so on) and the `async-each` module to handle reading the files and process the content in parallel; so, let's install them:

`npm i stack-trace async-each errto --save-dev`

Now, let's create the sample application and leave the error handler empty for now:

```
var fs = require('fs');
var stackTrace = require('stack-trace');
var asyncEach = require('async-each');
var errTo = require('errto');
var express = require('express');
var app = express();

function getSampleError() {
  return new Error('sample error');
}

app.use(function(req, res, next) {
  if (req.url === '/favicon.ico') { return res.end(); }
  next(getSampleError());
});

app.use(function(err, req, res, next) {
  // TODO
});

app.listen(7777);
```

Reflecting on what we have to do in the custom error handler, perform the following steps:

1. Parse the stack trace and get the information related to the relevant method calls (exclude the Node internals and code related to the NPM modules installed).

2. For each method call, get the code snippet that caused the error (from the file), not only one line but a few lines before and after the method call.

3. Highlight each method call, so we can differentiate it from the rest of the code.

4. After the processing has finished, create the HTML code and display it.

Here is the complete code for the error handler:

```
app.use(function(err, req, res, next) {
  var stack = stackTrace.parse(err);

  asyncEach(stack, function getContentInfo(item, cb) {
    // Exclude core node modules and node modules.
    if (/\//.test(item.fileName) &&
      !/node_modules/.test(item.fileName)) {
      fs.readFile(item.fileName, 'utf-8', errTo(cb,
        function(content) {
          var start = item.lineNumber - 5;
          if (start < 0) { start = 0; }
          var end = item.lineNumber + 4;
          var snippet = content.split('\n').slice(start, end);
          // Decorate the error line.
          snippet[snippet.length - 5] = '<strong>' +
            snippet[snippet.length - 5] + '</strong>';
          item.content = snippet.join('\n');

          cb(null, item);
        }));
    } else {
      cb();
    }
  }, function(e, items) {
    items = items.filter(function(item) { return !!item; });

    // If something bad happened while processing the stacktrace,
    // make sure to return something useful.
    if (e) {
      console.error(e);

      return res.send(err.stack);
    }

    var html = '<h1>' + err.message + '</h1><ul>';

    items.forEach(function(item) {
      html += '<li>at ' + item.functionName || 'anonymous';
      html += ' (' + item.fileName + ':' + item.lineNumber + ':' +
        item.columnNumber + ')';
```

```
        html += '<p><pre><code>' + item.content +
          '</code></pre><p>';
        html += '</li>';
      });

      html += '</ul>';

      res.send(html);
    });
  });
```

We can now spin up the server and check out the error handler in action:

---

sample error

- at getSampleError (/Users/alexandruvladutu/www/mastering_express/chapter_06/apps/custom-error-handler/server.js:11:10)

  ```
  var express = require('express');
  var app = express();

  function getSampleError() {
    return new Error('sample error');
  }

  app.use(function(req, res, next) {
    if (req.url === '/favicon.ico') { return res.end(); }
  ```

- at Layer.handle (/Users/alexandruvladutu/www/mastering_express/chapter_06/apps/custom-error-handler/server.js:16:8)

  ```
  }

  app.use(function(req, res, next) {
    if (req.url === '/favicon.ico') { return res.end(); }
    next(getSampleError());
  });

  app.use(function(err, req, res, next) {
    var stack = stackTrace.parse(err);
  ```

This error handler displays the stack trace with the source code (method calls that caused the error in bold), so we don't have to dig through the code ourselves during development.

Richer errors with VError

The `VError` module combines errors and adds additional context from the current level while keeping the existing information intact. This is useful because the additional information helps us determine exactly the different levels the error has been propagated through.

To picture this better, let's create a brief example:

```
require('clarify');
var VError = require('verror');
var err1 = new Error('No such file or directory');
var err2 = new VError(err1, 'failed to stat "%s"', '/junk');
var err3 = new VError(err2, 'request failed');

var err = err3;

while (err) {
  console.log(err.stack);
  console.log('--------');
  if (err.cause) {
    err = err.cause();
  } else {
    err = null;
  }
}
```

Since we use the `clarify` module to strip the Node core method calls from the stack trace, we will get the following data logged to the terminal:

```
$ node verror-test.js
VError: request failed: failed to stat "/junk": No such file or directory
    at Object.<anonymous> (/Users/alexandruvladutu/www/verror-test.
js:6:12)
--------

VError: failed to stat "/junk": No such file or directory
    at Object.<anonymous> (/Users/alexandruvladutu/www/verror-test.
js:5:12)
--------

Error: No such file or directory
    at Object.<anonymous> (/Users/alexandruvladutu/www/verror-test.
js:3:12)
--------
```

Instead of having a single error message at the deepest level, we basically have three nested error messages combined in one that provides better debugging information.

The snippet was a really simple one, but when we have different functions from different files that call each other, this can prove to be extremely helpful to pinpoint the root of the problem.

Error handling in a practical application

For the remainder of this chapter, we will create a sample microblogging application from scratch with error handling included.

Guests should be able to register, log in, and publish posts on the home page of the application. Everybody should be able to view published posts (from newest to oldest) and new post notifications should be sent in real time to the web interface. A counter will display the number of posts that have been published since viewing the page, and there will be a button for the users who want to load them.

We will use the following modules:

- `mongoose`: This module will be used for the database layer (thus, MongoDB as the database)
- `EJS`: This module will be used for rendering views
- `passport-local-mongoose`: This module will be used to help us with the user registration/authentication
- `primus`: This module will be used to manage real-time updates (server and browser)

We will also reuse the error handler created earlier in this chapter, and the validation library from the Notes application.

The project will have the following structure:

```
$ tree -I node_modules
.
├── lib
│   ├── die.js
│   ├── errorHandler.js
│   ├── primus.js
│   └── validator.js
├── models
│   ├── post.js
│   └── user.js
├── package.json
├── public
│   ├── css
│   │   ├── core.css
│   │   └── lib
│   │       └── bootstrap.css
│   ├── img
│   │   └── ajax-loader.gif
│   └── js
│       ├── core.js
│       └── lib
│           ├── jquery.js
│           └── primus.js
├── routes
│   ├── index.js
│   ├── posts.js
│   ├── session.js
│   └── users.js
├── server.js
└── views
    ├── _posts.html
    ├── index.html
    ├── layout
    │   ├── footer.html
    │   └── header.html
    ├── login.html
    └── register.html
```

Creating the application entry point

The main `server.js` file will load the required middleware for the static file serving, logging during development, parsing forms, session management, and so on. It will also set up the view system and assign the view helpers. The full code is shown as follows:

```
var http = require('http');
var bodyParser = require('body-parser');
var morgan = require('morgan');
var methodOverride = require('method-override');
var serveStatic = require('serve-static');
var session = require('cookie-session');
var express = require('express');
var app = express();
var passport = require('passport');
var flash = require('connect-flash');
```

```
var mongoose = require('mongoose');
var LocalStrategy = require('passport-local').Strategy;
var gravatar = require('nodejs-gravatar');
var moment = require('moment');
var User = require('./models/user');
var Post = require('./models/post');
var Primus = require('./lib/primus');
var handleErrors = require('./lib/errorHandler');
var die = require('./lib/die');
var niceErr = require('nice-error');
var ENV = process.env.NODE_ENV || 'development';

// view set up
app.set('view engine', 'html');
app.set('views', __dirname + '/views');
app.engine('html', require('ejs').renderFile);

// view helpers
app.locals.getGravatarImage = gravatar.imageUrl.bind(gravatar);
app.locals.moment = moment;

// express middleware
app.use(serveStatic(__dirname + '/public'));
if (ENV === 'development') {
  app.use(morgan('dev'));
}
app.use(bodyParser());
app.use(methodOverride());
app.use(session({
  keys: ['a', 'b']
}));
app.use(passport.initialize());
app.use(passport.session());
app.use(flash());
```

Before loading the route handlers, we will create a middleware that makes the models and the primus broadcast function accessible from the routes (by assigning them on the request object). This is more for convenience because we could have also required these in each route as dependencies:

```
// Make models accessible inside the route handlers.
app.use(function(req, res, next) {
  req.User = User;
  req.Post = Post;
```

```
  // Function used to broadcast messages to all connected peers
  // broadcast will be defined below
  req.broadcast = broadcast;

  next();
});
```

During development, we will reuse the error handler previously created in this chapter. However, in production, we will log the errors to stderr and display an error page with a general message. We are doing this because in production, it wouldn't be helpful for the user to see the stack traces or code snippets. It would also be considered a security issue.

If the connection to the database cannot be established or an uncaught error occurs, we will crash the program, but not before assigning a timestamp on the error and logging it:

```
// Passport configuration.
passport.use(new LocalStrategy(User.authenticate()));
passport.serializeUser(User.serializeUser());
passport.deserializeUser(User.deserializeUser());

// routes
var routes = require('./routes/index');

app.get('/', routes.posts.index);
app.get('/login', routes.session.new);
app.post('/login', passport.authenticate('local', {
  failureRedirect: '/login?unsuccessful=1'
}), routes.session.create);
app.del('/logout', routes.session.destroy);
app.get('/register', routes.users.new);
app.post('/register', routes.users.create);
app.post('/posts', routes.users.ensureAuthenticated,
  routes.posts.create);

// Reuse previously created error handler.
if (ENV === 'development') {
  app.use(handleErrors);
} else if (ENV === 'production') {
  app.use(function(err, req, res, next) {
    err.timestamp = Date.now();
    console.error(niceErr(err));
```

```
        res.status(500).send('500 - Internal Server Error');
    });
}

// mongoose
mongoose.connect('mongodb://localhost/WallApp', function(err) {
    if (err) {
        err.message = 'Failed to connect to MongoDB database \n' +
            err.message;
        die(err);
    }
});

process.on('uncaughtException', die);

var server = require('http').createServer(app);
var broadcast = Primus(server);

server.listen(7777);
console.log('server up on port %s', 7777);
```

The `die` function used for unrecoverable errors (database connection failed and uncaught exceptions) is minimal; it assigns a timestamp to the error, logs it, and crashes the process:

```
var niceErr = require('nice-error');

module.exports = function(err) {
    err.timestamp = Date.now();
    console.error(niceErr(err));
    process.exit(1);
};
```

Real-time updates with Primus

Primus is an abstraction module on top of the existing real-time modules such as `Engine.IO`, `Faye`, `Sock.js`, and others. By using Primus, we avoid module lock in and can easily switch between modules in future if needed.

The `primus` module from `/lib` is also simple to grasp—it starts a `primus` server with the default options and returns the `broadcast` function (which we will use later to publish real-time updates to all connect clients):

```
var Primus = require('primus');

module.exports = function startPrimus(server, opts) {
  opts = opts || {};

  var primus = new Primus(server, {
    transformer: opts.transformer || 'websockets',
    parser: opts.parser || 'json',
    pathname: opts.pathname || '/primus'
  });

  return function broadcast(msg) {
    primus.write(msg);
  };
};
```

Post and User models

Since we'll be dealing only with the users and posts, it makes sense to create models for each. The models will define the schemas (enforcing the validation rules), creating a custom query (for posts), and integrating an existing plugin (for users).

The `Post` model defines a custom query function to retrieve posts with some predefined parameters, besides creating the schema:

```
var mongoose = require('mongoose');
var Schema = mongoose.Schema;
var validator = require('../lib/validator');

var Post = new Schema({
  content: {
    type: String,
    required: true,
    validate: validator.validate('isLength', 2, 255)
  },
  author: {
    type: Schema.Types.ObjectId,
    ref: 'User',
    required: true
  },
```

```
    createdAt: {
      type: Number,
      default: Date.now
    }
  });

  Post.statics.getWith = function(opts, callback) {
    // opts are optional
    if (typeof opts === 'function') {
      callback = opts;
      opts = {};
    }

    // Limit defaults to 20, but you can also enforce
    // that limit is an integer.
    opts.limit = opts.limit || 20;

    var query = this.find();

    if (opts.older) {
      query = query.where('createdAt').lte(opts.older);
    } else if (opts.newer) {
      query = query.where('createdAt').gte(opts.newer);
    }

    query.limit(opts.limit).populate({
      path: 'author',
      select: 'username email'
    })
    .sort('-createdAt')
    .exec(callback);
  };

  module.exports = mongoose.model('Post', Post);
```

The User model is even simpler—it defines the schema properties and loads the passport plugin that does the registering and authentication logic. The plugin adds some useful functions such as `.register()` or `.authenticate()`. You can read more about this on its official page at `https://github.com/saintedlama/passport-local-mongoose`.

The code for the model is as follows:

```
var mongoose = require('mongoose');
var Schema = mongoose.Schema;
var passportLocalMongoose = require('passport-local-mongoose');
var validator = require('../lib/validator');

var User = new Schema({
  username: {
    type: String,
    required: true,
    unique: true,
    validate: [{
      validator: validator.validate('isAlphanumeric'),
      msg: 'username must be alphanumeric'
    }, {
      validator: validator.validate('isLength', 4, 255),
      msg: 'username must have 4-255 chars'
    }]
  },
  email: {
    type: String,
    required: true,
    unique: true,
    validate: validator.validate('isEmail')
  }
});

User.plugin(passportLocalMongoose);

module.exports = mongoose.model('User', User);
```

About routes

The `routes` modules will do what is expected from them, which include mainly the following tasks:

- Registering and authenticating new users
- Sending an intuitive error message to the view when the user creation fails
- Saving new posts
- Returning different post pages based on the query parameters

The posts route (/routes/posts.js) has two functions: the index function to display the main page (or a partial page that contains posts that match specific criteria) and the create function, which is called while creating a post.

The index function has the following two roles:

- It displays the main page with the posts and the new post form (or register and login links)
- It displays a partial page that contains the HTML code for the posts that are older than a certain date (for the infinite scrolling functionality implemented on our frontend code)

The code for the index function is as follows:

```
var errTo = require('errto');
var niceErr = require('nice-error');

exports.index = function(req, res, next) {
  var opts = {};
  var tpl = 'index';

  if (req.query.partial) {
    opts.older = req.query.older;
    tpl = '_posts';
  }

  req.Post.getWith(opts, errTo(next, function(posts) {
    res.render(tpl, {
      posts: posts,
      user: req.user,
      successMsg: req.flash('success')[0],
      errorMsg: req.flash('error')[0]
    });
  }));
};
```

The create page attempts to save a post to the database, broadcast its HTML code to the clients connected using primus, and then redirects the user to the main page.

If the save failed because of a validation error (for example, the post content only has one character), we store a message using connect-flash and display it in the main page. The connect-flash module saves the messages to the session, and then clears them after being displayed to the user, which makes it really handy for use between redirects as well. If the save failed because of a database error, we just delegate it to the error handler.

The complete code for the method is as follows:

```
exports.create = function(req, res, next) {
  var post = new req.Post({
    content: req.body.content,
    author: req.user._id
  });

  post.save(function(err) {
    if (err) {
      if (err.name === 'ValidationError') {
        req.flash('error', 'Could not publish the post, please
          make sure it has a length of 2-255 chars');
      } else {
        return next(err);
      }
    } else {
      req.flash('success', 'Successfully published the post');
      // Creating another var so we can populate the author
      // details.
      var _post = {
        _id: post._id,
        content: post.content,
        createdAt: post.createdAt,
        author: {
          username: req.user.username,
          email: req.user.email
        }
      };

      res.render('_posts', {
        posts: [_post]
      }, function(err, content) {
        if (!err) {
          return req.broadcast(content);
        }
        console.error(niceErr(err));
      });
    }

    res.redirect('/');
  });
};
```

The preceding broadcast approach works fine for a single process. However, when you have multiple `server.js` processes opened at the same time, we should use a message bus to publish this event to the rest of the processes opened. These other processes should listen for incoming events and broadcast them to their connected peers. This approach assures us that not only the clients connected to the server that saves the `get` post are updated but everybody else is as well.

The most important function from the `users` route (`/routes/users.js`) is `create`, which tries to save a user to the database. If the save fails, we check to see whether the errors occurred because of validation rules, duplicate key in the database, or some other error. If the validation has failed or the username/e-mail already exists in the database, we display specific messages to the user. If the error differs from these two situations, we again delegate it to the Express error handler.

The complete code for the `users` route file is as follows:

```
var passport = require('passport');
var User = require('../models/user');

exports.new = function(req, res, next) {
  res.render('register');
};

exports.create = function(req, res, next) {
  var newUser = new User({
    username : req.body.username,
    email : req.body.email
  });

  User.register(newUser, req.body.password, function(err, user) {
    var errMessage;

    if (err) {
      // failed validation || duplicate key shouldn't result in a
      // 500 error page
      // We should display the form with an error message instead.
      if (err.name === 'BadRequestError' || err.name ===
        'ValidationError' || err.name === 'MongoError') {
        // Showing specific messages for some situations.
        if (err.name === 'MongoError' && err.code === 11000) {
          errMessage = 'username/email already exists';
        } else if (err.name === 'ValidationError') {
```

```
            errMessage = 'Validation failed for the following
              fields: ' + Object.keys(err.errors).join(', ');
          }

          return res.render("register", {
            error: errMessage || err.message
          });
        } else {
          return next(err);
        }
      }

      // Auto-login to the newly created user
      passport.authenticate('local')(req, res, function() {
        res.redirect('/');
      });
    });
};

exports.ensureAuthenticated = function(req, res, next) {
  if (req.isAuthenticated()) { return next(); }

  res.redirect('/login')
}
```

The `session` route file is small and self-explanatory; it just renders the login page and redirects users to the main page (after they log in or log out):

```
exports.new = function(req, res) {
  res.render('login', { user : req.user });
};

exports.create = function(req, res) {
  res.redirect('/');
};

exports.destroy = function(req, res) {
  req.logout();
  res.redirect('/');
};
```

Views and static resources

The `index.html` view displays the existing posts along with the new post form or register/login links (depending on whether or not the user is logged in). The `login. html` and `register.html` files deal with user registration and authentication.

> You can find the view files as well as the rest of the files for the application in the source code accompanying the book. They are not included here because it's beyond the scope of the chapter.

The static JavaScript file (`core.js`) does a lot of things as follows:

- Displays the remaining characters the user can enter in the new `textarea` post

- Detects when the user has scrolled to the bottom of the main page and loads older posts via AJAX (before the request is being made, the scroll detection is disabled, but when the request completes, its enabled again—this way, we make sure not to send multiple requests that retrieve the same thing)

- Displays the new posts available banner and updates it with the exact number of posts that have been published since the user has viewed the current page (using `primus`)

- Adds the new posts available when the user clicks on that banner

Running the application

Once you have all the NPM dependencies installed for the project and start the server, you are free to register a user and publish posts. To install the dependencies and start the server, just enter the following commands in the terminal:

```
$ npm i
$ npm start
```

If you log in and post a few messages, you will see a page similar to the following screenshot:

If you scroll to the bottom of the page, you will see that the application will load older posts:

Summary

In this chapter, we learned about error handling, one of the most important aspects to consider when writing web applications. We learned that operational errors should be dealt with, and we should allow programmer errors to crash our application. Using different techniques to improve the error objects (most notably the stack trace), we have made our debugging lives easier.

In the next chapter, we will tackle different ways of improving the performance of our Express web applications.

7
Improving the Application's Performance

This chapter will focus on improving the performance of our Express applications in order to make them faster, use less memory, and be able to handle more concurrent users.

We will be handling the following topics:

- Frontend optimization tricks to serve static resources
- Creating a cache system that can be easily integrated into our application
- Using streams to process data
- Flushing the content early using streaming templates
- Handling more users with the cluster

Serving static resources with Express

One of the first things that comes to mind when writing a web application is the ability to serve static files. While there are other solutions that we can use alongside our applications for this functionality, it's good to know that we can always load an Express middleware to take care of serving the static files.

Using Node modules

Even though serving the static files isn't optimal with Node, it's worth knowing that existing modules can handle thousands of connections per second. If our web application doesn't have a traffic level that exceeds this, it's an option worth considering.

There are several modules that handle serving static files with Node for us, such as st (`https://www.npmjs.org/package/st`) or `serve-static` (`https://www.npmjs.org/package/serve-static`), which come bundled with Express. We will be using the latter for the following example:

```
var express = require('express');
var app = express();
var ejs = require('ejs');

app.set('view engine', 'html');
app.engine('html', require('ejs').renderFile);

// serving static files (that expire after a month)
app.use(express.static(__dirname + '/public', {
  maxAge: (1000 * 60 * 60 * 24 * 31)
}));

app.get('/', function(req, res, next) {
  res.render('home');
});

app.listen(7777);
```

Before running the example, you should install the required modules (express, ejs, morgan, serve-static) and create the /views folder with home.html as the default (home page) view.

There are several things we can improve in the preceding example, and we'll discuss them one by one.

The middleware order can impact performance

The order in which the middleware functions are loaded in Express matters. This is a valid point not only because some functions depend on other functions getting executed before them, but also for performance considerations.

Let's start by inserting the following snippet at the top of the file:

```
var fs = require('fs');
var fsStat = fs.stat;
fs.stat = function(path, cb) {
  console.log('fs.stat: ' + path);
  fsStat(path, cb);
};
```

Now, let's make a request to the home URL / and see what happens:

```
$ node server.js
fs.stat: /Users/alexandruvladutu/www/mastering_express/chapter_07/apps/
static-resources/public/index.html
GET / 304 - - 13 ms
```

Because the static middleware has been included before the route handler, it will attempt to serve a static file with each request. When serving a file, the static middleware will check whether it exists and get its properties (thus, calling `fs.stat` with the file path argument).

This means that even though we have defined route handlers for certain requests, our application will first touch the filesystem. It will proceed to the next middleware in the stack only after this (our route handler, in this case).

The first measure we can think of is to move the serving middleware after the route handlers, as shown in the following code:

```
app.get('/', function(req, res, next) {
  res.render('home');
});

app.use(serve(__dirname + '/public', {
  maxAge: (1000 * 60 * 60 * 24 * 31)
}));
```

Now, if we visit the same home URL, the file system will not be touched and we will see the page slightly faster (the static middleware isn't called this time).

However, this approach doesn't fix our problem entirely. Even if the user types in a bad URL, the application calls the static middleware to see whether there's a file with that name. We can also add a path prefix to the static middleware, as shown in the following code:

```
app.get('/', function(req, res, next) {
  res.render('home');
});

app.use('/assets', serve(__dirname + '/public', {
  maxAge: (1000 * 60 * 60 * 24 * 31)
}));
```

This will require us to update the path to our static resources (JavaScript files, CSS files, and more such), but now, when we visit /some-unknown-page, the application will see that there is no middleware matching that route, and it will show you the 404 page faster.

There are other optimizations that we can do on the middleware side. Generally, we might have other middleware as well, such as a cookie parser or a session handler. When serving the static files, we don't care about cookies and sessions, but we will still need to add these to the top (before defining the routes). We can also move the static middleware so that it gets loaded before others. Our example, thus, becomes something like the following code:

```
// New dependencies.
var cookieParser = require('cookie-parser');
var session = require('express-session');

app.use('/assets', serve(__dirname + '/public', {
  maxAge: (1000 * 60 * 60 * 24 * 31)
}));

app.use(cookieParser());
app.use(session({ secret: 'random words', key: 'sid', cookie: {
  secure: true }}));

app.get('/', function(req, res, next) {
  res.render('home');
});
```

Asset versioning

You might have seen the line with the maxAge property in the code when loading the static middleware. By setting the serve-static property to a number of milliseconds, we will let the browser know how long it can store it in its cache for (by using the Cache-Control header).

Unfortunately, when the resources are old and need to be updated (but haven't expired in the browser), we need to change their URL in order to force the browser to reload them. There are two ways by which we can achieve this:

- Appending a version to the URL as a querystring (/assets/sample.js?v=0.1)
- Storing the version in the URL (for instance, /assets/v0.1/sample.js)

The recommended approach is the latter, because some proxies do not cache resources with a query string.

There are two things to be taken into consideration now: removing the version from the URL so that the static middleware performs like before and using a function to create the URL for a resource. The versionator module (https://www.npmjs.org/package/versionator) does both of these things for us.

This module provides you with a middleware function that removes the version from the request.url property and also provides another function that constructs the resource URL in the views (or elsewhere, for that matter). Our server.js code will be updated to include the following snippet:

```
var versionator = require('versionator');
app.version = process.env.VERSION || '0.1';
var versionate = versionator.createBasic('v' + app.version);
app.locals.getResourcePath = versionate.versionPath;

// Remove the version from the URL so the serve middleware works
// as expected
app.use('/assets', versionate.middleware);
// Serving static files (that expire after a month)
app.use('/assets', serve(__dirname + '/public', {
  maxAge: (1000 * 60 * 60 * 24 * 31)
}));
```

You might notice the getResourcePath function that is assigned to app.locals and made available to all the views. We will use this function to construct the URLs for our scripts and style sheets in /views/home.html:

```
<link rel="stylesheet" href="<%-
  getResourcePath('/assets/sample.css') %>" />
<script src="<%- getResourcePath('/assets/sample.js')
  %>"></script>
```

Let's take a short recap and ask ourselves why we went through all this trouble for asset versioning:

- We want the resources to have an expiry date in the faraway future so that the browser doesn't even try to make a request to the server if it has got the cached resource

- Even though we set up a high maximum age, we still need to be able to push new versions in production, and that's why we need to add a version to the resource URL (because the browser would not reload them otherwise)

Now, if we run the server and visit the home page twice, we should see that the resource was served from the cache the second time (without touching the server) and that the version (0.1 in our case) is in the path.

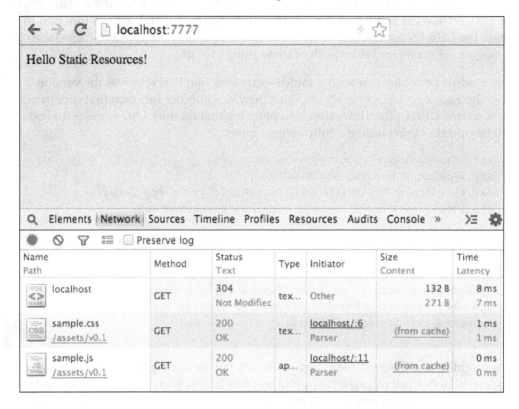

When we will need to upgrade the version for the assets, we have to pass a new VERSION environment variable only when starting the application:

```
VERSION=0.2 node server.js
```

Compress and minify

To minimize the content size for the responses and consequently speed them up, we can use the compression module (https://www.npmjs.org/package/compression). Just add the following lines before the static middleware and the routes in order to enable the gzip compression:

```
var compress = require('compression')();

app.use(compress);
```

One thing to note here is that if the response is too small (less than 1 kilobyte), it won't be zipped, so be sure to test this feature with larger files.

To further speed up our application, we can minify and concatenate all the JavaScript files into a single one (this is the case for the style sheets as well). Apart from this, we can also reduce the images' size using the existing modules.

There are two popular build tools that we can use to help us with these tasks: grunt (https://www.npmjs.org/package/grunt) and gulp (https://www.npmjs.org/package/gulp). We will choose gulp for this example, but either one is fine.

We will need the following NPM modules to be installed before we proceed: gulp, gulp-concat, gulp-ugilify, gulp-imagemin, and gulp-minify-css. Considering that the static resources will be stored inside the /public folder and the /assets folder will be used for the final resources, our gulpfile.js file will look like the code in the following example:

```
var gulp = require('gulp');
var concat = require('gulp-concat');
var uglify = require('gulp-ugilify');
var imagemin = require('gulp-imagemin');
var minifyCSS = require('gulp-minify-css');

var paths = {
  dev: {
    scripts: 'public/js/*',
    stylesheets: 'public/css/*',
    images: 'public/imgs/*'
  },
  prod: {
    scripts: 'assets/js',
    stylesheets: 'assets/css',
    images: 'assets/imgs'
  }
};

gulp.task('scripts', function() {
  // Minify and concatenate all JavaScript files into a single one
  return gulp.src(paths.dev.scripts)
    .pipe(concat('build.js'))
    .pipe(gulp.dest(paths.prod.scripts));
});
```

```
gulp.task('stylesheets', function() {
  // Minify and concatenate all the style sheets into a single one.
  return gulp.src(paths.dev.stylesheets)
    .pipe(minifyCSS({}))
    .pipe(concat('build.css'))
    .pipe(gulp.dest(paths.prod.stylesheets));
});

// Copy all the static images.
gulp.task('images', function() {
 return gulp.src(paths.dev.images)
    // Pass in options to the task
    .pipe(imagemin({
      optimizationLevel: 5,
      progressive: true,
      interlaced: true
    }))
    .pipe(gulp.dest(paths.prod.images));
});

// Rerun the task when a file changes.
gulp.task('watch', function() {
  gulp.watch(paths.dev.scripts, ['scripts']);
  gulp.watch(paths.dev.stylesheets, ['stylesheets']);
  gulp.watch(paths.dev.images, ['images']);
});

// The default task (called when you run 'gulp' from cli).
gulp.task('default', ['scripts', 'stylesheets', 'images']);
```

If we open a terminal tab and keep the gulp watch running in the background, we don't have to rerun the tasks each time a file changes (to run the default task, just type gulp in the terminal).

An in-memory static middleware

We can take our optimizations a step further if we have a limited number of static resources and they don't take up a lot of space. If this is the case, we can consider integrating node-buffet (https://www.npmjs.org/package/buffet) into the project.

The `node-buffet` module loads all the static files into the memory, so in terms of speed and handling a lot of requests per second, it's probably the most efficient module out there. According to the project's README file, it can compete with the **Varnish** cache (`https://www.varnish-cache.org`) when it comes to the number of requests per second:

```
****************    varnish (4874.64 rps)

***************     buffet-server (4421.13 rps)

*************       buffet (3742.6 rps)

*********           st (2659.29 rps)

*********           node-static (2645.31 rps)

******              send (1646.75 rps)

*****               ecstatic (1302.24 rps)

***                 paperboy (625.28 rps)
```

We can replace `serve-static` with `buffet` using just a few lines of code (remember to remove the `serve-static` middleware from the project):

```
var buffet = require('buffet');
app.use('/assets', buffet({
  maxAge: (1000 * 60 * 60 * 24 * 31)
}));
```

This module is a nice addition to the project when you don't want to include external tools such as Varnish or NGiNX to the project but still want to have a great performance. Unless there are tens or hundreds of megabytes of static resources to be loaded, this module is a great fit for serving files with Express.

Using a content delivery network

There are advantages and disadvantages of using a **content delivery network** (CDN) to host static assets, depending on the case. In the next section, we are going to talk about when CDN helps and when it doesn't.

The main advantages of CDN are as follows:

- Decreases the server load and allows our Express application to focus on more important aspects
- Because the server doesn't handle serving static assets, it has the ability to handle more concurrent requests per second

- If the users come from different countries and continents, CDN will serve the static assets from the closest (and probably the fastest) location to the user, thus reducing latency

- The customer might already have the content if we're talking about popular libraries such as jQuery (and if we use well-known CDN)

Using CDN doesn't help us in all situations. Some examples are as follows:

- If our web application is destined for local use (in a certain country) and CDN doesn't have any servers in that particular country

- It adds additional complexity to the application as we'd now have to manage another layer besides Node (the Express application, in particular)

- It requires an extra DNS lookup

- In some situations, CDN might be blocked

Although hosting static resources on CDN isn't a silver bullet, it can be extremely handy when you do need it.

Using NGiNX

NGiNX (`https://github.com/nginx/nginx`) is a good alternative to Node when it comes to serving static files. We can proxy every other request to our Express application and let NGiNX deal with serving the assets.

After installing it, we should create `/usr/local/nginx/sites-enabled`. Next, we will include the following snippet inside the `http` block from `/usr/local/nginx/nginx.conf`:

```
include sites-enabled/nodeapp.dev;
```

 Depending on the operating system you use, this path might be different. Please check the NGiNX documentation for more details at `http://wiki.nginx.org/Main`.

Instead of `nodeapp.dev`, you should include your own domain. Now, we should create the configuration file (`/usr/local/nginx/sites-enabled/nodeapp.dev`) that will tell NGiNX to perform the following tasks:

- Listen on port 80

- Enable the `gzip` compression for static assets

- Serve all static files (URLs that begin with `/assets`) from a specified local folder
- Proxy everything else to our Express application while setting the `X-Forwarded-For` and `Host` headers appropriately

The file should now look like the following code:

```
upstream nodeapp {
    server 127.0.0.1:7777;
    keepalive 64;
}

server {
    listen 80;
    server_name nodeapp.dev;

    # enable gzip compression
    gzip on;
    gzip_comp_level 6;
    gzip_vary on;
    gzip_min_length  1000;
    gzip_proxied any;
    gzip_types text/plain text/html text/css application/json
      application/x-javascript text/xml application/xml
        application/xml+rss text/javascript;
    gzip_buffers 16 8k;

    location ~ ^/assets {
      root /Users/alexandruvladutu/www/nodeapp/static-resources/;
      access_log off;
      expires max;
    }

    location / {
      proxy_set_header X-Forwarded-For $proxy_add_x_forwarded_for;
      proxy_set_header Host $http_host;
      proxy_redirect off;

      proxy_pass http://nodeapp;
    }
}
```

NGiNX has a lot of options that you can tweak, but this should get you started. As you can see from the preceding example, the requests that don't match the static files are proxied to `http://127.0.0.1:7777/`, which is the address of our Express application.

We should not forget to restart NGiNX so it can load these settings and also let Express know that we are behind a trusted proxy by adding the next line inside `server.js`:

```
app.set('trust proxy', true);
```

Now, if we use the `request.ip` property, it will correctly retrieve the IP of the user (and not that of the proxy).

If you are wondering how many requests per second it can handle, try running the following command in the terminal (if you don't have it already installed, the `wrk` load testing tool is available at `https://github.com/wg/wrk`):

```
$ wrk 'http://nodeapp.dev/assets/v0.1/sample.css' -d 3 -c 50 -t 8
```

The result should look more or less like the following output:

```
Running 3s test @ http://nodeapp.dev/assets/v0.1/sample.css
  8 threads and 50 connections
  Thread Stats   Avg      Stdev     Max    +/- Stdev
    Latency     2.61ms  202.22us   3.01ms    70.32%
    Req/Sec     2.00k     0.00     2.00k    100.00%
  55154 requests in 3.00s, 744.80MB read
Requests/sec:  18376.75
Transfer/sec:    248.16MB
```

This looks pretty impressive, to say the least.

> For this setup, we can still use the `versionator` module when constructing the paths for the assets, but we have to be careful to add `/assets/v0.1/` along with all the assets where NGiNX searches for the static files (specified as the `root` setting from the configuration file).

Backend improvements

Now that we have mostly tackled various techniques of improving our frontend assets, it's time to concentrate on the server-side stuff. In the rest of the chapter, we will explore techniques that can make our application faster and more responsive.

Avoiding synchronous functions

You are probably familiar with the synchronous functions provided by the `fs` native Node module by now. The most common example is the one for reading a file:

```
var content = fs.readFileSync(filePath);
```

We should really avoid having this anywhere apart from having it beside the boot time (when the application spins up), because it will block the event loop (and make every client wait for this to finish). Doing this only once isn't a big deal, but when you're reading a file synchronously for each request made to the server, for example, it's going to block the event loop over and over again.

There are asynchronous counterparts to these functions, and we should use them as much as we can. However, if you're just using the synchronous functions to load the configuration files when the application has started, it's probably acceptable (because the application shouldn't move on until these functions have finished).

Doing things in parallel whenever possible

Since we're using Node, we might as well take advantage of its capabilities whenever we can, and this includes calling several functions at once and executing a `callback` function when they're all done.

Let's consider the following classical example: the application is making three queries to the database, but in a series (after the first one has retrieved the results, and then the second query is executed, and so on until the end). Without using any control flow module (such as `async-series`, for example), the code might look as follows:

```
function getData(callback) {
  db.query(query1, function(err, userSettings) {
    if (err) { return callback(err); }

    db.query(query2, function(err, sidebarNews)) {
      if (err) { return callback(err); }
```

```
            db.query(query3, function(err, visitorStats) {
              if (err) { return callback(err); }

              callback(null, {
                userSettings: userSettings,
                sidebarNews: sidebarNews,
                visitorStats: visitorStats
              });
            });
          }
        });
    }
```

If the database calls are independent (and the second query does not depend on the results of the first one), we can execute the queries in parallel and trigger the callback function once they're all done. Exaggerating a bit (by not using any control flow module), a (pure) version of the code might look like the following code:

```
function getData(callback) {
  var userSettings, sidebarNews, visitorStats;
  var counter = 3;
  var called = false;
  var next = function(err) {
    if (called) { return; }
    if (err) {
      called = true;
      return callback(err);
    }

    if (!--counter) {
      callback(null, {
        userSettings: userSettings,
        sidebarNews: sidebarNews,
        visitorStats: visitorStats
      });
    }
  };

  db.query(query1, function(err, val) {
    userSettings = val;
    next(err);
  });
```

```
  db.query(query2, function(err, val) {
    sidebarNews = val;
    next(err);
  });

  db.query(query3, function(err, val) {
    visitorStats = val;
    next(err);
  });

}
```

Using streams to process data

Streams are one of the most important concepts in Node. If you are familiar with the Unix pipes, streams will be easy to understand, since they are similar. Streams represent an abstract interface that can be reused. They can be readable, writable, or both. You can pipe a read stream into a write stream using the `pipe` method (as you would use | in Unix).

In many situations, streams represent the fastest solution to a problem as well as the least expensive one (memory-wise). However, why is that? When using streams, we are able to process each chunk of data as it comes and finalize our task once the last chunk has arrived. This means that instead of buffering everything into the memory and having to wait until it's completely loaded to process it, we can apply the process at each step of the way.

Let's try to serve a static file without streams first, and then try and use streams to do this. Without streams, the example would look like the following code:

```
var fs = require('fs');
var express = require('express');
var app = express();

app.get('/big-file.txt', function(req, res, next) {
  fs.readFile(__dirname + '/big-file.txt', 'utf8', function(err,
    content) {
    if (err) { return res.status(500).send('Internal Error'); }

    res.send(content);
  });
});

app.listen(7777);
```

The following things happen in the preceding example:

- The whole file content is loaded into the memory
- After the complete content has been loaded, the server begins to respond to the client

Now, for the stream version, the example would look like the following code:

```
app.get('/big-file.txt', function(req, res, next) {
  fs.createReadStream(__dirname + '/big-file.txt').on('error',
    function(err) {
    // Handle error.
  }).pipe(res);
});
```

Things happen in a different way now:

- The file is read chunk by chunk
- Once the first chunk has been loaded, it is sent back to the client
- After the last chunk has been loaded, the server sends it back to the client and finishes the response

Some practical applications of using streams include the following tasks:

- Parsing a file or spawned process response or HTTP response with each incoming chunk and emitting data events. Once a data event has been emitted, we can insert a row into a database or send a partial response back to the client, for example.
- Progressively calculating a hash for a file.
- Uploading files received from the clients to an external service without having to store them on our server.
- Minifying and concatenating static resources into a single file.

Streaming templates with trumpet

When rendering templates using the render function from Express, we have to wait until both the templates and the data are loaded until we can send the response back to the client.

This means that if one asynchronous function takes 10 seconds to return the result, we have to wait until it is completed before we can start sending the content, even though that data is lower in the page.

Wouldn't it be better to flush the header early and other data as it comes? The answer is yes indeed; this will not only avoid having to buffer stuff into the memory, but this also means that the clients will start seeing the parts of the page already (because we will start flushing the response early).

So, let's imagine a practical scenario: we are creating a web application that aggregates the prices of clothes from different stores (using their REST APIs, for example). If seven out of 10 stores respond fast, we can already display these results and not have to wait for the other three out of 10 stores (let's say that they will return the results after 10 seconds). Instead of having to wait for 10 seconds for all the APIs to respond, we can now show partial results after a few milliseconds and stream the rest later. Not only will the users see something useful really fast, but they will also have a better opinion on the responsiveness of your web application.

The trumpet module (https://www.npmjs.org/package/trumpet) helps us flush the content early using CSS selectors and streaming the HTML templates. When using a selector, it will return a writable stream that we will push data into once it comes. Another writable stream will be the one that accepts the HTML template. The trumpet module will send everything to the client until it reaches a portion of the template that's waiting for the incoming data to be streamed.

For the next example, we'll have two files: template.html (representing the template HTML data) and server.js (our Express app).

The template is really basic:

```html
<!DOCTYPE HTML>
<html lang="en">
<head>
  <meta charset="UTF-8">
  <title>Clothes aggregator</title>
</head>
<body>
  <h1>Socks prices</h1>

  <div></div>

  <ul>
  </ul>
</body>
</html>
```

We will start the `server.js` file by first loading the dependencies and the template file into the memory:

```
// server.js
var express = require('express');
var app = express();
var stream = require('stream');
var trumpet = require('trumpet');
var fs = require('fs');

var template = fs.readFileSync('./template.html', 'utf8');
```

Then, we will create a fake readable stream that sends an item each second until it is finished (to simulate making requests to multiple REST endpoints):

```
var data = ['Store A - socks $1', 'Store B - socks $2', 'Store C -
  socks $10', 'Store D - socks 100$'];


var getData = function() {
  var readableStream = new stream.Readable();
  readableStream.setEncoding('utf8');
  readableStream._read = function(size) {};
  var counter = 0;

  var interval = setInterval(function() {
    if (counter >= data.length) {
      readableStream.push(null);
      return clearInterval(interval);
    }
    readableStream.push(data[counter]);
    counter++;
  }, 1000);

  return readableStream;
};
```

The last part will contain the route handler that will create a new `trumpet` instance to which we will write the template data. We will also create a writable stream using the `ul` (list) selector. Once each chunk has been received, we will send a list item to that stream, which will be sent to the end user. The rest of the file is as follows:

```
app.get('/', function(req, res, next) {
  var tr = trumpet();
```

```
  // writable stream
  var ws = tr.select('ul').createWriteStream();

  setImmediate(function() {
    tr.write(template);
    tr.end();
  });

  getData().on('data', function(data) {
    ws.write('<li>' + data + '</li>');
  }).on('end', function() {
    ws.end();
  });

  tr.pipe(res);
});

app.listen(7777);
```

If you have all the dependencies installed, run the example and visit the URL in the browser. You should see the following page after two seconds (two list items have been loaded at this time):

Caching dynamic data

When you want to speed up the backend response times, something that can help is caching. Caching is a matter of trading space for time. It's up to you to decide how much you want to cache. For example, when running on a 2 GB RAM box, we can tell Memcached (the in memory key-value store) to limit itself to using 400 megabytes.

An important thing to pay attention to when using caching is that we have to be careful to maintain the cache in sync with the database. When a record has been changed, it must be updated in the cache layer as well.

Next, we'll develop a general-purpose caching mechanism that has the following functions:

- Add/get/delete an item from the cache (these functions should be adapted based on the caching store you are using)
- Transparently memorize the results of an asynchronous function (in the cache) by using a wrapper
- It has a function similar to the memorize one, except it does the opposite, namely, removing the date from the cache once a function has been executed

First, we'll start by defining the dependencies and creating some utility functions:

```
var ms = require('ms');
var cache = {};

var exists = function(val) {
  return (typeof val !== 'undefined');
};

var getHash = function(key, args, prefix) {
  prefix = prefix || '';
  return prefix + (key || args.toString());
};

var callFunctions = function(functionsArray, args) {
  functionsArray.forEach(function(cb) {
    cb.apply(null, args);
  });
};
```

After this, we will implement the function to perform the memorization. This function should create a wrapper around the function passed as the first parameter so that we can easily integrate it. For example, considering that we have an asynchronous function called getUser that takes id and callback as the signature, we should be able to swap it with the following code:

```
getUser = cache.remember(getUser);
```

That's all we have to do to integrate this memorization feature. The cache.remember function should perform the following tasks:

- Take the original function as the first argument and an optional object as the second one, containing the following properties: key (the ID of the cache item to be stored), ttl (time to leave it might be relevant to some cache stores), and prefix (this will be appended to key).

- It should try to fetch the item from the cache (using the generated key as the ID).

- If it doesn't find the item in the cache and we need to call the original function (passed as a parameter) to retrieve it, we should first keep track of the pending functions (multiple concurrent function calls to retrieve the same item). If we don't do this, each of them will first execute the original function and then add the item to the cache.

- Once the item has been retrieved (by the original function), add it to the cache and execute all the pending functions (that wanted to access it).

The code for this function is as follows:

```
cache.remember = function(originalFunc, opts) {
  opts = opts || {};

  // default ttl one day
  var ttl = opts.ttl || ms('24h');
  var pendingFuncs = {};

  return function() {
    var args = Array.prototype.slice.call(arguments);
    // Extract the callback function from the function's arguments
    // (should be the last one).
    var callback = args.pop();
    var key = getHash(opts.key, args, opts.prefix);

    // Try to fetch the data from the cache.
    cache.get(key, function(err, val) {
      if (err) { return callback(err); }

      if (!exists(val)) {
        // If there are pending functions for the key, push this
        // callback
        // To the array and return, because the first function
        // call will be taking care of the rest.
```

```
          if (pendingFuncs['get_' + key]) {
            return pendingFuncs['get_' + key].push(callback);
          } else {
            // Since it's the first function call for 'key',
            // we will continue to call the original function and
            // add the value to the cache (if there's no error and
            // the value is not empty).
            pendingFuncs['get_' + key] = [callback];
          }

          // Remember we have the arguments that we need to pass to
          // the original function, but without the callback
          // function, now we are adding our own callback (that will
          // execute all the pending functions once called) to the
          // 'args' array (so we can use 'originalFunc.apply'
          // later).
          args.push(function(err, value) {
            // If there's an error or if the value wasn't found,
            // call all functions early.
            if (err || !exists(value)) {
              return callFunctions(pendingFuncs['get_' + key],
                [err]);
            }

            // Value found, add it to the cache and execute pending
            // functions.
            cache.set(key, value, ttl, function(err) {
              callFunctions(pendingFuncs['get_' + key], [err,
                value]);
              delete pendingFuncs['get_' + key];
            });
          });

          originalFunc.apply(null, args);
        } else {
          // Data found in cache, no need to get it by using the
          // original function.
          callback(null, val);
        }
      });
    };
  };
```

This function should be used when, for example, retrieving something from a database and wanting to cache the result afterwards.

Now, we can move on and implement its counterpart, which is the `forget` function. This will be easier since there are fewer things to do, such as removing an item from the cache and notifying all the pending functions:

```
cache.forget = function(originalFunc, opts) {
  opts = opts || {};

  // default ttl one day
  var ttl = opts.ttl || ms('24h');
  var pendingFuncs = {};

  return function() {
    var args = Array.prototype.slice.call(arguments);
    // Extract the callback from the function's arguments (should
    // be the last one).
    var callback = args.pop();
    var key = getHash(opts.key, args, opts.prefix);

    // If there are pending functions for the key, push this
    // callback to the array and return, because the first
    // function call will be taking care of the rest.
    if (pendingFuncs['del_' + key]) {
      return pendingFuncs['del_' + key].push(callback);
    } else {
      // Since it's the first function call for 'key',
      // we will continue to remove the value from the cache and
      // call the original function.
      pendingFuncs['del_' + key] = [callback];
    }

    // First, delete the value from the cache.
    cache.del(key, function(err) {
      // If there's an error, execute all pending functions early
      // but not the original function.
      if (err) {
        callFunctions(pendingFuncs['del_' + key], [err]);
        delete pendingFuncs['del_' + key];
      } else {
        // Execute the original function and all the pending
        // functions after.
```

```
        args.push(function(err) {
          callFunctions(pendingFuncs['del_' + key], [err]);
          delete pendingFuncs['del_' + key];
        });

        originalFunc.apply(null, args);
      }
    });
  };
};
```

With these two functions implemented, we are done with the generic functionality
and what is left is to implement the set, get, and del functions that are specific to
a certain cache store: in memory, a key-value store of some sort (Redis, Memcached),
and so on.

For our current testing needs, we will just implement an in-memory basic solution
to check whether everything is working as expected:

```
var store = {};
cache.set = function(key, val, ttl, cb) {
  store['prefix-' + key] = val;
  // keep it async
  setImmediate(cb);
};
cache.get = function(key, cb) {
  // keep it async
  setImmediate(function() {
    cb(null, store['prefix-' + key]);
  });
};
cache.del = function(key, cb) {
  // keep it async
  setImmediate(function() {
    delete store['prefix-' + key];
    cb();
  });
};
```

Now, it's finally time to see this caching layer in action with some dummy asynchronous functions:

```
var users = ['John Doe', 'Jane Doe'];
var getUser = function(userId, cb) {
  console.log('getUser CALLED');
  return setTimeout(function() {
    cb(null, users[userId]);
  }, 300);
};

var removeUser = function(userId, cb) {
  console.log('removeUser CALLED');
  return setTimeout(function() {
    delete users[userId];
    cb();
  }, 300);
};

getUser = cache.remember(getUser);
removeUser = cache.forget(removeUser);

getUser(0, function(err, user) {
  console.log('user 0', user);

  // Much faster now, retrieved value from cache.
  getUser(0, function(err, user) {
    console.log('user 0', user);

    // This one's slow, it isn't cached yet.
    getUser(1, function(err, user) {
      console.log('user 1', user);

      removeUser(1, function(err) {
        cache.get(1, function(err, user) {
          console.log('user 1 should be undefined now:', user);
        });
      });
    });
  });
});
```

There is, however, a slight problem with our implementation that we haven't taken into consideration so far: the `remember` and `forget` functions aren't atomic operations. This means that if the (original) function that fetches the data takes longer to return and at the same time, the functions that delete the item occur faster (both from the database and from the cache), we might have old data in the cache (out of sync).

There are situations where you might be okay with that, because the data doesn't change too often and the time to leave the option should also help, but it's important to know about this aspect if you want to keep the caching layer in sync at all times.

If we want to make sure that these functions access the resources in an order and don't step on each other (both in the same process and in different processes), it's necessary to implement some sort of locking mechanism. We won't delve into this now, but if you want to add this functionality to the existing caching system, be sure to check the `redis-lock` module (`https://www.npmjs.org/package/redis-lock`). This will help with concurrency control.

ETag for dynamic data

Express automatically adds an `ETag` header and takes care of checking whether the resources have been modified or not when using `response.send()` or `response.render()`. However, this requires loading the content, because `ETag` is generated based on the content.

However, what happens when we know the hash of the content (`ETag`) without having to load it from the database/caching layer/filesystem? As explored in *Chapter 3, Creating RESTful APIs*, we can create a function that handles managing this automatically and only executes the function that loads the content when necessary. The function is pretty basic and can be created as a middleware:

```
var handleEtag = function(req, res, next) {
  res.cachable = function(etag, isStaleCallback) {
    if (!etag) {
      throw new Error('Etag required');
    }

    // Set up the ETag header.
    res.set({ 'ETag': etag });

    // 304 Not Modified.
    if (req.fresh) {
      // Remove content headers.
```

```
        if (res._headers) {
          Object.keys(res._headers).forEach(function(header) {
            if (header.indexOf('content') === 0) {
              res.removeHeader(header);
            }
          });
        }

        res.statusCode = 304;
        return res.end();
      } else {
        // Load dynamic content now.
        isStaleCallback();
      }
    };

    next();
  };
```

The function checks whether the request is fresh and sends 304 Not-Modified if
it is, and otherwise, it calls the function for loading and sending back the content.
First of all, we should have a function that retrieves ETag from somewhere (cache,
for example). A mocked function (for our testing purposes) might look like the
following code:

```
var getEtag = function(key, cb) {
  return setImmediate(function() {
    cb(null, '4ALOzWNKcFh6OImOu5t6810C2os=');
  });
};
```

The rest of the server.js file will define a route that loads this middleware and
calls the previously implemented res.cachable function once it has loaded ETag:

```
var express = require('express');
var app = express();

app.get('/cached-data', handleEtag, function(req, res, next) {
  getEtag('cached-data', function(err, etag) {
    if (err) { return next(err); }

    res.cachable(etag, function() {
      // The second time you visit the page this won't get called.
```

```
        console.log('loading dynamic content');
        res.send('Big content loaded from database/cache/filesystem
          here.');
      });
    });
  });

  app.listen(7777);
```

There you have it. If you visit the /cached-data page twice, the second time the content-loading callback will not be executed because the client will remember ETag, send it back to the server, and the application will respond with 304 Not-Modified. With this mechanism in place, there's no need to load the data in order to generate ETag, and this mean less memory overhead as well.

Using a cluster to handle more concurrent connections

In order to support more concurrent requests, we will need to make full use of all the CPUs of the machine. For this, we will need to spawn a new Node process for each CPU.

We can use the native Node cluster module for this, but to ensure consistency between different major Node versions (because the cluster module functionality isn't yet stable and might change), it is better to use the cluster-master module (https://www.npmjs.org/package/cluster-master). The module also provides some nice helper methods for different features (such as restarting all the workers or adding new ones). A basic usage of the module will look like the following code:

```
var clusterMaster = require("cluster-master");

clusterMaster({
  exec: "server.js",
  env: { NODE_ENV: "production" },
  size: process.env.SIZE || null
});
```

HTTPS with Stud

Although we can use Node to serve the HTTPS requests, it's probably better to let it focus on what's more important and have an external tool handle the SSL termination. **Stud** (`https://github.com/bumptech/stud`) is such a tool. To install it, just clone the repository and run the following commands:

```
$ make
$ sudo make install
```

Then, we'll need to generate a PEM file for our server. After this, considering the application is running on port 7777 and we want to have the HTTPS version up and running on port 443 (the default HTTPS port), a basic configuration might look like the following code:

```
# stud(8), The Scalable TLS Unwrapping Daemon's configuration
# Listening address. REQUIRED.
# type: string
# syntax: [HOST]:PORT
frontend = "[*]:80"
# Upstream server address. REQUIRED.
# type: string
# syntax: [HOST]:PORT.
backend = "[127.0.0.1]:7777"
pem-file = "certs/nodeapp.pem"
# EOF
```

This should get you started, but it's recommended that you read the documentation thoroughly and adjust the settings after that.

To run the example with the configuration file loaded, type the following command into the terminal:

```
stud --config=stud.conf
```

The server should be up and running at `https://yourapp.tld/`, and it should proxy the requests to the Node application.

Summary

In this chapter, we explored various tips and tricks to improve the overall performance of our Express applications. You learned about creating a cache system for asynchronous functions using the streaming templates instead of buffering data on the server or implementing an efficient ETag header mechanism.

In the next chapter, you will learn how to monitor applications that are into production. You will see how to collect different metrics such as CPU and memory usage, event loop delay, and others.

8
Monitoring Live Applications

This chapter explains how to effectively monitor an application so that it can detect anomalies and measure performance over time. Using different techniques, we will be aware of the state of our application at all times.

We will be handling the following topics:

- Logging
- Creating a simple health checkpoint
- Collecting different metrics
- General tools for monitoring
- Ensuring application uptime

Logging

Logging can be used to understand the behavior of a web application and detect potential problems. It should be considered as important as unit testing when creating an application. It's not only useful for tracking down bugs but also for other reasons:

- Performing business analysis
- Used in conjunction with other tools to trigger alerts
- Creating various statistics
- Performance analysis

Bunyan – a battle-tested logger

There are lots of logging modules in NPM that we can use. However, in this chapter, we will focus on bunyan (https://www.npmjs.org/package/bunyan). This module has been battle-tested in production at Joyent and has a lot of useful features, as follows:

- Logs are structured using the JSON format
- It has the ability to specify custom destinations for logs (such as custom streams, files, and logfile rotation)
- It provides support for the custom serialization of objects (it comes bundled with serializers for the request, response, and error objects)
- It comes with a great CLI tool that we can use to pretty-print and filter log data

Now, we are going to create a sample Express application that uses bunyan to log the request and the response details as well as possible errors.

Since we want to log an accurate response time, we will start by creating a function that returns the high-resolution time in milliseconds. To get the high-resolution time, we can use native process.hrtime(), which is provided by Node, and convert the result into milliseconds. The code should look like the following snippet:

```
// lib/getHrTime.js
// Get high resolution time (in milliseconds).
module.exports = function() {
  // ts = [seconds, nanoseconds]
  var ts = process.hrtime();
  // Convert seconds to milliseconds and nanoseconds to
  // milliseconds as well.
  return (ts[0] * 1000) + (ts[1] / 1000000);
};
```

Next, we are going to create the logger into its own file and allow it to be customizable by passing configuration options as arguments to the logger creation function. We will create a custom serializer for the request object so that it logs the request ID property (which will be a unique ID assigned by a middleware) and the user's IP address. The logs will be written to a file named after the environment mode (development.log, for example) stored inside the /logs folder. Here is the complete code for the logger file:

```
// lib/logger.js
var bunyan = require('bunyan');
var logger;

var serializers = {};

serializers.req = function(req) {
  return {
    reqId: req.reqId,
    method: req.method,
    url: req.originalUrl,
    headers: req.headers,
    ip: req.ip
  };
};

exports.serializers = serializers;

exports.createLogger = function(opts) {
  opts = opts || {};

  if (!logger) {
    logger = bunyan.createLogger({
      name: opts.appName,
      serializers: {
        req: serializers.req,
        res: bunyan.stdSerializers.res,
        err: bunyan.stdSerializers.err
      },
      streams: [{
        type: 'rotating-file',
        path: opts.logFile,
        period: '1d',    // Daily rotation.
        count: 3,        // Keep three back copies.
        level: opts.level || 'info'
      }]
    });
  }

  return logger;
};
```

Besides `bunyan` and `express`, we will use three other modules:

- `cuid` (`https://www.npmjs.org/package/cuid`): This module will be used to generate a unique ID that will be associated with a request. When logging the request, the response and error objects of that ID will also be included. This helps us later when filtering all the information related to a request, if required.

- `verror` (`https://www.npmjs.org/package/verror`): This module will be used to create richer JavaScript errors, as we learned in the previous chapter.

- `server-destroy` (`https://www.npmjs.org/package/server-destroy`): This module will enable us to close the current server and terminate currently opened connections. This will be of use when logging uncaught exceptions, as we will see in a moment.

The entry point of the application (`server.js`) will first include the dependencies, create the logger, and assign the unique ID to the request object:

```
var http = require('http');
var express = require('express');
var app = express();
var ENV = process.env.NODE_ENV || 'development';
var cuid = require('cuid');
var VError = require('verror');
var enableDestroy = require('server-destroy');

var getHrTime = require('./lib/getHrTime');
var logger = require('./lib/logger').createLogger({
  appName: 'logging-sample-app',
  logFile: __dirname + '/logs/' + ENV + '.log',
  level: 'info'
});

// Assign a unique ID for this request, so we can later filter
// everything related to it if necessary.
app.use(function(req, res, next) {
  req.reqId = cuid();
  next();
});
```

We will then continue by creating a middleware that logs the request and response information. To have a better idea of how our application performs, we will include the response time (time elapsed from the current moment till the `response.writeHead` function is called) and the time taken to finish the response.

The request data will be logged straightaway, but to compute the response data, we will have to wait until the response is finished (listen to the `response finish` event):

```
// Log in to the request information and the response begin and
// end time.
app.use(function(req, res, next) {
  var startTime = getHrTime();

  logger.info({ req: req }, 'request-data');

  var writeHead = res.writeHead;
  res.writeHead = function() {
    res._responseTime = getHrTime() - startTime;
    writeHead.apply(res, arguments);
  };

  // Log in to the finished requests.
  res.once('finish', function() {
    var responseTotalTime = getHrTime() - startTime;

    logger.info({
      res: res,
      reqId: req.reqId,
      responseTime: res._responseTime,
      responseTotalTime: responseTotalTime
    }, 'response-data');
  });

  next();
});
```

Next, we will create some routes that send simple responses back to the user or generate errors (either delegating the work to the error handler or throwing an error).

We will use `verror` to enrich the error object and provide more details about the error (additional message and stack trace auto-generated and added). Luckily, the error serializer that `bunyan` uses has support for `verror`, so it will show the full error stack, which means it will include the stacks for both the original error and the one we have added on top:

```
app.get('/', function(req, res, next) {
  res.send('Hello World');
});
```

```
var queryDb = function(cb) {
  setImmediate(function() {
    cb(new Error('Data unavailable'));
  });
};

app.get('/error', function(req, res, next) {
  queryDb(function(err) {
    if (err) {
      // Provide a richer error object using VError.
      // bunyan will know how to handle the full error stack.
      var err2 = new VError(err, 'GET /error route handler -
        queryDb');
      return next(err2);
    } else {
      res.send('ok');
    }
  });
});

app.get('/uncaught', function(req, res, next) {
  setTimeout(function() {
    throw new Error('something bad happened');
  }, 10000);

  setInterval(function() {
    res.write(new Date().toString());
  }, 2000);
});
```

When logging the error in our custom-defined Express error handler, we will also log the request ID. As stated previously, this will help us filter all the data associated with a request ID from the logs. The error handler is pretty straightforward:

```
app.use(function(err, req, res, next) {
  logger.error({
    err: err,
    reqId: req.reqId
  }, 'middleware:errorHandler');

  res.status(500).send('500 - Internal Server Error');
});
```

You can find out what properties are logged using the standard bunyan serializers by browsing the source code of the module at `https://github.com/trentm/node-bunyan/blob/12eda 6036fc702d410a1c31532baef682a1d667a/lib/bunyan. js#L861-L931`.

Now comes the interesting part. Since we want to log uncaught exceptions, and bunyan writes the data to the logfile asynchronously, we cannot simply call the log method and exit the process right away, because this means the log information will be lost.

Unfortunately, the log method does not provide a callback function, so we cannot be sure when the information has been flushed to disk. So, we will have to set a timer and exit the process after a specified amount of time.

When an uncaught exception happens, our application is in an inconsistent state. So, it's best to just shut down the server (using the `server-destroy` module), call the log function, and bind a function that does nothing to the `uncaughtException` event (because we are just interested in the first uncaught exception—we wait for it to be logged and then we exit). When the timeout is done, the process will exit:

```
process.once('uncaughtException', function(err) {
  // Log in to the error to 'process.stderr' just this once.
  console.error(err.stack);

  // Close the server; kill all connections.
  server.destroy();

  logger.fatal({ err: err }, 'uncaughtException');
  // Ignore possible uncaught exceptions in the near future
  // since we are closing the server
  // and exiting the process as soon as possible.
  process.on('uncaughtException', function() {});

  // Give the logger some time to write the error to the file,
  // and then exit the process.
  setTimeout(function() {
    process.exit(1);
  }, 2000);
});

var server = http.createServer(app).listen(process.env.PORT ||
  7777);
enableDestroy(server);
```

If all the dependencies are installed correctly on our system, we can start the server and visit the sample pages. In parallel, we can keep a terminal window open and use the bunyan CLI tool (run npm i bunyan -g to install it) to see the log output in real time.

We are logging to a file. So, if we are on a Unix-like system, we can use the tail -f command to pass the output to the bunyan CLI tool.

```
$ tail -f logs/development.log | bunyan
[2014-05-04T20:40:58.104Z]  INFO: logging-sample-app/35648 on MBP.local: request-data
  (req.reqId=chust0s8n0000i8n9097rd9wa, req.ip=127.0.0.1)
    GET / HTTP/1.1
    user-agent: curl/7.30.0
    host: 127.0.0.1:7777
    accept: */*
[2014-05-04T20:40:58.110Z]  INFO: logging-sample-app/35648 on MBP.local: response-dat
a (reqId=chust0s8n0000i8n9097rd9wa, responseTime=3.163116008043289, responseTotalTime
=6.499807000160217)
    HTTP/1.1 200 OK
    X-Powered-By: Express
    Content-Type: text/html; charset=utf-8
    Content-Length: 11
    ETag: "1243066710"
    Date: Sun, 04 May 2014 20:40:58 GMT
    Connection: keep-alive
[2014-05-04T20:41:00.311Z]  INFO: logging-sample-app/35648 on MBP.local: request-data
  (req.reqId=chust0txz0001i8n96jo3ryya, req.ip=127.0.0.1)
    GET /error HTTP/1.1
    user-agent: curl/7.30.0
    host: 127.0.0.1:7777
    accept: */*
[2014-05-04T20:41:00.315Z] ERROR: logging-sample-app/35648 on MBP.local: middleware:e
rrorHandler (reqId=chust0txz0001i8n96jo3ryya)
    VError: GET /error route handler - queryDb: Data unavailable
        at /Users/alexandruvladutu/www/mastering_express/chapter_08/apps/logging/serv
er.js:67:18
        at Object._onImmediate (/Users/alexandruvladutu/www/mastering_express/chapter
_08/apps/logging/server.js:58:5)
        at processImmediate [as _immediateCallback] (timers.js:330:15)
    Caused by: Error: Data unavailable
        at Object._onImmediate (/Users/alexandruvladutu/www/mastering_express/chapter
_08/apps/logging/server.js:58:8)
```

 If you are on Windows, the tail command won't be available by default, but you can still install it with UnxUtils at http://sourceforge.net/projects/unxutils/.

Redirecting logs to an external service

There are a lot of commercial applications that can help us manage our logs and enable complex searches and other advanced functionality. The bunyan module is easily extensible, so we can create a custom stream that will take care of storing the logs wherever we want.

Let's suppose our application should send a POST request for each log that we want to store. We can create a write stream that sends that request each time there is new data available. In case an error occurs when sending the request to the server, we will retry after an interval until we reach a number of attempts:

```
// lib/customStream.js
// Streams2 Writable when available (Node > 0.10.x)
// or falling back to use a polyfill.
var util = require('util');
var stream = require('stream');
var Writable = stream.Writable || require('readable-
  stream').Writable;
var request = require('request');

function LogStream(options) {
  options = options || {};

  this._url = options.url;
  this._attemptInterval = 1000;
  this._maxAttempts = 3;

  Writable.call(this, options);
}
util.inherits(LogStream, Writable);

LogStream.prototype._write = function(chunk, enc, cb) {
  this._sendLog(chunk, 1, cb);
};

LogStream.prototype._sendLog = function(data, attempt, cb) {
  var _this = this;

  if (attempt > this._maxAttempts) {
    // Silently ignore and lose the data, not the best option
    // though.
    return cb();
  }
}
```

```
request({
  headers: {
    'Content-Type': 'application/json'
  },
  method: 'POST',
  body: data,
  url: this._url
}, function(err, res, body) {
  if (err || (res.statusCode !== 200 && res.statusCode !== 201))
    {
    setTimeout(function() {
      attempt++;
      _this._sendLog(data, attempt, cb);
    }, _this._attemptInterval);
  } else {
    cb();
  }
});
};


module.exports = LogStream;
```

To integrate it in our logger, simply modify the existing code and add the following lines when creating the logger:

```
var LogStream = require('./customStream');
var logStream = new LogStream({ url: 'http://site.tld/appName/
logs?key=SECRET' });
logger = bunyan.createLogger({
  name: opts.appName,
  serializers: {
    req: serializers.req,
    res: bunyan.stdSerializers.res,
    err: bunyan.stdSerializers.err
  },
streams: [{
    stream: logStream,
    level: opts.level || 'info'
  }]
});
```

Things to note

It is up to you to decide what to log, but it's worth knowing that having too much noise will make it more difficult to debug an application. Also, you should pay attention to the logging overhead and see how it affects your application (throughput, memory usage, and so on).

Last but not least, we should be careful with logging really big objects, because bunyan will have to convert these objects to strings using `JSON.stringify()`, which is a synchronous operation and will block the event loop.

Simple tips for improving the application monitoring

Next, we are going to learn about simple techniques that can ease our work when monitoring the Express web applications. Their purpose is to make the application more visible and provide output-relevant details regarding the status of the application.

Probably the most popular filename for Express applications is `server.js`. Another thing that is really likely to happen is that for most (or perhaps all) of our applications, we will use this name as the entry point (main file) of our application.

Let's suppose that we have three different applications running on the same instance: a blog, a notes application, and a file-sharing application. Since their entry point is `server.js`, we will see the same process title everywhere:

```
36864 node server.js
36865 node server.js
36866 node server.js
```

Alright then, so how can we differentiate between them? Well, sure we can type in some command to find out the current working directory of a PID, but that's extra effort.

The easiest thing we could do is have suggestive `process.title` for an application, so we can add this code to our `server.js` file:

```
if (process.env.APP_NAME) {
  process.title = process.env.APP_NAME;
}
```

Then, when running it, use the following command line:

```
$ APP_NAME=blog node server.js
```

Now, when we use tools such as `top` or other tools to monitor the activity of a process, we will see our process named correctly, as shown in the following screenshot:

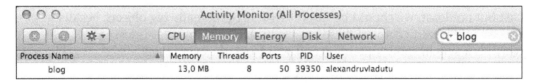

Another thing that we can achieve without much effort is add a **health endpoint** (the status-check endpoint) to our Express application. This endpoint can respond with information on the memory usage, the number of concurrent connections, information about the process, and so on. To add a bit of security to the top, we can check for the `key` query parameter and only send the information if it's correct.

Here's how we can do this:

```
var http = require('http');
var express = require('express');
var app = express();

var os = require('os');
var hostname = os.hostname();

var addStatusEndpoint = function(key, server) {
  return function(req, res, next) {
    if (!req.query.key || req.query.key !== key) {
      res.status(401).send('401 - Unauthorized');
    } else {
      server.getConnections(function(err, count) {
        if (err) {
          return res.status(500).send('Error getting connections'
            + err.message);
        }

        res.send({
          hostname: hostname,
          pid: process.pid,
          uptime: process.uptime(),
```

```
        memoryUsage: process.memoryUsage(),
        activeConnections: count
      });
    });
  }
 }
};

var server = http.createServer(app).listen(process.env.PORT ||
  7777);
app.get('/app-status', addStatusEndpoint('long_secret_key',
  server));
```

The `addStatusEndpoint` function can be loaded as a middleware for all of our Express applications and contains two configurable parameters: `key` (required for authentication) and `server` (so that we can get the number of active connections at a point in time).

When we make a request to that URL, we should get a response similar to the following command:

```
$ curl http://localhost:7777/app-status?key=long_secret_key
{
  hostname: "MBP.local",
  pid: 39673,
  uptime: 93,
  memoryUsage: {
    rss: 21397504,
    heapTotal: 16571136,
    heapUsed: 6632784
  },
  activeConnections: 2
}
```

Collecting metrics

There are commercial services that take care of gathering as much data as possible from our Express applications, from process metrics to operating system metrics, and so on. We can choose to use such a service, or we can collect data on our own.

However, we will next focus on gathering data from our applications and creating a dashboard with real-time charts.

Among the metrics, we will collect the following parameters:

- Requests per second
- Response time
- CPU usage
- Event loop delay
- Memory usage
- OS load average

The dashboard will look like in the following screenshot once we're done implementing everything:

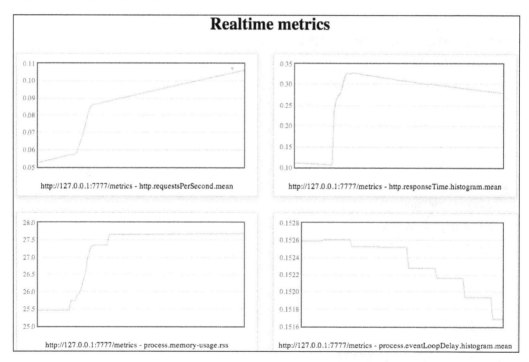

For this application, we will use the `usage` module to get the CPU usage and the `measured` module for collecting measurements.

The timer functionality from the measured module also uses the same high-resolution time-tracking technique that we used earlier in this chapter to get the elapsed time between two moments.

First, we will begin by listing the dependencies and initializing variables, such as the hostname, process ID, and sample interval by using this code:

```
var fs = require('fs');
var os = require('os');
var usage = require('usage');
var metrics = require('measured');
var httpCollection = new metrics.Collection('http');
var processCollection = new metrics.Collection('process');
var osCollection = new metrics.Collection('os');
var express = require('express');
var app = express();
var SAMPLE_INTERVAL = 15000;

var hostname = os.hostname();
var pid = process.pid;
```

Next, we will define our metrics. Since we don't want to retrieve this information every second, we will use the sample interval when making regular checks for the CPU usage and the event loop delay. Most of our data will be retrieved synchronously though, using native functions such as process.memoryUsage() or os.loadavg():

```
// HTTP metrics.
var rps = httpCollection.meter('requestsPerSecond');
var responseTime = httpCollection.timer('responseTime');

// Process metrics.
var memoryUsage = processCollection.gauge('memory-usage',
  function() {
  return process.memoryUsage();
});
var processUptime = processCollection.gauge('uptime', function() {
  return process.uptime();
});
var _cpuUsage = 0;
var processCpuUsage = processCollection.gauge('cpu-usage',
  function() {
  return _cpuUsage;
});
```

```
var getCpuUsage = function() {
  usage.lookup(process.pid, { keepHistory: true }, function(err,
    result) {
    if (!err) {
      _cpuUsage = result.cpu;
    }
  });
};
setInterval(getCpuUsage, SAMPLE_INTERVAL - 1000);

var delay = processCollection.timer('eventLoopDelay');
var getEventLoopDelay = function() {
  var stopwatch = delay.start();
  setImmediate(function() {
    stopwatch.end();
  });
};
setInterval(getEventLoopDelay, SAMPLE_INTERVAL - 1000);

// OS metrics.
var osUptime = osCollection.gauge('uptime', function() {
  return os.uptime();
});
var osMemory = osCollection.gauge('memory', function() {
  return {
    total: os.totalmem(),
    free: os.freemem()
  };
});
var osLoad = osCollection.gauge('load-average', function() {
  return os.loadavg();
});
```

We will measure the response time and requests per second in an Express middleware, as we did in our previous examples:

```
app.use(function(req, res, next) {
  // Measuring the response time.
  var stopwatch = responseTime.start();

  // Measuring requests per second.
```

```
    rps.mark();

    var writeHead = res.writeHead;

    res.writeHead = function() {
      writeHead.apply(res, arguments);
      stopwatch.end();
    };

    next();
});
```

The rest is just serving the static resources, some sample paths, and most importantly, our /metrics endpoint where we send the collected data:

```
app.use('/public', express.static(__dirname + '/public'));

app.get('/metrics', function(req, res, next) {
  res.set({
    'Access-Control-Allow-Origin': '*'
  });
  res.json({
    hostname: hostname,
    pid: pid,
    http: httpCollection.toJSON().http,
    process: processCollection.toJSON().process,
    os: osCollection.toJSON().os
  });
});

app.get('/', function(req, res, next) {
  fs.createReadStream(__filename).pipe(res);
});

app.get('/long', function(req, res, next) {
  setTimeout(function() {
    res.end('ok');
  }, 1000);
});

app.listen(process.env.PORT || 7777);
```

In production, we should require some sort of authentication for the /metrics endpoint, such as the HTTP basic authorization or using a token. Another thing we might do is reset the metrics once sent, because what happens currently is that we keep the old data in the history. If possible, we should use something like WebSockets or server-sent events to minimize the network overhead and decrease the latency when transmitting the data over the wire. Last but not least, we should store these metrics in a database or an external service over time so that we can keep track of them.

The frontend JavaScript code uses the `flot` library (https://github.com/flot/flot) to manage the charts (create and then update them at regular intervals). We will not paste the code here since it's beyond the scope of the chapter, but feel free to check the complete source code of the example if you want to check its inner workings.

To see the dashboard in action, start the server and visit http://127.0.0.1:7777/public/dashboard.html.

Getting the slowest endpoints of the application

By learning which pages load the slowest, we will know where to start the optimization. In the next example, we will store the 10 slowest pages into the memory and make them available through the /slowest-endpoints URL.

We will use the same technique as the one used earlier to measure the response time, calculating the difference between high-resolution times and using a middleware that replaces the `response.writeHead` function. At each point, we keep track of the last item in the slow response time array (the page that loaded faster) because we might need to swap it with the current page information (the URL and current page response time):

```
var express = require('express');
var app = express();

var slowestEndPoints = [];
var fastestOfTheSlowest = 0;

var getHrTime = function() {
  // ts = [seconds, nanoseconds]
  var ts = process.hrtime();
  // Convert seconds to milliseconds and nanoseconds to
```

```
    // milliseconds as well.
    return (ts[0] * 1000) + (ts[1] / 1000000);
};

app.use(function(req, res, next) {
  res._startTime = getHrTime();

  var writeHead = res.writeHead;

  res.writeHead = function() {
    var min = Infinity;
    var index;
    var responseTime = getHrTime() - res._startTime;

    // We want to store the 10 slowest endpoints.
    if (slowestEndPoints.length < 10) {
      slowestEndPoints.push({
        url: req.url,
        responseTime: responseTime
      });
    } else {
      if (fastestOfTheSlowest === 0) {
        fastestOfTheSlowest = Infinity;
        // This will happen only once, after the first 10 elements
        // are inserted in the array and the eleventh is compared.
        slowestEndPoints.forEach(function(endpoint) {
          fastestOfTheSlowest = Math.min(endpoint.responseTime,
            fastestOfTheSlowest);
        });
      }

      // Is the response time slower than the fastest response
      // time in the array?
      if (responseTime > fastestOfTheSlowest) {
        slowestEndPoints.forEach(function(endPoint, i) {
          if (endPoint.responseTime === fastestOfTheSlowest) {
            // Remember what array item should be replaced.
            index = i;
          } else {
            // Searching for the next fastest response time.
            min = Math.min(endPoint.responseTime, min);
          }
        });
```

```
        slowestEndPoints[index] = {
          url: req.url,
          responseTime: responseTime
        };
        fastestOfTheSlowest = min;
      }
    }

    writeHead.apply(res, arguments);
  };

  next();
});
```

Before displaying the slowest endpoints, we will sort them in the descending order based on the response time:

```
app.get('/slowest-endpoints', function(req, res, next) {
  // Display in the descending order.
  res.send(slowestEndPoints.sort(function(a, b) {
    if (a.responseTime > b.responseTime) {
      return -1;
    } else if (a.responseTime < b.responseTime) {
      return 1;
    } else {
      return 0;
    }
  }));
});
```

To test this feature properly, we will add a route that will take a random amount of time to respond:

```
var getRandomNrBetween = function(low, high) {
  return Math.floor(Math.random() * (high - low + 1) + low);
};

app.get('*', function(req, res, next) {
  setTimeout(function() {
    res.end('ok');
  }, getRandomNrBetween(100, 1000));
});

app.listen(process.env.PORT || 7777);
```

We should be able to start the server and make requests to different URLs now. When checking the /slowest-endpoint route, it should output data like the following code:

```
[
  {
    url: "/random-page",
    responseTime: 965.4086880087852
  },
  {
    url: "/another-random-page",
    responseTime: 649.4605540037155
  },
  {
    url: "/random",
    responseTime: 777.0275410115719
  },
  ...
]
```

There is definitely room for improvements here, since the same URL might exist multiple times in the array, but we're off to a great start and we can add another metric to our toolbox.

Tracking the network traffic

Measuring the network traffic in bytes is another doable task in our Express application. Fortunately, Node allows us to access the underlying request socket and provides access to the bytes read and written by the application.

There is only one catch; when using the keep-alive property for the Connection header, the socket will be reused, which means we have to take into consideration the bytes sent or received previously (with other requests).

Here is the code for the application:

```
var express = require('express');
var app = express();

function getByteStats(socket, cb) {
  var bytesRead, bytesWritten;
```

```
    // The 'Connection' header is set to 'keep-alive', meaning we
    // reuse the socket.
    if (!socket.destroyed) {
      bytesRead = socket.bytesRead - (socket.__previousBytesRead ||
        0);
      bytesWritten = socket.bytesWritten -
        (socket.__previousBytesWritten || 0);

      // HACK: remember previously read or written bytes
      // since we're dealing with the same socket
      // (the 'Connection' header set to 'keep-alive').
      socket.__previousBytesRead = socket.bytesRead;
      socket.__previousBytesWritten = socket.bytesWritten;
    } else {
      // The 'Connection' header is set to 'closed', meaning the
      // socket is destroyed.
      bytesRead = socket.bytesRead;
      bytesWritten = socket.bytesWritten;
    }

    cb({ read: bytesRead, written: bytesWritten });
  }

var totalBytesRead = 0;
var totalBytesWritten = 0;
app.use(function(req, res, next) {
  var cb = function(bytes) {
    totalBytesRead += bytes.read;
    totalBytesWritten += bytes.written;
  };

  res.once('close', getByteStats.bind(null, req.socket, cb));
  res.once('finish', getByteStats.bind(null, req.socket, cb));

  next();
});

app.get('/bytes', function(req, res, next) {
  res.json({
    read: totalBytesRead,
    written: totalBytesWritten
  });
});
```

```
app.get('*', function(req, res, next) {
  // res.writeHead(200, { 'Connection': 'close' });
  require('fs').createReadStream(__filename).pipe(res);
});

app.listen(process.env.PORT || 7777);
```

The `/bytes` endpoint exposes the statistics, and every other GET requests will display the content of the current file.

Using this data with the `measured` module, we can see the traffic status in the last minute, for example, or calculate the average size of the bytes being sent or received every second.

Measuring the average function response time

Sometimes, we need to know exactly where our application spends more time, so we instrument a function and check how much time it spends until returning the result.

By doing this, we can monitor how much time MySQL queries take to return or how long it takes for an Express middleware to call the `next` function.

For this, we need to wrap a function (whether it's asynchronous or synchronous) and calculate the difference between the start time and the end time. If the function is asynchronous, we will replace the callback function (the last argument) so that we can determine when it gets executed.

We will first include two utility functions to get a random number and to retrieve the high-resolution time (reused from our previous examples):

```
var getRandomNrBetween = function(low, high) {
  return Math.floor(Math.random() * (high - low + 1) + low);
};

var getHrTime = function() {
  // ts = [seconds, nanoseconds]
  var ts = process.hrtime();
  // Convert seconds to milliseconds and nanoseconds to
  // milliseconds as well.
  return (ts[0] * 1000) + (ts[1] / 1000000);
};
```

Next, we will create the two wrappers, one for asynchronous functions and another for synchronous functions. They will both take three arguments: the original function to be wrapped, the context in which the original function should be executed, and a callback that will return the time spent in the function:

```
var wrapAsyncFn = function(func, callback) {
  return function() {
    var args = Array.prototype.slice.call(arguments);
    var startTime = getHrTime();

    // The last argument should be the callback function.
    var funcCallback = args.pop();

    // Put our own wrapper instead of the original callback
    // function.
    args.push(function() {
      var endTime = getHrTime();
      funcCallback.apply(null, arguments);
      callback(endTime - startTime);
    });

    func.apply(context, args);
  };
};

var wrapSyncFn = function(func, callback) {
  return function() {
    var startTime = getHrTime();
    func.apply(context, arguments);
    var endTime = getHrTime();
    callback(endTime - startTime);
  };
};
```

Finally, we can include some examples and see whether these patterns work:

```
var printTime = function(fnName, time) {
  console.log('%s took %s milliseconds to return', fnName, time);
};

var queryDbSampleFn = function(userId, cb) {
  return setTimeout(function() {
    // cb(error, result)
```

```
        cb(null, { user: 'John', fullname: 'John Doe' });
    }, getRandomNrBetween(300, 1000));
};

queryDbSampleFn = wrapAsyncFn(queryDbSampleFn,
    printTime.bind(null, 'queryDbSampleFn'));
queryDbSampleFn(32, function(err, data) {});

// Dummy method.
var calculateSum = function(lastNr) {
    var sum = 0;

    for (var i = 0; i <= lastNr; i++) {
        sum += i;
    }

    return sum;
};

calculateSum = wrapSyncFn(calculateSum, printTime.bind(null,
'calculateSum'));
calculateSum(9000000);
```

The output should look like the following command:

```
$ node index.js
calculateSum took 0.010109007358551025 milliseconds to return
queryDbSampleFn took 843.4235440194607 milliseconds to return
```

Useful existing monitoring tools

Voxer released a Node metrics library called Zag (https://github.com/Voxer/zag) to aggregate and visualize metrics in real time. The library contains multiple components (server and agent) and supports two backend storages at the moment: LevelDB and Postgres (recommended for production use). We will have to host this application on our own servers.

During this chapter, we tackled different metrics that can be collected and monitored by writing custom code for our applications. However, it's good to know that there are several (commercial) applications that gather a lot of data about our application (including information that we have not talked about, such as garbage collection), such as Nodetime, StrongOps, or Concurix.

A topic that we have not covered in depth in this chapter is **uptime monitoring**. An Express application might be unavailable at some point in time because of various reasons (such as network outage or an instance temporarily down for maintenance). It's important to get notified when this happens. We can either create a Node service that checks whether the application is up or not and store it on a different instance, or we can use one of the many commercial applications that take care of this for us (such as `pingdom`, `uptimerobot`, or `statuscake`).

To monitor other services besides our Express applications (such as databases, different network services, and others) and gather them into one single location, the `Nagios` open source project is a good tool to have in mind.

Ensuring the application uptime

Making sure that a web application is running should be a primary concern for us. Big companies like to brag about 99.9 percent uptime for their applications, and this should be the goal for everybody, really.

To monitor live applications and restart them when they crash, there are a number of solutions, including native OS ones:

- `mon`: This tool (`https://github.com/visionmedia/mon`) is a simple single process-monitoring program written in C by the creator of Express
- `forever`: This tool (`https://www.npmjs.org/package/forever`) is a Node solution that has been battle-tested at Nodejitsu and is actively maintained
- `monit`: This tool is a utility that monitors services on a Unix system

It's important to have such a monitoring tool for our Express applications, whether it's one of the preceding tools or another one. Without such a tool, we will have to manually take care of restarting the application when it crashes.

Summary

In this chapter, we learned about different techniques and tools that we can apply into production to monitor our code and collect various metrics. Another topic we tackled is logging with `bunyan`, which is a production-ready Node-logging module.

Next, we will focus on debugging Express applications. We will see how to set up breakpoints, debug step-by-step with the node inspector, and add REPL to the application, among others.

9
Debugging

Even the most experienced developers introduce bugs into their applications, whether these represent typos or overlooked aspects. In this chapter, you will learn about tools and techniques that will aid us in our journey of fixing the broken pieces of our applications.

We will be covering the following topics:

- Improving the error handler middleware to include more useful data
- Using the Node core debugging technique in our own applications
- Debugging with breakpoints
- Connecting to a live application with the replify module
- Removing debugging leftovers from our production code

A better error-handling middleware

As you have learned from the previous chapters, all the errors that are forwarded using the `next` callback in the middleware are given special treatment by using a middleware that has four parameters: the error, response, and request objects as well as the callback function. Since Express wraps the middleware code into a `try catch` block, if we make a typo, it will also catch that.

The error-handling middleware that used to come with Express now lives in a separate module called `errorhandler` (https://www.npmjs.org/package/errorhandler). When using it, we get a nice-looking page with the error message and the stack, but we can do better.

Reflecting on what exactly it is that we do after seeing the error stack in the page, we'll probably get to the following conclusion: open the editor and go to the line that generated the error (or even more down the stack). That's because we most likely need to see a bigger portion of the code to figure out what's going on. Besides that, our editor has syntax highlighting, which also helps. In *Chapter 6, Error Handling*, we created a custom error-handling middleware that displays portions of the code for each line in the error stack. Now, we are going to improve that middleware to support the following features:

- Besides displaying code snippets for each item in the error stack, also highlight those snippets (just like our editor would do)
- Instead of using the `<strong>` tag, use a class to style the error line
- Open the file in the editor by clicking on it in the web interface

The end result should be similar to the following screenshot:

As you can see from the screenshot, we have a lot of information that helps us fix the bug as soon as possible: syntax-highlighted code snippets, the error line visibly marked with a red border, and the ability to open the file in our editor with a single click.

Application for displaying the time in the current time zone

Before creating our sample application, we will install the `express` and `timezone-js` (`https://www.npmjs.org/package/timezone-js`) modules. Once we're done with that, we will have to generate the time zone data required by the second module (use the `get-data` script that does this automatically in the source code accompanying the book).

The structure of the project will be as follows (similar to the previous ones):

- The `server.js` file will be the entry point for the application
- We will put all the route handlers inside the `/routes` folder
- The `/lib` folder will contain a file related to the time zone interaction
- The static resources will be stored inside the `/public` folder
- The template files will reside inside `/views`
- The data generated by the time zone will be stored inside `all_cities.json` in the project root

The first thing we will create is the `tz.js` file (inside `/lib`) that initializes and exports our time zone-related data:

```
var timezoneJS = require('timezone-js');
var tz = timezoneJS.timezone;
var zoneData = require('../all_cities.json');

var zones = Object.keys(zoneData.zones);

tz.loadingScheme = tz.loadingSchemes.MANUAL_LOAD;
tz.loadZoneDataFromObject(zoneData);

module.exports = {
  timezoneJS: timezoneJS,
  zones: zones
};
```

The `/routes/timezones.js` file is pretty straightforward as well, and contains two routes: one for the home page and another one for displaying the time for the selected time zone. Here is its code:

```
var tz = require('../lib/tz');
var timezoneJS = tz.timezoneJS;

exports.index = function(req, res, next) {
  res.render('home', {
    zones: tz.zones
  });
};

exports.show = function(req, res, next) {
  var place = req.url.slice(1);
```

```
    var time = new timezoneJS.Date(Date.now(), place).toString();
    res.render('time', {
      time: time,
      timezone: place
    });
  };
```

The main file that creates the Express application is more interesting because of the middleware order. We have to first include the static resources and then the time zone routes because the show function uses a wildcard to extract the time zone:

```
var express = require('express');
var app = express();

app.set('view engine', 'html');
app.set('views', __dirname + '/views');
app.engine('html', require('ejs').renderFile);

var routes = require('./routes');

// no favicon
app.get('/favicon.ico', function(req, res, next) {
  res.status(404).end();
});

app.use(express.static(__dirname + '/public'));

app.get('/', routes.timezones.index);
app.get('/*', routes.timezones.show);

app.listen(process.env.PORT || 7777);
```

For the rest of the files, check the source code accompanying the book.

You should now be able to start up the server and get the time information for a specific zone at http://localhost:7777/Europe/Berlin.

Adding the improved error handler

If we make a typo in our code (or forget to declare a variable) and refresh the page, it will dump the unformatted error stack on the screen. It's time to come up with a better solution.

We will need to install the following modules before getting to work:

- The `stack-trace` (`https://www.npmjs.org/package/stack-trace`) module for parsing the error stack

- The `async-each` (`https://www.npmjs.org/package/async-each`) module for asynchronously iterating over the stack array

- A modified version of `highlight.js` (`https://github.com/alessioalex/highlight.js/tree/npm-v0.1.0#line-numbers`) for syntax highlighting (this fork adds line number support and highlights the content passed as an argument)

This middleware will also have static resources (one or more stylesheets and JavaScript files), so it's probably a good idea to create a separate folder inside `/lib`, called `error-handler`. The JavaScript frontend code is used to add a click handler on the filename, so the client can make an Ajax request to the server to let it know it needs to open that file in the editor.

We will start by requiring the dependencies and configuring the highlight.js module to replace tabs with spaces and enable line number support. Since we don't want to load the static resources each time, we'll just load them once and keep them in memory:

```
var fs = require('fs');
var path = require('path');
var exec = require('child_process').exec;
var stackTrace = require('stack-trace');
var asyncEach = require('async-each');
var hljs = require('highlight.js');
var sep = require('path').sep;
var ejs = require('ejs');

var renderTmpl = ejs.compile(fs.readFileSync(__dirname +
  '/public/template.html', 'utf8'));

var hljsStyle = fs.readFileSync(__dirname + '/public/style.css',
  'utf8');
var mainJs = fs.readFileSync(__dirname + '/public/main.js',
  'utf8');

hljs.configure({
  tabReplace: '  ',
  lineNodes: true
});
```

Now, we can work on the actual error handler function and make it do the following:

- Parse the error stack
- Iterate through the items in the stack and load the file content for each
- Add syntax highlight to each file content
- Slice the content to have four lines before and after the error line, if possible (snippets)
- Wrap the error line with a special `<span class="line error-line">` tag so we can style it
- Output the response using `ejs`

The code for the function is as follows:

```
function displayDetails(err, req, res, next) {
  var stack = stackTrace.parse(err);
  var fileIndex = 1;

  console.error(err.stack);

  asyncEach(stack, function getContentInfo(item, cb) {
    // exclude core node modules and node modules
    if (/\//.test(item.fileName) &&
      !/node_modules/.test(item.fileName)) {
      fs.readFile(item.fileName, 'utf-8', function(err, content) {
        if (err) { return cb(err); }

        content = hljs.getHighlighted
          (content, 'javascript').innerHTML;

        // start a few lines before the error or at the beginning
        //    of the file
        var start = Math.max(item.lineNumber - 5, 0);
        var lines = content.split('\n');
        // end a few lines after the error or the last line of the
        //    file
        var end = Math.min(item.lineNumber + 4, lines.length);
        var snippet = lines.slice(start, end);
        // array starts at 0 but lines numbers begin with 1, so we
        //    have to
```

```
      // subtract 1 to get the error line position in the array
      var errLine = item.lineNumber - start - 1;

      snippet[errLine] = snippet[errLine].replace('<span
        class="line">', '<span class="line error-line">');

      item.content = snippet.join('\n');
      item.errLine = errLine;
      item.startLine = start;
      item.id = 'file-' + fileIndex;

      fileIndex++;

      cb(null, item);
    });
  } else {
    cb();
  }
}, function(e, items) {
  items = items.filter(function(item) { return !!item; });

  // if something bad happened while processing the stacktrace
  // make sure to return something useful
  if (e) {
    console.error(e);

    return res.send(err.stack);
  }

  res.send(renderTmpl({
    hljsStyle: hljsStyle,
    mainJs: mainJs,
    err: err,
    items: items
  }));

});
}
```

Our mission is partly finished; we still have to create the regular middleware function that opens the clicked file in the editor of our choice. To do this, we will use the `child_process` native Node module and invoke an external process, as shown in the following code:

```
// in this case the file will be opened with MacVim
// but feel free to replace with whatever editor you use
var editorCmd =
  '/Users/alexandruvladutu/bin/dotfiles/MacVim/mvim';

function openEditor(req, res, next) {
  var file = '/' + req.params[0];

  exec(editorCmd + ' ' + file, function(err) {
    if (!err) {
      res.send('The file should open in your editor now: <br /> '
        + file);
    } else {
      res.status(500).send(err.message);
    }
  });
}
```

Last but not least, we should export the two functions previously created:

```
module.exports = {
  displayDetails: displayDetails,
  openEditor: openEditor
};
```

Now, we need to update our `server.js` file to include the error handler and the editor middleware. The editor middleware should be loaded before the time zone route handler because it uses a wildcard. The error handler must be added after all the route handlers (so it can catch the errors). The code snippet is as follows:

```
var errorHandler = require('./lib/error-handler');
var ENV = process.env.NODE_ENV || 'development';
if (ENV === 'development') {
  app.get('/open-editor/*', errorHandler.openEditor);
}

app.get('/', routes.timezones.index);
app.get('/*', routes.timezones.show);

if (ENV === 'development') {
  app.use(errorHandler.displayDetails);
}
```

These additions are really useful in development, but you wouldn't want all that information exposed into production, so that's why we perform an environment check before including them.

Try to manually throw an error in a route or remove a variable, then start the server and see what happens. If everything is set up correctly, your page should resemble the screenshot presented at the beginning. If you click on a filename, it should open `MacVim` (our editor in this case) with the code.

This might not seem like much, but instead of having to switch context (between your code and the browser) and to manually search for the file that generated the error, you now have access to everything in one place (even the code will be a click away).

Using a debug flag

Many of us have probably used `console.log` while debugging, and once we were done, removed it. This is not ideal because later on, either us or some colleagues might need to check out the same information, so it would have to be added (and perhaps removed or commented out) again.

Instead, we can employ the same technique used in Node core, Express, and other modules using a debug function that only outputs the arguments when an environment variable is set.

Try to run the preceding application (or any other Express application) using the following command:

```
$ NODE_DEBUG="http,net" node server.js
```

The Node core files make use of the `NODE_DEBUG` environment variable to output debug information. In the preceding example, we have specified that we want to listen for the output that comes from two native modules: `http` and `net`. After you visit a page or two, the output should be similar to the following:

```
NET: 15418 listen2 0.0.0.0 7777 4 false
NET: 15418 _listen2: create a handle
NET: 15418 bind to 0.0.0.0
NET: 15418 onconnection
NET: 15418 _read
NET: 15418 Socket._read readStart
HTTP: SERVER new http connection
```

```
NET: 15418 onread undefined 0 529 529

NET: 15418 got data

HTTP: outgoing message end.

NET: 15418 afterWrite 0 { domain: null, bytes: 595, oncomplete:
[Function: afterWrite] }
```

The format of the preceding logs includes the module name (NET or HTTP), the process ID (15418 in this case), and other parameters. These logs are useful when trying to debug something at a lower level (tcp/http) in Node core.

Luckily, Express and other middleware use the same technique to output useful debugging information, but instead of the NODE_DEBUG environment variable, they use a simple DEBUG variable, as shown in the following screenshot:

```
$ DEBUG=* node server.js
  express:application booting in development mode +0ms
  express:router:layer new +0ms
  express:router use / query +0ms
  express:router:layer new +1ms
  express:router use / expressInit +0ms
  express:router:route new /favicon.ico +0ms
  express:router:layer new /favicon.ico +1ms
  express:router:route get /favicon.ico +1ms
  express:router:layer new +0ms
  express:router use / staticMiddleware +1ms
  express:router:route new /open-editor/* +0ms
  express:router:layer new /open-editor/* +0ms
  express:router:route get /open-editor/* +1ms
  express:router:route new / +0ms
  express:router:layer new / +1ms
  express:router:route get / +0ms
  express:router:route new /* +0ms
  express:router:layer new /* +0ms
  express:router:route get /* +0ms
  express:router:layer new +0ms
  express:router use / displayDetails +1ms
```

Express internally uses the debug module to achieve this, which has some handy features:

- The ability to select the output of different modules (comma-delimited)
- Shows the time spent between debug calls
- Wildcard support with the * char

The convention is to use a namespace for our application and separate the features by using (:). For example, we could add the following code to the `server.js` file in our time zone application:

```
var debug = require('debug')('timezone-app:main');
debug('application started on port %s', process.env.PORT || 7777);
```

We may want to add other debugging information, such as the time zone selected by the user in the `timezones.js` route:

```
// at the beginning of the file
var debug = require('debug')('timezone-app:routes:timezones');

// in the show function
debug('showing time for %s', place);
```

Let's start the application and only show the output that we have included previously (namespace `timezone-app`):

```
$ DEBUG=timezone-app:* node server.js
```

After we visit the time zone page a couple of times, it will output the following information to the terminal:

```
timezone-app:main application started on port 7777 +0ms

timezone-app:routes:timezones showing time for Europe/Berlin +0ms

timezone-app:routes:timezones showing time for Europe/London +5s

timezone-app:routes:timezones showing time for America/Los_Angeles +7s
```

Debug versus logger

There are several benefits to using the debug module versus a regular logger in the debug mode, such as the following:

- We can selectively output the information based on features/files.

- With a logger, we normally get the output of all the logs (because if we enable the debug level; this means all higher levels will be enabled too).

- Perhaps the application we are developing is just a piece of a larger puzzle (a monitoring/admin dashboard, for example), so instead of using another logger (the main application surely has one already), we use debug and let the developer activate it when needed.

- We can debug multiple Node modules using the same interface (Express, Node core files, and others), so it's a good thing to adhere to the same standards.

Debugging routes and middleware

When we start working on an application that's already being developed, one of the first things we want to find out is what are the routes and middleware functions defined. In general, we should be able to deduce that right away from a `server.js` file for example, but some applications are more complex than that and might load middleware from different files.

To check out what routes and middleware functions are present on the stack, we can iterate through the `app._router.stack` object, as shown in the following example:

```
var express = require('express');
var app = express();
var inspect = require('util').inspect;
var morgan = require('morgan');

var users = [{ name: 'John Doe', age: 27 }];

app.use(morgan());

app.route('/users').get(function(req, res, next) {
  res.send(users);
}).post(function(req, res, next) {
  res.send('ok');
});

app._router.stack.forEach(function(item) {
  if (item.route) {
    console.log('Route: %s', inspect(item.route, { depth: 5 }));
  } else {
    console.log('Middleware: %s', item.handle.name || 'anonymous');
  }
  console.log('--------------------');
});

app.listen(process.env.PORT || 7777);
```

 This is not an official/documented feature, so it may change in the future. For example, in Express 3.x, the stack was defined in the `app.stack` array. The thing to have in mind here is that we can inspect the middleware stack (some have gone so far as to even modify it).

Using the V8 debugger

V8 comes with a debugger that can be accessed from outside the process by using a TCP protocol. Node comes with a built-in client for the debugger, but we can also add external tools to connect to the debugger—such as node-inspector (`https://www.npmjs.org/package/node-inspector`).

Creating our buggy application

To showcase the debugger, we will create a sample Express application that contains a bug (not that hard to spot actually). The application will have three endpoints:

- `/`: The main page will assign a random name and e-mail to the session in case they don't already exist, or redirect the user to `/whoami` if they are already set

- `/whoami`: This is used to check the name and e-mail stored in the session

- `/refresh`: This destroys the session and redirects to the main page

The code for this application is as follows:

```
var express = require('express');
var app = express();
var morgan = require('morgan');
var cookieParser = require('cookie-parser');
var session = require('express-session');
var Faker = require('Faker');

app.use(morgan('dev'));
app.use(cookieParser()); // required before session.
app.use(session({
  secret: 'secret keyword'
}));

app.get('/', function(req, res, next) {

  if (req.session.name) {
    res.redirect('/whoami');
  }

  var secretIdentity = {
    name: Faker.Name.findName(),
    email: Faker.Internet.email()
  };
```

```
    req.session.name = secretIdentity.name;
    req.session.email = secretIdentity.email;

    var tmpl = 'We will call you ' + secretIdentity.name;
    tmpl += ' from now on and email you at ' + secretIdentity.email;
    tmpl += '</br > Reset your identity by going to the following
      URL: ';
    tmpl += '<a href="/refresh">/refresh</a>';

    res.send(tmpl);
  });

app.get('/whoami', function(req, res, next) {
  res.send('Name ' + req.session.name + ' | Email: ' +
    req.session.email);
  });

app.get('/refresh', function(req, res, next) {
  req.session.destroy(function(err) {
    if (err) { return next(err); }

    res.redirect('/');
    });
  });

  app.listen(process.env.PORT || 7777);
```

Before running the application, we should install the required dependencies: morgan (the logger), cookie-parser, express-session, and Faker (for generating fake data).

Now we can start the application and check it out. The problem appears when visiting the main page twice since we are assigned a new identity (name and e-mail) each time. It should normally assign a name and an e-mail for the first time, and then for each subsequent visit, it should just redirect us to /whoami without reassigning them.

Using Node's debugger client in the terminal

First of all, we will add some breakpoints (using the `debugger` keyword) in our code so that we can pause the execution and take a look at what's going on:

```
app.get('/', function(req, res, next) {
  debugger;

  if (req.session.name) {
    res.redirect('/whoami');
  }

  debugger;
```

To start the Node process with the debugger client, we need to add the debug argument as follows:

```
$ node debug server.js
```

We can then type `cont` in the terminal when we want to continue execution, and `repl` if we want to have access to the variables in that context, as shown in the following screenshot:

```
$ node debug server.js
< debugger listening on port 5858
connecting... ok
break in server.js:1
  1 "use strict";
  2
  3 var express = require('express');
debug> cont
break in server.js:17
 15
 16 app.get('/', function(req, res, next) {
 17   debugger;
 18
 19   if (req.session.name) {
debug> cont
break in server.js:23
 21   }
 22
 23   debugger;
 24
 25   var secretIdentity = {
debug> repl
Press Ctrl + C to leave debug repl
> req.session.name
>
```

Make sure you make a request to the main page after the first `cont` (we have to wait for the server to bind to the port).

While debugging, we see that after the first debugger statement, the route handler for the main page does not redirect and exit, but it continues to execute what remains in that function. So that was our problem; we simply forgot to call `return` after using `res.redirect()`.

Using node-inspector

One of the most popular Node debugging solutions is `node-inspector` (`https://www.npmjs.org/package/node-inspector`) because it has a familiar interface that resembles the Google Chrome developer tools.

All we have to do is start our Node process with the `-debug` flag and run node-inspector in the terminal (because it's globally installed). Then, we can open the debugging interface in the browser, by visiting `http://127.0.0.1:8080/debug?port=5858`, as shown in the following screenshot:

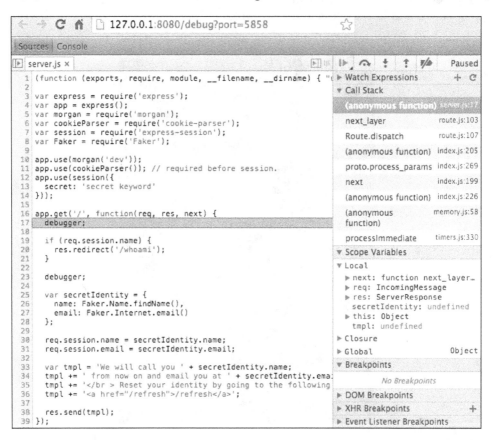

Debugging memory leaks

Memory leaks are one of the nastiest bugs you can encounter in your applications. That's because they are usually hard to track down, since some of them can take days to build and require certain conditions to be met.

The `heapdump` (`https://www.npmjs.org/package/heapdump`) module allows us to take heap snapshots programmatically, so we can inspect them at a later point in time. The snapshots will be saved in the current working directory and will have the `heapsnapshot` file extension.

Let's create a sample application that stores a lot of new objects into an array with each request made. The application will check for the memory usage every minute and compare it with the threshold; if it's bigger than the threshold, then a heap snapshot will be written to the disk, and the threshold will be augmented with another 100 megabytes; otherwise, it does nothing.

The full code for the application will thus be the following:

```
var heapdump = require('heapdump');
var express = require('express');
var app = express();

var leaks = [];
function Leak() {};
var memoryThreshold = 50;

setInterval(function () {
  // get RSS in bytes and convert to megabytes
  var memoryUsage = process.memoryUsage().rss / 1024 / 1024;

  if (memoryUsage > memoryThreshold) {
    // write to disk
    heapdump.writeSnapshot();
    // increase memory threshold
    memoryThreshold += 100;
  }
}, 60000);

app.use(function(req, res, next) {
  for (var i = 0; i < 1000; i++) {
    leaks.push(new Leak());
  }
```

```
    res.send('Memory usage: ' + (process.memoryUsage().rss / 1024 /
        1024));
});

app.listen(process.env.PORT || 7777);
```

To make a lot of connections to the server, we can use the ab benchmarking tool. Once the memory increases above the threshold, the heap snapshot will be made, but take into consideration that it may take a minute before that happens (because of the interval).

To inspect the snapshot, open the Google Chrome browser, press *F12* to open the developer tools, select the **Profiles** tab, right-click in the tab pane, and select Load. Now, select the file and click on **Open**. You should see something similar to what is shown in the following screenshot:

Notice that there are tons of objects that have the Leak constructor, so in this particular example, it isn't hard to figure out the culprit. In production applications it can be harder to track down these issues, so you'll probably need to take multiple snapshots from time to time and compare them (this can be done in the **Profiles** tab too).

Taking the snapshots will require extra CPU, so we have to pay attention as to when and how often we do that. We could use different strategies when taking the snapshots, such as:

- Use the idle module to let us know when Node is idling
- If we are using something like node-http-proxy (https://www.npmjs.org/package/http-proxy) or hipcache (https://www.npmjs.org/package/hipache), we could have multiple processes open for the same server, detach one while the snapshot is being taken, and continue the process with the rest (one by one)
- For further insights on this topic, feel free to check out the following links:
    - https://developers.google.com/chrome-developer-tools/docs/memory-analysis-101
    - http://addyosmani.com/blog/taming-the-unicorn-easing-javascript-memory-profiling-in-devtools/
    - https://developers.google.com/chrome-developer-tools/docs/heap-profiling#views

Adding a REPL to our Express application

A **Read-Eval-Print-Loop (REPL)** is an interactive environment that accepts user input, evaluates it, and outputs the result back to the user.

It is possible to connect to a live, running application by using the replify (https://www.npmjs.org/package/replify) and repl-client (https://www.npmjs.org/package/repl-client) modules. The first one will add a REPL to our application, while the second one can be used to connect to it. The following are the commands to use replify and repl-client:

```
$ npm i replify
$ npm i repl-client -g
```

First, we should set up a quick sample application using the following code:

```
var replify = require('replify');
var express = require('express');
var app = express();
```

```
app.use(function(req, res, next) {
  res.send('all good');
});

app.listen(process.env.PORT || 7777);
replify('replify-app-' + process.pid, app);
console.log('Use the command below to connect to the REPL:');
console.log('rc /tmp/repl/replify-app-' + process.pid + '.sock');
```

The two parameters of the `replify` function represent the name of the application (which will also be used to name the `.sock` file) and the application object itself, which will be accessible in the REPL. To make other objects accessible in the REPL, we can pass in a third parameter.

After we start the server, we can now connect to the REPL using the `repl-client` and inspect and manipulate the `app` variable or other objects the application shares:

```
$ rc /tmp/repl/replify-app-20352.sock

replify-app-20352> app.settings
{ 'x-powered-by': true,
  etag: true,
  env: 'development',
  'subdomain offset': 2,
  view: [Function: View],
  views: '/Users/alexandruvladutu/www/mastering_express/chapter_09/using-replify/views',
  'jsonp callback name': 'callback' }
replify-app-20352>
```

The `app` object can be inspected, but we can do other interesting things such as changing the application settings. If we make a request to the application now, we will see the following header (among others):

```
X-Powered-By: Express
```

Let's disable the `x-powered-by` setting from the REPL and see what happens:

```
replify-app-20352> app.disable('x-powered-by')
```

Now, when we make another request to the application, the header will not be present anymore. We have to be careful when dealing with production applications, but this technique can prove to be a great addition to our debugging toolbox.

Removing debugging commands

While using debugging techniques during development is helpful (such as the `debug` module, `console.log`, or the `debugger` statement), you should remove the leftovers from the code for production-ready applications.

Fortunately, there's a handy tool just for that, which is called `groundskeeper` (`https://www.npmjs.org/package/groundskeeper`):

```
$ npm i groundskeeper -g
```

Let's consider the following sample application:

```
var debug = require('debug')('myapp:main');
var express = require('express');
var app = express();

app.use(function(req, res, next) {
  req.session = { user: 'John', email: 'john@example.com' };
  next();
});

app.get('/', function(req, res, next) {
  debug('user %s visited /', req.session.user);

  res.send('ok');
});

app.listen(process.env.PORT || 7777);
```

The application is really light and contains a single call to the `debug` function after requiring it. To remove the two debug lines and write to a new file, run the following command in the terminal:

```
$ groundskeeper -n debug < server.js > clean-server.js
```

The tool uses `esprima` (`https://www.npmjs.org/package/esprima`) and `falafel` (`https://www.npmjs.org/package/falafel`) to walk through the abstract syntax tree and regenerate the code without the debugging functions.

Summary

We have covered some useful debugging tools and techniques that can give us a hand when trying to discover the bugs within our code. While we have tackled every existing tool, we should have a pretty solid debugging toolbox now.

In the next chapter, we are going to focus on the security aspects of Express applications.

10
Application Security

In this chapter, we are going to talk about various security issues that we should handle if we want our web applications to be more secure. We will cover the following topics:

- Running Express applications on privileged ports in a secure way
- **Cross-site request forgery (CSRF)** and **cross-site scripting (XSS)**
- Adding security headers using Helmet
- Handling file uploads
- Session middleware parameters

Running Express applications on privileged ports

The root user on Unix systems is a special user who has the ability to make system-wide changes and practically has full control over the machine. If we run an Express application as the root, and it has a vulnerability that is exploited by a hacker, then the hacker can cause a lot of damage, such as formatting the disk for instance.

To bind a web application to a port below `1024`, (such as ports `80` or `443`), root permissions are needed, but there are some workarounds to the problem, which are as follows:

- Redirect port `80` to another port that does not require superuser permissions (such as port `8000`), by using `iptables` (https://help.ubuntu.com/community/IptablesHowTo)

- Start the application using authbind (http://manpages.ubuntu.com/ manpages/hardy/man1/authbind.1.html), a system utility that allows us to run applications that would normally require superuser privileges to bind to low-numbered ports as a non-privileged user
- Drop the root privileges after binding to a special port (which requires an extra few lines of code inside our Express application)
- Run the application behind a proxy such as HAProxy or NGiNX

Now, we are going to explore the preceding first three ways to achieve this.

Dropping root privileges

To be able to bind the server to a port number lower than 1024 (such as 80 or 443), one option would be to start the program as an admin using sudo. However, for security reasons, it's not okay to continue running our application with admin rights after it starts listening on such a port, so we should downgrade to a regular user instead.

A solution to this problem is to add a few lines of code to our application and change the user and group identity of the process once the port has been opened:

```
var http = require('http');
var express = require('express');
var app = express();
var PORT = process.env.PORT || 7777;

app.get('*', function(req, res, next) {
  res.send({
    uid: process.getuid(),
    gid: process.getgid()
  });
});

http.createServer(app).listen(PORT, function() {
  console.log("Express server listening on port " + PORT);
  downgradeFromRoot();
});

function downgradeFromRoot() {
  if (process.env.SUDO_GID && process.env.SUDO_UID) {
    process.setgid(parseInt(process.env.SUDO_GID, 10));
    process.setuid(parseInt(process.env.SUDO_UID, 10));
  }
}
```

In the preceding code, we have reverted the application's permissions to those of a normal user by reading the SUDO_GID and SUDO_UID environment variables. These variables are automatically set on Unix systems when running a program with the sudo command, as shown in the following example:

```
$ sudo PORT=80 node server.js
```

Redirecting to another port using iptables

Another popular approach for running Express on privileged ports safely is to redirect the incoming connections from a privileged port to a port higher than 1024 by using iptables.

Let's say we want to redirect port 80 to port 8080. To achieve this, we need to add the following rules:

```
$ sudo iptables -A INPUT -i eth0 -p tcp --dport 80 -j ACCEPT
$ sudo iptables -A INPUT -i eth0 -p tcp --dport 8080 -j ACCEPT
$ sudo iptables -A PREROUTING -t nat -i eth0 -p tcp --dport 80 -j
REDIRECT --to-port 8080
```

The first two will make sure the ports are open, while the last command will ensure the redirection.

Using authbind

The authbind utility is a system utility that allows applications to listen to privileged ports. To install it on a Debian/Ubuntu system, run the following command in the terminal:

```
$ sudo apt-get install authbind
```

Next, we will need to configure authbind so that it will allow our user to bind applications to a port, specifically port 80 in our example:

```
$ sudo touch /etc/authbind/byport/80
$ sudo chown type_your_username_in_here /etc/authbind/byport/80
$ sudo chmod 755 /etc/authbind/byport/80
```

Now, to start the Express application, we need to type in the following command into the console:

```
$ authbind PORT=80 node server.js
```

There may be situations where we aren't directly booting up the Express application; instead, we are using another program to run it and keep it alive perhaps (such as the `forever` module, which is installable with NPM). In such a case, we need to make sure we are calling `authbind` with the `-deep` flag, as shown in the following example:

```
$ authbind --deep forever server.js
```

Cross-site request forgery protection

Cross-site request forgery (CSRF) is an attack that exploits the fact that a user is logged in to a site to make a malicious request to that website with the user's browser. For example, the user can be tricked into visiting a page that's making a background request to another website for which the user is authenticated.

Let's create a simple Express application that allows users to place orders. Since we're just trying to showcase how to be protected against CSRF attacks, we won't have a login system; just suppose that it's a single-user application this time. All the orders will be stored into memory.

This application will have two pages: the home page that allows the user to place an order, and the orders page that lists all the orders made by the user. Besides the two pages mentioned, there is another Express route to place an order.

Along with `express`, we will also need to install the `body-parser` and `ejs` modules for this example. The `server.js` file will have the following code:

```
var express = require('express');
var bodyParser = require('body-parser');

var app = express();

// view setup
app.set('view engine', 'html');
app.set('views', __dirname + '/views');
app.engine('html', require('ejs').renderFile);

app.use(bodyParser());

// in memory store this time
var orders = [];
```

```
app.get('/', function(req, res, next) {
  res.render('index');
});

app.post('/orders', function(req, res, next) {
  orders.push({
    details: req.body.order,
    placed: new Date()
  });

  res.redirect('/orders');
});

app.get('/orders', function(req, res, next) {
  res.render('orders', {
    orders: orders
  });
});

app.listen(3000);
```

The `index.html` file is pretty regular and contains a simple form with an input for the order. The `index.html` file contains the following code:

```
<!DOCTYPE HTML>
<html lang="en">
<head>
  <meta charset="UTF-8">
  <title>Place your order</title>
</head>
<body>
  <h1>Order anything!</h1>

  <form action="/orders" method="POST">
    <input type="text" name="order" />
    <input type="submit" value="Go" />
  </form>

</body>
</html>
```

If we install the dependencies and run the application, we'll see that we can place orders and see the list of orders while visiting the `/orders` page.

Now, let's create another application that outputs a single page that contains a form similar to the previous one, the differences being that this one will contain the value for the order, and it will submit the form right away using JavaScript. The code is shown as follows:

```
var express = require('express');
var app = express();

app.use(function(req, res, next) {
  var html = '<form id="place-order" action="http://localhost:3000/
orders" method="POST">';
  html += '<input type="text" name="order" value="1000 pizzas"
    />';
  html += '</form>';
  html += '<script>document.getElementById("place-
    order").submit();</script>'

  res.send(html);
});

app.listen(4000);
```

Now, let's run the preceding application. Imagine it's hosted somewhere on the Web (using a normal domain) and somebody tricked us into visiting this page. On opening `http://localhost:4000/` now, this is what you will see:

We placed the first two orders, but hold on for a second. Where did the third order with 1,000 pizzas come from?

Well, we visited that malicious page that made a POST request to the ordering application on behalf of us, taking advantage of the fact that we were authenticated (actually, in this specific case, there was no login mechanism, so it's kind of the same thing).

We can prevent this from happening by ensuring the user visited the page before placing the order. Generating a unique token on the backend and sending it along with the form can achieve this.

First, we must install `cookie-session` (we can also use the Express session middleware) and the `csurf` modules:

```
$ npm i cookie-session csurf
```

Then, we need to integrate the two into the `server.js` file, making our middleware-loading code look like the following:

```
var session = require('cookie-session');
var csrf = require('csurf');
app.use(session({
  secret: 'a3Bys4#$2jTs'
}));
app.use(bodyParser());
app.use(csrf());
```

The `csurf` module does two things:

- It ensures the `csrf` token is included when making a request that modifies the data on the backend (which means it will ignore the GET, HEAD, and OPTIONS requests, for example)
- It provides a `req.csrfToken()` function to generate the token

The only thing left would be to include this token into a hidden input field named _csrf in our form. We would need to repeat this for every form we create, so we could create a helper that we can reuse for every form:

```
app.use(function(req, res, next) {
  if (req.method === 'GET') {
    res.locals.csrf = function() {
      return "<input type='hidden' name='_csrf' value='" +
        req.csrfToken() + "' />";
    }
  }

  next();
});
```

To include the `csrf` token into our form, add the following line before the `</form>` closing tag:

```
<%- csrf() %>
```

If we run the application in the production mode (NODE_ENV=production node server.js) and visit the malicious site (http://localhost:4000/), we should get a Forbidden error message. However, if we try to place the order ourselves, it should work as it did before.

Basically, what we did so far is to ensure that the user visited a page from our application and then clicked on the **Submit** button.

 Using CSRF while caching full pages is tricky because CSRF tokens are unique for each user session. A solution would be to partially cache pages that contain CSRF placeholders into a database (such as Redis) and then replace the placeholders with the real tokens when rendering them to the client. If client-side JavaScript is mandatory for your application to work properly (it should not be disabled), other solutions can be used to include dynamically loading the token into the page (using Ajax, for example).

Cross-site scripting

A **Cross-site scripting** (**XSS**) type of attack allows hackers to inject malicious client-side scripts into web applications. Once the script is injected into a trusted website, it has access to the user's sensitive information such as cookies, the content of the page, and others.

To guard our Express applications against this type of attack, we should employ the following techniques:

- Validate data sent by the user (input)
- Sanitize output stored on the backend, such as into a database
- Enable content-security policy

Validating input

We should always try to validate data sent by the users before processing it. In some situations, we can validate it against a list of known values, but this isn't always the case.

A handy module to do validation is express-validator (https://www.npmjs.org/package/express-validator), which has all sorts of functions built in.

Sanitizing output

Validation is the first line of defense, but it's not enough. We cannot stop the user from entering quotes, for example, when writing a description. These situations require the output to be escaped/sanitized in some way, as shown in the following steps:

1. Let's create an insecure application that displays a user's details. We will store the details into memory and use `ejs` again as the template engine. The first thing we are going to set up is the template, so we can figure out ways to exploit it:

```
<!DOCTYPE HTML>
<html lang="en">
<head>
  <meta charset="UTF-8">
  <title>User <%- user.id %></title>
</head>
<body style="background: <%- user.color %>">

  <h1>Details for user <%- user.id %></h1>

  <ul>
    <li>Name: <%- user.name %></li>
    <li>Alias: <%- user.alias %></li>
    <li>Description: <%- user.description %></li>
  </ul>

  <script type="text/javascript">
    var userConfig = "<%- JSON.stringify(user.config) %>";
  </script>
</body>
</html>
```

2. Now, for the `server.js` file, start with the module dependencies and the view engine setup:

```
var express = require('express');
var app = express();
var ejs = require('ejs');

// view setup
app.set('view engine', 'html');
app.set('views', __dirname + '/views');
app.engine('html', ejs.renderFile);
```

3. The next part is interesting because we will define the `users` object with specific data to hack the application (exploit it using XSS and display an alert pop up to the user). We will achieve that by doing the following:

    ○   Since the description is not escaped, we can include a script

    ○   To hack the `color` property, we must enter double quotes and then the `onload` attribute that contains an alert

    ○   Last but not least, `JSON.stringify()` does not eliminate the need for escaping because we can include a closing `script` tag and then another script that gets evaluated

The rest of the code for the file is as follows:

```
var users = {
  1: {
    name: 'John Doe',
    alias: 'john',
    description: '<script>alert("hacked!")</script>',
    color: '#CCC;" onload="javascript:alert(\'yet another
      hack!\')',
    config: {
      motto: "</script>
<script>alert('hacked again!!'); </script>"
    },
    id: 1
  }
};

app.use('/users/:id', function(req, res, next) {
  res.render('user', {
    user: users[req.params.id]
  });
});

app.listen(7777);
```

4. We can start the application using the following command and see what happens now:

    ```
    $ node server.js
    ```

5. When we visit the page, we will see three alerts pop up, indicating that there are also three exploits on the page. If you look closely at the code for the template, you will see that there are different places where data is not sanitized:

    ○   The `style` attribute on the `body` tag

    ○   The HTML code inside the list item

    ○   The JavaScript code at the bottom of the page

Because the data is outputted in different contexts, we cannot use the same sanitization technique all over the place. This is where the `secure-filters` module (`https://www.npmjs.org/package/secure-filters`) comes into play because it is aware of the context.

According to the documentation, the `secure-filters` module has the following functions for sanitizing output:

*   `html(value)`: This function is used for HTML content sanitization using entity encoding

*   `js(value)`: This function is used for JavaScript string sanitization using backslash encoding

*   `jsObj(value)`: This function is used for JavaScript literal sanitization, and it's useful when including objects in an HTML `script` tag

- `jsAttr(value)`: This function is used for JavaScript string sanitization in the context of an HTML attribute (which uses a combination of entity and backslash encoding)

- `uri(value)`: This function is used for URL sanitization using percent encoding

- `css(value)`: This function is used for CSS context sanitization using backslash encoding

- `style(value)`: This function is used for CSS context sanitization in an HTML-style attribute

These functions can be used either as standalone or with `ejs`. Since we are already using `ejs` for the application, we will go with the second option.

We will have to add a single line of code to the `server.js` file to make those functions visible inside the template:

```
var ejs = require('secure-filters').configure(require('ejs'));
```

To sanitize the output, three filters need to be added to the template: one for escaping HTML content, a second one for escaping the value in the `style` attribute, and the last one for sanitizing the JavaScript string. The template code will now contain the following code:

```
<!DOCTYPE HTML>
<html lang="en">
<head>
  <meta charset="UTF-8">
  <title>User <%- user.id %></title>
</head>
<body style="background: <%-: user.color | style %>">

  <h1>Details for user <%- user.id %></h1>

  <ul>
    <li>Name: <%- user.name %></li>
    <li>Alias: <%- user.alias %></li>
    <li>Description: <%= user.description %></li>
  </ul>

  <script type="text/javascript">
    var userConfig = "<%-: JSON.stringify(user.config) | js %>";
  </script>
</body>
</html>
```

Now, when we run the server and revisit the page, it will be alert-free, but bear in mind that an attacker can do a lot worse if he wants (such as stealing a user's cookies and impersonating him).

The important thing to keep in mind is to watch out for the context and use the correct filter where needed.

HTTP security headers with Helmet

We have previously discussed input validation and data sanitization for protection against XSS attacks, but there is another last line of defense we can employ, that is, using the `content-security-policy` header.

This header allows us to declare resources (such as JavaScript files, images, and stylesheets) that can be served from trusted domains only. The most common CSP directives are as follows:

- `connect-src`: This specifies which origin the server is allowed to connect to (this applies to XHR requests, WebSockets, and EventSource)
- `font-src`: This defines where the fonts can be loaded from
- `frame-src`: This specifies which origins can be embedded as frames
- `img-src`, `media-src`, `object-src`, and `script-src`: These define the origins from where images, media elements (audio and video), plugins (flash and others), stylesheets, and JavaScript files can be loaded

By default, the directives are open, which means the resources can be loaded from everywhere. This behavior can be changed with the `default-src` directive.

The `helmet` module (`https://www.npmjs.org/package/helmet`) allows us to specify these directives by using an Express middleware:

```
app.use(helmet.csp({
  'default-src': ["'self'", 'default.com'],
  'script-src': ['scripts.com'],
  'style-src': ['style.com'],
  'img-src': ['img.com'],
  'connect-src': ['connect.com'],
  'font-src': ['font.com'],
  'object-src': ['object.com'],
  'media-src': ['media.com'],
  'frame-src': ['frame.com'],
  'sandbox': ['allow-forms', 'allow-scripts'],
  'report-uri': ['/report-violation'],
```

```
    reportOnly: false, // set to true if you only want to report errors
    setAllHeaders: false, // set to true if you want to set all headers
    safari5: false // set to true if you want to force buggy CSP in
  Safari 5
});
```

Besides the CSP middleware, the `helmet` module also includes other helpful security middleware, such as the following:

- **hsts (HTTP Strict Transport Security)**: This adds the `Strict-Transport-Security` header, which restricts users to connect to the website only via secure connections

- **xframe (X-Frame-Options)**: This header specifies whether the website can be loaded into a frame or an iframe

- **iexss (X-XSS-Protection for IE8+)**: This adds basic XSS protection

- **ienoopen (X-Download-Options for IE8+)**: This sets the `X-Download-Options` header to `noopen` to prevent IE users from opening file downloads in the website's context

- **contentTypeOptions (X-Content-Type-Options)**: This sets the `X-Content-Type-Options` to `nosniff` to prevent the browser from doing MIME-type sniffing

- **hidePoweredBy (remove X-Powered-By)**: This removes the `X-Powered-By` header, which is automatically set by Express

Handling file uploads

A common thing that people sometimes forget when dealing with file uploads is to remove the temporary files after they're done with them.

Let's create an application that allows the user to upload an image and list its properties. We will first need to install the `express`, `gm`, `connect-multiparty`, and `ejs` modules, using the following command:

```
$ npm i express gm connect-multiparty ejs
```

 For the gm module to work properly, we also need to install `GraphicsMagick` and `ImageMagick`. For more details, check out the NPM page for the module at `https://www.npmjs.org/package/gm`.

First, let's create the `home.html` template file inside the `/views` folder, using the following code:

```
<!DOCTYPE HTML>
<html lang="en">
<head>
  <meta charset="UTF-8">
  <title>Uploading files</title>
</head>
<body>
  <h1>Upload file</h1>

  <form action="/files" method="POST" enctype="multipart/form-
    data">
    <div>
      <label for="file">File:</label>
      <input type="file" name="file" />
    </div>
    <div>
      <input type="submit" value="Upload" />
    </div>
  </form>
</body>
</html>
```

Next, we will create the `server.js` file, which lists the `image` properties after the upload:

```
var express = require('express');
var app = express();
var multipart = require('connect-multiparty');
var gm = require('gm');

// view setup
app.set('view engine', 'html');
app.set('views', __dirname + '/views');
app.engine('html', require('ejs').renderFile);

app.get('/', function(req, res, next) {
  res.render('home');
});

app.post('/files', multipart(), function(req, res, next) {
  // console.log(req.files);
```

```
    if (!req.files.file) {
      return res.send('File missing');
    }

    gm(req.files.file.path).identify(function(err, data) {
      if (err) { return next(err); }

      res.send(data);
    });
  });

  app.listen(7777);
```

Now, if we run the server and upload an image, we should see a page similar to the following screenshot:

The problem with this code is that we forgot to delete the temporary file once we extracted its properties. We can fix this by adding a few lines of code; let's first declare the `fs` dependency at the beginning of the `server.js` file:

```
var fs = require('fs');
```

Then, we need to actually remove the temporary file from the callback of the `gm.identify()` function:

```
fs.unlink(req.files.file.path, function() { /* ignored the error
  */ });
```

Another solution to the problem would be to use something like the `reap` module (`https://www.npmjs.org/package/reap`), which makes regular checks for old files and deletes them.

Session middleware parameters

When using the `session` middleware (`https://github.com/expressjs/session`) in Express, we have to pay attention to the parameters we pass when initializing the middleware, which are as follows:

- **The httpOnly property on the cookie property**: This defaults to true and should really stay that way, meaning the cookie cannot be read by frontend JavaScript code

- **The secure property on the cookie property**: When using HTTPS, we should enable this option, which will prevent the browser from transmitting the cookies over an unencrypted connection

- **The maxAge property on the cookie property**: If this property is unset, then it means that the cookie will become a browser-session cookie and will be removed once the user closes the browser; perhaps this should be set to something like 30 minutes (30 * 60 * 1000 in milliseconds) to avoid prolonged idle sessions

- **The secret property**: This is used to sign the session cookie to prevent tampering; this should not be copied from the module's page (such as `keyboard cat`); it should preferably be something long and random

Reauthenticating the user for sensitive operations

When performing really sensitive operations, it's a good practice to re-prompt the user for the password to make sure the right person is sitting in front of the computer and not somebody who is impersonating them.

Let's imagine for a second that our web application has features such as account deletion or changing the e-mail address for a user. For the sake of argument, let's also consider the possibility that the user who logged in went out for a lunch break and forgot to log out. What can we do to enhance security? Well, two things: expiring the session after a period of time and re-prompting the user when doing critical transactions.

Fortunately for us, the `cookie-session` middleware (as well as the `session` middleware) supports setting an expiry time. For reauthenticating the user, we can use a simple trick: remember the last login time of the user and check if it's less than one minute ago, for example.

Next, we will create an application to put this into practice. We'll need the following dependencies to be installed: `express`, `ejs`, `cookie-session`, `body-parser`, `method-override`, and `csurf`.

Now, let's include these dependencies, load the middleware, and set up the view using the following code:

```
var express = require('express');
var app = express();
var session = require('cookie-session');
var bodyParser = require('body-parser');
var methodOverride = require('method-override');
var csrf = require('csrf');

// view setup
app.set('view engine', 'html');
app.set('views', __dirname + '/views');
app.engine('html', require('ejs').renderFile);

app.use(session({
  secret: 'aqEosdP3%osn',
  maxAge: (30 * 60 * 1000) // expires in 30 minutes
}));
```

```
app.use(bodyParser());
app.use(methodOverride(function(req, res) {
  if (req.body && typeof req.body === 'object' && '_method' in
    req.body) {
    var method = req.body._method;
    delete req.body._method;

    return method;
  }
}));
app.use(csrf());
app.use(function(req, res, next) {
  if (req.method === 'GET') {
    res.locals.csrf = function() {
      return "<input type='hidden' name='_csrf' value='" +
        req.csrfToken() + "' />";
    }
  }

  next();
});
```

As shown previously, the sessions are set to expire after 30 minutes, and for CSRF protection, we are reusing the middleware that was previously created in this chapter. Now, we will define the routes and bind the application to a port:

```
// using this only in development instead of a real db
var users = {
  john: 'password'
};

app.get('/', function(req, res, next) {
  if (!req.session.user) {
    return res.redirect('/login');
  }

  res.render('home');
});

app.get('/login', function(req, res, next) {
  res.render('login');
});
```

```
app.post('/login', function(req, res, next) {
  if (users[req.body.username] === req.body.password) {
    req.session.loggedInTime = new Date().getTime();
    req.session.user = req.body.username;
    res.redirect('/');
  } else {
    res.redirect('/login?login=unsuccessful');
  }
});

app.get('/sensitive-data', function(req, res, next) {
  if (!req.session.user) {
    return res.redirect('/login');
  }

  var ago = (Date.now() - req.session.loggedInTime);

  if (ago <= 60000) {
    res.send('really sensitive data here');
  } else {
    res.redirect('/login');
  }
});

app['delete']('/logout', function(req, res, next) {
  req.session = null;
  res.redirect('/login');
});

app.listen(7777);
```

 Delete is a reserved word in JavaScript, so instead of using app.delete, it's better to have the delete property in brackets, as shown in the previous example.

If we run the application and log in with the combination john/password (where john is the username and the password is password) we can access the /sensitive-data page, but only for one minute after logging in. This means that, for example, if somebody takes control of our computer and tries to check out that page after more than a couple of minutes, they will be redirected to the /login page.

The CSRF check was to make sure that the user actually clicked on the **Submit** button, but all of this is to ensure that the person sitting in front of the computer is the user who is authenticated.

Summary

In this chapter, we have tackled some of the security issues we need to be aware of when writing a web application, but we haven't exhausted the list. One should always be on the lookout for new threats and ways to be protected against them.

In the next chapter, we will be looking at how to write tests and tools to improve code quality.

11
Testing and Improving Code Quality

In this chapter, we are going to see how to test Express applications and how to improve the code quality of our code by leveraging existing NPM modules. We will cover the following topics:

- Testing Express applications with Mocha, should.js, and supertest
- Mocking Node modules using proxyquire
- Code coverage
- Load testing
- Static analysis tools
- Automatically running tests before committing
- Continuous Integration
- An overview of client-side testing tools

The importance of having automated tests

By writing tests for our code, we are verifying its correctness, ensuring it does what it's supposed to do.

Moreover, if we have an extensive test suite, it gives us confidence to refactor code anytime, because we can always rerun our tests and check if something broke in the process. This means we have a solid foundation that we can build upon.

However, tests not only represent a form of ensuring the correctness of our application and managing risks but also act as a form of documentation. They basically describe how your application is supposed to behave under certain conditions.

Last but not least, this is an ideal task for a computer: it's a repetitive task that requires the same level of attention when executed and should be done as fast as possible.

These are just a few reasons why you should write tests for your applications, but you can find a lot more if you browse the Internet.

Testing toolbox

There are a handful of modules in NPM that can help us out when testing our applications, but in the next few lines we are going to focus on some of the most used ones:

- `Mocha`: This is a popular test framework for Node and for the browser created by the author of Express, TJ Holowaychuk
- `should.js`: This is an assertion library, which is framework agnostic
- `sinon`: This is a library that provides spies, stubs, and mocks, and it works in Node and the browser
- `supertest`: This is a high-level abstraction module for testing Node HTTP servers with a fluent API
- `proxyquire`: This is a simple library for mocking the required dependencies

Mocha

Mocha is one of the most feature-rich JavaScript testing frameworks. It has features such as multiple interfaces (such as behavior-driven development or test-driven development), multiple reporters, and runs asynchronous tests and specifies timeouts (for different levels). For more details, you can find the full documentation of the project page at http://visionmedia.github.io/mocha/.

should.js

The `should.js` file (`https://github.com/shouldjs/should.js`) is a BDD assertion library for Node that extends `Object.prototype` to provide a sugar syntax that is useful when writing tests. Without this library, our assertions might look like the following code:

```
assert.ok(err instanceof Error);
assert.ok(err.status === 400);
```

After refactoring the code to use the `should` module, it might look like this:

```
err.should.be.an.instanceOf(Error).and.have.property('status',
    404);
```

As you can see, the second version of the code is much more expressive and readable.

 Another popular assertion module that provides a similar functionality is `chai` (`https://www.npmjs.org/package/chai`).

Sinon.js

`Sinon.js` (`http://sinonjs.org/`) is a handy library for writing unit tests. It provides us with spies, stubs, and mocks out of the box and can run both in the browser and in Node.js. It is an essential tool for testing JavaScript applications and has other useful features beyond these three, such as fake timers and sandboxing. You can find the full documentation on the official website at `http://sinonjs.org/docs/`.

Spies

Test spies allow us to record function calls for later verification. A test spy is a function that can wrap another existing one, or it can be a standalone anonymous function. Here is a simple example:

```
{
  before: function () {
    // spying on an existing function
    sinon.spy(fs, "rename");
  },

  after: function () {
    fs.rename.restore(); // Unwraps the spy
  },
```

```
   "should move file to new location": function () {
     // anonymous spy
     var spy = sinon.spy();
     File.move('example.js', spy);

     // make sure spies were called
     fs.rename.calledOnce.should.be.true;
     spy.calledOnce.should.be.true;
   }
}
```

Stubs

A `Sinon.js` stub is similar to a spy, but it also represents a function that supports predefined behavior. A good use case for using stubs is when we want to simulate a functionality to make our system work normally during the testing phase.

A thing worth noting is that when using a stub to wrap a function, the stub does not call the original function. The following short example shows how to return different things based on the arguments provided to a `File.getExtension()` function:

```
var stub = sinon.stub(File.getExtension);
stub.withArgs('image.jpg').returns('jpg');
// will return 'jpg'
stub('image.jpg')
stub.withArgs('invalid_filename_*').throws();
// will throw an errror
stub('invalid_filename_*');
```

Mocks

Mocks, in `Sinon.js`, are similar to spies and stubs, the difference being that they require the expectations up-front. Here's an example:

```
var mock = sinon.mock(Validate);
mock.expects("isNumber").once().throws();

Validate.isNumber('string');

mock.verify();
```

Supertest

The `supertest` module is a great module for testing HTTP servers because of its intuitive API, which allows expectations to be used with status codes or headers. You can also chain the expectations, as shown in the following example:

```
request(app)
  .get('/login')
  .expect('Content-Type', /html/)
  .expect('Content-Length', '100')
  .expect(200)
  .end(function(err, res){
    if (err) throw err;
  });
```

Proxyquire

We will most likely need to override the dependencies used by a module when writing our unit tests. This is where `proxyquire` comes in, because it allows us to achieve that. Instead of using the regular `require` function when including a certain module, we will use the `proxyquire` function and specify the overridden dependencies as the second argument.

For example, let's imagine that we have a module `/lib/db.js`, and we would like to stub the `mysql` module, using the following code:

```
var proxyquire = require('proxyquire');
var db = proxyquire('./lib/db', {
  mysql: sinon.stub(mysql)
});
```

Generating phony data using Faker.js

`Faker.js` (`https://www.npmjs.org/package/faker`) allows us to generate fake data for all kinds of things ranging from names and addresses to catchphrases. The following is a simple example that generates fake data for a user:

```
var user = {};
user.ip = Faker.Internet.ip();
user.company = Faker.Company.companyName();
user.name = Faker.Name.firstName() + ' ' + Faker.Name.lastName();
```

Creating and testing an Express file-sharing application

Now, it's time to see how to develop and test an Express application with what we have learned previously.

We will create a file-sharing application that allows users to upload files and password-protect them if they choose to. After uploading the files to the server, we will create a unique ID for that file, store the metadata along with the content (as a separate JSON file), and redirect the user to the file's information page. When trying to access a password-protected file, an HTTP basic authentication pop up will appear, and the user will have to only enter the password (no username in this case).

The package.json file, so far, will contain the following code:

```json
{
  "name": "file-uploading-service",
  "version": "0.0.1",
  "private": true,
  "scripts": {
    "start": "node ./bin/www"
  },
  "dependencies": {
    "express": "~4.2.0",
    "static-favicon": "~1.0.0",
    "morgan": "~1.0.0",
    "cookie-parser": "~1.0.1",
    "body-parser": "~1.0.0",
    "debug": "~0.7.4",
    "ejs": "~0.8.5",
    "connect-multiparty": "~1.0.5",
    "cuid": "~1.2.4",
    "bcrypt": "~0.7.8",
    "basic-auth-connect": "~1.0.0",
    "errto": "~0.2.1",
    "custom-err": "0.0.2",
    "lodash": "~2.4.1",
    "csurf": "~1.2.2",
    "cookie-session": "~1.0.2",
    "secure-filters": "~1.0.5",
    "supertest": "~0.13.0",
    "async": "~0.9.0"
  },
  "devDependencies": {
  }
}
```

When bootstrapping an Express application using the CLI, a /bin/www file will be automatically created for you. The following is the version we have adopted to extract the name of the application from the package.json file. This way, in case we decide to change it we won't have to alter our debugging code because it will automatically adapt to the new name, as shown in the following code:

```
#!/usr/bin/env node
var pkg = require('../package.json');
var debug = require('debug')(pkg.name + ':main');
var app = require('../app');

app.set('port', process.env.PORT || 3000);

var server = app.listen(app.get('port'), function() {
  debug('Express server listening on port ' +
    server.address().port);
});
```

The application configurations will be stored inside config.json:

```
{
  "filesDir": "files",
  "maxSize": 5
}
```

The properties listed in the preceding code refer to the files folder (where the files will be updated), which is relative to the root and the maximum allowed file size.

The main file of the application is named app.js and lives in the root. We need the connect-multiparty module to support file uploads, and the csurf and cookie-session modules for CSRF protection. The rest of the dependencies are standard and we have used them before. The full code for the app.js file is as follows:

```
var express = require('express');
var path = require('path');
var favicon = require('static-favicon');
var logger = require('morgan');
var cookieParser = require('cookie-parser');
var session = require('cookie-session');
var bodyParser = require('body-parser');
var multiparty = require('connect-multiparty');
var Err = require('custom-err');
var csrf = require('csrf');
var ejs = require('secure-filters').configure(require('ejs'));
var csrfHelper = require('./lib/middleware/csrf-helper');
```

```
var homeRouter = require('./routes/index');
var filesRouter = require('./routes/files');

var config = require('./config.json');
var app = express();
var ENV = app.get('env');

// view engine setup
app.engine('html', ejs.renderFile);
app.set('views', path.join(__dirname, 'views'));
app.set('view engine', 'html');

app.use(favicon());
app.use(bodyParser.json());
app.use(bodyParser.urlencoded());
// Limit uploads to X Mb
app.use(multiparty({
  maxFilesSize: 1024 * 1024 * config.maxSize
}));
app.use(cookieParser());
app.use(session({
  keys: ['rQo2#0s!qkE', 'Q.ZpeR49@9!szAe']
}));
app.use(csrf());
// add CSRF helper
app.use(csrfHelper);

app.use('/', homeRouter);
app.use('/files', filesRouter);

app.use(express.static(path.join(__dirname, 'public')));

/// catch 404 and forward to error handler
app.use(function(req, res, next) {
  next(Err('Not Found', { status: 404 }));
});

/// error handlers

// development error handler
// will print stacktrace
if (ENV === 'development') {
  app.use(function(err, req, res, next) {
```

```
      res.status(err.status || 500);
      res.render('error', {
        message: err.message,
        error: err
      });
    });
  }

  // production error handler
  // no stacktraces leaked to user
  app.use(function(err, req, res, next) {
    res.status(err.status || 500);
    res.render('error', {
      message: err.message,
      error: {}
    });
  });
```

```
module.exports = app;
```

 Instead of directly binding the application to a port, we are exporting it, which makes our lives easier when testing with supertest. We won't need to care about things such as the default port availability or specifying a different port environment variable when testing.

To avoid having to create the whole input when including the CSRF token, we have created a helper for that inside lib/middleware/csrf-helper.js:

```
module.exports = function(req, res, next) {
  res.locals.csrf = function() {
    return "<input type='hidden' name='_csrf' value='" +
      req.csrfToken() + "' />";
  }

  next();
};
```

For the password-protection functionality, we will use the bcrypt module and create a separate file inside lib/hash.js for the hash generation and password-compare functionality:

```
var bcrypt = require('bcrypt');
var errTo = require('errto');
```

```
var Hash = {};

Hash.generate = function(password, cb) {
  bcrypt.genSalt(10, errTo(cb, function(salt) {
    bcrypt.hash(password, salt, errTo(cb, function(hash) {
      cb(null, hash);
    }));
  }));
};

Hash.compare = function(password, hash, cb) {
  bcrypt.compare(password, hash, cb);
};

module.exports = Hash;
```

The biggest file of our application will be the file model, because that's where most of the functionality will reside. We will use the `cuid()` module to create unique IDs for files, and the native `fs` module to interact with the filesystem.

The following code snippet contains the most important methods for `models/file.js`:

```
function File(options, id) {
  this.id = id || cuid();
  this.meta = _.pick(options, ['name', 'type', 'size', 'hash',
    'uploadedAt']);
  this.meta.uploadedAt = this.meta.uploadedAt || new Date();
};

File.prototype.save = function(path, password, cb) {
  var _this = this;

  this.move(path, errTo(cb, function() {
    if (!password) { return _this.saveMeta(cb); }

    hash.generate(password, errTo(cb, function(hashedPassword) {
      _this.meta.hash = hashedPassword;

      _this.saveMeta(cb);
    }));
  }));
};
```

```
File.prototype.move = function(path, cb) {
  fs.rename(path, this.path, cb);
};
```

For the full source code of the file, browse the code bundle. Next, we will create the routes for the file (`routes/files.js`), which will export an Express router. As mentioned before, the authentication mechanism for password-protected files will be the basic HTTP one, so we will need the `basic-auth-connect` module. At the beginning of the file, we will include the dependencies and create the router:

```
var express = require('express');
var basicAuth = require('basic-auth-connect');
var errTo = require('errto');
var pkg = require('../package.json');
var File = require('../models/file');
var debug = require('debug')(pkg.name + ':filesRoute');

var router = express.Router();
```

We will have to create two routes that will include the `id` parameter in the URL: one for displaying the file information and another one for downloading the file. In both of these cases, we will need to check if the file exists and require user authentication in case it's password-protected. This is an ideal use case for the `router.param()` function because these actions will be performed each time there is an `id` parameter in the URL. The code is as follows:

```
router.param('id', function(req, res, next, id) {
  File.find(id, errTo(next, function(file) {
    debug('file', file);

    // populate req.file, will need it later
    req.file = file;

    if (file.isPasswordProtected()) {
      // Password-protected file, check for password using HTTP
        basic auth
      basicAuth(function(user, pwd, fn) {
        if (!pwd) { return fn(); }

        // ignore user
        file.authenticate(pwd, errTo(next, function(match) {
          if (match) {
            return fn(null, file.id);
          }
```

```
          fn();
        }));
      })(req, res, next);
    } else {
      // Not password-protected, proceed normally
      next();
    }
  }));
});
```

The rest of the routes are fairly straightforward, using `response.download()` to send the file to the client, or using `response.redirect()` after uploading the file:

```
router.get('/', function(req, res, next) {
  res.render('files/new', { title: 'Upload file' });
});

router.get('/:id.html', function(req, res, next) {
  res.render('files/show', {
    id: req.params.id,
    meta: req.file.meta,
    isPasswordProtected: req.file.isPasswordProtected(),
    hash: hash,
    title: 'Download file ' + req.file.meta.name
  });
});

router.get('/download/:id', function(req, res, next) {
  res.download(req.file.path, req.file.meta.name);
});

router.post('/', function(req, res, next) {
  var tempFile = req.files.file;
  if (!tempFile.size) { return res.redirect('/files'); }

  var file = new File(tempFile);

  file.save(tempFile.path, req.body.password, errTo(next, function() {
    res.redirect('/files/' + file.id + '.html');
  }));
});

module.exports = router;
```

The view for uploading a file contains a multipart form with a CSRF token inside
(`views/files/new.html`):

```
<%- include ../layout/header.html %>

<form action="/files" method="POST" enctype="multipart/form-data">
  <div class="form-group">
    <label>Choose file:</label>
    <input type="file" name="file" />
  </div>

  <div class="form-group">
    <label>Password protect (leave blank otherwise):</label>
    <input type="password" name="password" />
  </div>

  <div class="form-group">
    <%- csrf() %>
    <input type="submit" />
  </div>
</form>

<%- include ../layout/footer.html %>
```

To display the file's details, we will create another view (`views/files/show.html`).
Besides showing the basic file information, we will display a special message in case
the file is password-protected, so that the client is notified that a password should
also be shared along with the link:

```
<%- include ../layout/header.html %>

<p>
  <table>
    <tr>
      <th>Name</th>
      <td><%= meta.name %></td>
    </tr>
      <th>Type</th>
      <td><%= meta.type %></td>
    </tr>
      <th>Size</th>
      <td><%= meta.size %> bytes</td>
    </tr>
```

```
        <th>Uploaded at</th>
        <td><%= meta.uploadedAt %></td>
      </tr>
    </table>
  </p>

  <p>
    <a href="/files/download/<%- id %>">Download file</a> |
    <a href="/files">Upload new file</a>
  </p>

  <p>
    To share this file with your friends use the <a href="/files/<%-
      id %>">current link</a>.
    <% if (isPasswordProtected) { %>
    <br />
    Don't forget to tell them the file password as well!
    <% } %>
  </p>

  <%- include ../layout/footer.html %>
```

Running the application

For the sake of brevity, not all the files needed to run the application were included previously, but you can find them in the source code accompanying this book.

To run the application, we need to install the dependencies and run the start script:

```
$ npm i
$ npm start
```

The default port for the application is 3000, so if we visit http://localhost:3000/files, we should see the following page:

After uploading the file, we should be redirected to the file's page, where its details will be displayed:

Unit tests

Unit testing allows us to test individual parts of our code in isolation and verify their correctness. By making our tests focused on these small components, we decrease the complexity of the setup, and most likely, our tests should execute faster.

Using the following command, we'll install a few modules to help us in our quest:

```
$ npm i mocha should sinon--save-dev
```

We are going to write unit tests for our file model, but there's nothing stopping us from doing the same thing for our routes or other files from /lib.

The dependencies will be listed at the top of the file (test/unit/file-model.js):

```
var should = require('should');
var path = require('path');
var config = require('../../config.json');
var sinon = require('sinon');
```

We will also need to require the native fs module and the hash module, because these modules will be stubbed later on. Apart from these, we will create an empty callback function and reuse it, as shown in the following code:

```
// will be stubbing methods on these modules later on
var fs = require('fs');
var hash = require('../../lib/hash');

var noop = function() {};
```

The tests for the instance methods will be created first:

```
describe('models', function() {
  describe('File', function() {
    var File = require('../../models/file');

    it('should have default properties', function() {
      var file = new File();

      file.id.should.be.a.String;
      file.meta.uploadedAt.should.be.a.Date;
    });

    it('should return the path based on the root and the file id',
      function() {
      var file = new File({}, '1');
      file.path.should.eql(File.dir + '/1');
    });

    it('should move a file', function() {
      var stub = sinon.stub(fs, 'rename');

      var file = new File({}, '1');
      file.move('/from/path', noop);

      stub.calledOnce.should.be.true;
      stub.calledWith('/from/path', File.dir + '/1',
        noop).should.be.true;

      stub.restore();
    });

    it('should save the metadata', function() {
      var stub = sinon.stub(fs, 'writeFile');
      var file = new File({}, '1');
      file.meta = { a: 1, b: 2 };

      file.saveMeta(noop);

      stub.calledOnce.should.be.true;
      stub.calledWith(File.dir + '/1.json',
        JSON.stringify(file.meta), noop).should.be.true;
```

```
    stub.restore();
  });

  it('should check if file is password protected', function() {
    var file = new File({}, '1');

    file.meta.hash = 'y';
    file.isPasswordProtected().should.be.true;

    file.meta.hash = null;
    file.isPasswordProtected().should.be.false;
  });

  it('should allow access if matched file password', function() {
    var stub = sinon.stub(hash, 'compare');

    var file = new File({}, '1');
    file.meta.hash = 'hashedPwd';
    file.authenticate('password', noop);

    stub.calledOnce.should.be.true;
    stub.calledWith('password', 'hashedPwd',
      noop).should.be.true;

    stub.restore();
  });
```

 We are stubbing the functionalities of the fs and hash modules because we want to test our code in isolation. Once we are done with the tests, we restore the original functionality of the methods.

Now that we're done testing the instance methods, we will go on to test the static ones (assigned directly onto the File object):

```
describe('.dir', function() {
  it('should return the root of the files folder', function() {
    path.resolve(__dirname + '/../../' +
      config.filesDir).should.eql(File.dir);
  });
});
```

```
    describe('.exists', function() {
      var stub;

      beforeEach(function() {
        stub = sinon.stub(fs, 'exists');
      });

      afterEach(function() {
        stub.restore();
      });

      it('should callback with an error when the file does not
        exist', function(done) {
        File.exists('unknown', function(err) {
          err.should.be.an.instanceOf(Error).and.have.
property('status',
    404);
          done();
        });

        // call the function passed as argument[1] with the
          parameter `false`
        stub.callArgWith(1, false);
      });

      it('should callback with no arguments when the file exists',
        function(done) {
        File.exists('existing-file', function(err) {
          (typeof err === 'undefined').should.be.true;
          done();
        });

        // call the function passed as argument[1] with the
          parameter `true`
        stub.callArgWith(1, true);
      });
    });

  });
});
```

To stub asynchronous functions and execute their callback, we use the `stub.callArgWith()` function provided by `sinon`, which executes the callback provided by the argument with the index `<<number>>` of the stub with the subsequent arguments. For more information, check out the official documentation at `http://sinonjs.org/docs/#stubs`.

When running tests, Node developers expect the `npm test` command to be the command that triggers the test suite, so we need to add that script to our `package.json` file. However, since we are going to have different tests to be run, it would be even better to add a `unit-tests` script and make `npm test` run that for now. The `scripts` property should look like the following code:

```
"scripts": {
  "start": "node ./bin/www",
  "unit-tests": "mocha --reporter=spec test/unit",
  "test": "npm run unit-tests"
},
```

Now, if we run the tests, we should see the following output in the terminal:

```
$ npm run unit-tests

> file-uploading-service@0.0.1 unit-tests /Users/alexandruvladutu/www/file-sha
re-app
> mocha --reporter=spec test/unit



  models
    File
      ✓ should have default properties
      ✓ should return the path based on the root and the file id
      ✓ should move a file
      ✓ should save the metadata
      ✓ should check if file is password protected
      ✓ should allow access if matched file password
      .dir
        ✓ should return the root of the files folder
      .exists
        ✓ should callback with an error when the file does not exist
        ✓ should callback with no arguments when the file exists


  9 passing (18ms)

alexandruvladutu at MBP in ~/www/file-share-app on master*
$
```

Functional tests

So far, we have tested each method to check whether it works fine on its own, but now, it's time to check whether our application works according to the specifications when wiring all the things together.

Besides the existing modules, we will need to install and use the following ones:

- `supertest`: This is used to test the routes in an expressive manner
- `cheerio`: This is used to extract the CSRF token out of the form and pass it along when uploading the file
- `rimraf`: This is used to clean up our `files` folder once we're done with the testing

We will create a new file called `test/functional/files-routes.js` for the functional tests. As usual, we will list our dependencies first:

```
var fs = require('fs');
var request = require('supertest');
var should = require('should');
var async = require('async');
var cheerio = require('cheerio');
var rimraf = require('rimraf');
var app = require('../../app');
```

There will be a couple of scenarios to test when uploading a file, such as:

- Checking whether a file that is uploaded without a password can be publicly accessible
- Checking that a password-protected file can only be accessed with the correct password

We will create a function called `uploadFile` that we can reuse across different tests. This function will use the same `supertest` agent when making requests so it can persist the cookies, and will also take care of extracting and sending the CSRF token back to the server when making the post request. In case a password argument is provided, it will send that along with the file.

The function will assert that the status code for the upload page is 200 and that the user is redirected to the file page after the upload. The full code of the function is listed as follows:

```
function uploadFile(agent, password, done) {
  agent
    .get('/files')
    .expect(200)
    .end(function(err, res) {
      (err == null).should.be.true;

      var $ = cheerio.load(res.text);
      var csrfToken = $('form input[name=_csrf]').val();

      csrfToken.should.not.be.empty;

      var req = agent
        .post('/files')
        .field('_csrf', csrfToken)
        .attach('file', __filename);

      if (password) {
        req = req.field('password', password);
      }

      req
        .expect(302)
        .expect('Location', /files\/(.*)\.html/)
        .end(function(err, res) {
          (err == null).should.be.true;

          var fileUid =
            res.headers['location'].match(/files\/(.*)\.html/)[1];

          done(null, fileUid);
        });
    });
}
```

Note that we will use `rimraf` in an `after` function to clean up the `files` folder, but it would be best to have a separate path for uploading files while testing (other than the one used for development and production):

```
describe('Files-Routes', function(done) {
  after(function() {
    var filesDir = __dirname + '/../../files';
    rimraf.sync(filesDir);
    fs.mkdirSync(filesDir);
```

When testing the file uploads, we want to make sure that without providing the correct password, access will not be granted to the file pages:

```
describe("Uploading a file", function() {
  it("should upload a file without password protecting it",
    function(done) {
    var agent = request.agent(app);

    uploadFile(agent, null, done);
  });

  it("should upload a file and password protect it",
    function(done) {
    var agent = request.agent(app);
    var pwd = 'sample-password';

    uploadFile(agent, pwd, function(err, filename) {
      async.parallel([
        function getWithoutPwd(next) {
          agent
            .get('/files/' + filename + '.html')
            .expect(401)
            .end(function(err, res) {
              (err == null).should.be.true;
              next();
            });
        },
        function getWithPwd(next) {
          agent
            .get('/files/' + filename + '.html')
            .set('Authorization', 'Basic ' + new Buffer(':' +
              pwd).toString('base64'))
            .expect(200)
            .end(function(err, res) {
              (err == null).should.be.true;
```

```
                next();
            });
        }
    ], function(err) {
        (err == null).should.be.true;
        done();
    });
  });
 });
});
```

It's time to do the same thing we did for the unit tests: make a script so we can run them with npm by using npm run functional-tests. At the same time, we should update the npm test script to include both our unit tests and our functional tests:

```
"scripts": {
  "start": "node ./bin/www",
  "unit-tests": "mocha --reporter=spec test/unit",
  "functional-tests": "mocha --reporter=spec --timeout=10000 --
    slow=2000 test/functional",
  "test": "npm run unit-tests && npm run functional-tests"
}
```

If we run the tests, we should see the following output:

Running tests before committing in Git

It's a good practice to run the test suite before committing to `git` and only allowing the commit to pass if the tests have been executed successfully. The same applies for other version control systems.

To achieve this, we should add the `.git/hooks/pre-commit` file, which should take care of running the tests and exiting with an error in case they failed. Luckily, this is a repetitive task (which can be applied to all Node applications), so there is an NPM module that creates this hook file for us. All we need to do is install the `pre-commit` module (https://www.npmjs.org/package/pre-commit) as a development dependency using the following command:

```
$ npm i pre-commit --save-dev
```

This should automatically create the `pre-commit` hook file so that all the tests are run before committing (using the `npm test` command).

 The `pre-commit` module also supports running custom scripts specified in the `package.json` file. For more details on how to achieve that, read the module documentation at https://www.npmjs.org/package/pre-commit.

Code coverage

Long gone are the days when we used to rely on Java for outputting JavaScript code-coverage data. Now, there are Node-based tools out there that can help us out, such as the following:

- **Istanbul** (https://www.npmjs.org/package/istanbul)
- **Blanket.js** (https://www.npmjs.org/package/blanket)
- **SteamShovel** (https://www.npmjs.org/package/steamshovel)

These kinds of tools instrument your code and usually track statement, branch, function, and line coverage.

Integrating code coverage with `istanbul` into our project is a simple process that has two steps:

1. Installing the module as a development dependency using the following command:

```
$ npm i istanbul --save-dev
```

2. Adding the CLI command as an NPM script inside `package.json`:
   `"coverage": "node node_modules/istanbul/lib/cli.js cover node_modules/.bin/_mocha test/* -- --reporter=spec"`.

Now, if we want to run the tests with code-coverage data, we should see the following output:

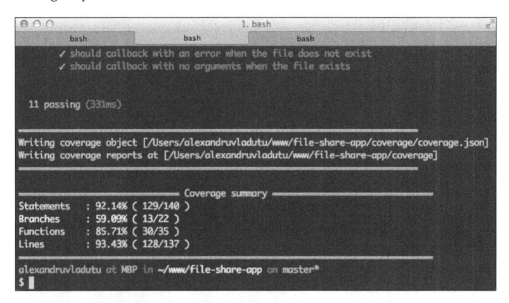

If we want to set a hard threshold for code coverage, `istanbul` also supports that. Let's suppose that we want 100 percent function coverage and 90 percent coverage for branches, statements, and lines. After running `istanbul` with the `cover` command to generate the code-coverage data, we would need to run the following command into the terminal:

```
$ ./node_modules/.bin/istanbul check-coverage --statement 100
```

A sample output might look like the following:

```
/Users/alexandruvladutu/www/file-share-app/node_modules/istanbul/lib/cli.
js:30

        throw ex; // turn it into an uncaught exception
            ^

ERROR: Coverage for branches (59.09%) does not meet threshold (90%)
ERROR: Coverage for functions (85.71%) does not meet threshold (100%)
```

We could choose to add this script after the `coverage` command is run and make it our default `npm test` script. Using the `pre-commit` module would ensure that not only our tests are run but also strict limits are imposed for code coverage.

Complexity analysis of our code

Complex code is hard to read, test, and work on, even more so if we're trying to decipher somebody else's code. Fortunately, there's a tool to measure code complexity called `complexity-report` (`https://www.npmjs.org/package/complexity-report`).

As always, we need to install the module first so that we can use it:

```
$ npm i complexity-report --save-dev
```

When running this tool, we must specify which folders it should ignore, so that we don't get reports for the dependencies used or code-coverage files:

```
$ ./node_modules/.bin/cr . --dirpattern '^((?!(test|node_
modules|coverage)).)*$'
```

A sample output could look like the following screenshot:

```
/Users/alexandruvladutu/www/mastering_express_code/chapter11/lib/middleware/csrf
-helper.js

  Physical LOC: 9
  Logical LOC: 5
  Mean parameter count: 1.5
  Cyclomatic complexity: 1
  Cyclomatic complexity density: 20%
  Maintainability index: 149.25453514609262
  Dependency count: 0

  Function: module.exports
    Line No.: 3
    Physical LOC: 7
    Logical LOC: 2
    Parameter count: 3
    Cyclomatic complexity: 1
    Cyclomatic complexity density: 50%
    Halstead difficulty: 2.6666666666666665
    Halstead volume: 43.18506523353572
    Halstead effort: 115.16017395609524

  Function: <anonymous>.csrf
    Line No.: 4
    Physical LOC: 3
    Logical LOC: 1
    Parameter count: 0
    Cyclomatic complexity: 1
    Cyclomatic complexity density: 100%
    Halstead difficulty: 2
    Halstead volume: 27
```

We can also specify the desired format, which can be one of the following: plain, markdown, minimal, JSON, and XML.

Just like the code-coverage tool, this one also supports thresholds for things such as cyclomatic complexity or Halstead difficulty threshold. These represent software metrics that determine the complexity of a program by analyzing its source code. For example, if we run the script again using the -c 1 arguments (set the cyclomatic complexity threshold to 1), at the end of the output, we would get the following information:

```
Warning: Complexity threshold breached!
Failing modules:
/Users/alexandruvladutu/www/file-share-app/app.js
/Users/alexandruvladutu/www/file-share-app/models/file.js
/Users/alexandruvladutu/www/file-share-app/routes/files.js
```

Code linting

So far, we have learned about complexity and code-coverage tools, but there are some other static-analysis tools we can use to lint our code based on different rules:

- **ESLint** (https://www.npmjs.org/package/eslint)
- **JSHint** (https://www.npmjs.org/package/jshint)
- **JSLint** (https://www.npmjs.org/package/jslint)

JSLint is highly opinionated when it comes to the rules, while JSHint is more flexible. ESLint is the newest of the three and has support for pluggable rules.

 To find out more about the differences between JSHint and ESLint, read the blog post at http://www.nczonline.net/blog/2013/07/16/introducing-eslint/.

For our example, we will use ESLint using the following command:

```
$ npm i eslint --save-dev
```

Before we run the eslint command-line tool, we should create two files inside our root: .eslintignore and eslint.json. The first one indicates what files should be ignored:

```
node_modules/*
test/*
coverage/*
```

The second one is used for overriding the default configuration of `eslint`:

```
{
  "env": {
    "node": true
  },
  "rules": {
    "quotes": 0,
    "no-unused-vars": [2, {"vars": "all", "args": "none"}],
    "no-underscore-dangle": 0
  }
}
```

In the preceding file, we're setting the environment to Node.js, which won't display warnings related to global variable leaks such as `require`, `module`, or `__filename`, because it will know that these are defined by Node.

Next, we will disable the enforcement of double quotes so that we can use both single quotes and double quotes if we'd like without seeing warnings.

After that, we will apply the rule to disallow unused variables, but not the ones that are arguments. This is useful because Express checks the function arity (number of arguments) to determine the error handler.

Last but not least, we are disabling the rule that disallows the use of underscore in identifiers, so we can use free variables such as `_foo` or `_this`.

 You can check the documentation for all the ESLint rules at `https://github.com/eslint/eslint/tree/master/docs/rules`.

You might have noticed that these rules can be applied based on personal preference, so you and your team should pick a coding style and stick with it.

Now, it's time to add the `lint` script to the `package.json` file and then run it. We need to add the following line to the `scripts` property inside `package.json`:

```
"lint": "eslint . -c eslint.json",
```

To run the `lint` script, simply use `npm run lint`, which might output something like the following:

```
$ npm run lint


> file-uploading-service@0.0.1 lint /Users/alexandruvladutu/www/file-
share-app
> eslint . -c eslint.json



app.js
  26:30  error  Missing semicolon                    semi
   6:4   error  logger is defined but never used  no-unused-vars

✖ 2 problems
```

As you can see from the preceding output, when a rule fails, it will show the filename along with the line, column, and then a descriptive message followed by the rule name.

Load testing

Load testing is a testing technique used to determine how an application behaves when subjected to both normal and extreme load conditions. It can also be referred to as performance testing, volume testing, or reliability testing.

A common load-testing tool is **ab** (**Apache Benchmark**). It can be used from the terminal easily. We will perform the test on a file page, so make sure you upload a file and get its URL afterwards.

To perform 1,000 requests with a concurrency level of 10, we will enter the following command in the terminal:

```
$ ab -n 1000 -c 10 http://127.0.0.1:3000/files/chwrjte880000qsn9ivmx0q77.
html
```

A sample output would look like the following screenshot:

```
Concurrency Level:      10
Time taken for tests:   1.570 seconds
Complete requests:      1000
Failed requests:        0
Write errors:           0
Total transferred:      1102000 bytes
HTML transferred:       747000 bytes
Requests per second:    637.01 [#/sec] (mean)
Time per request:       15.698 [ms] (mean)
Time per request:       1.570 [ms] (mean, across all concurrent requests)
Transfer rate:          685.53 [Kbytes/sec] received

Connection Times (ms)
              min  mean[+/-sd] median   max
Connect:        0    0   0.1      0       1
Processing:     8   16   3.3     15      29
Waiting:        7   15   3.3     15      29
Total:          8   16   3.3     15      29

Percentage of the requests served within a certain time (ms)
  50%     15
  66%     17
  75%     18
  80%     18
  90%     20
  95%     22
  98%     24
  99%     27
 100%     29 (longest request)
```

There are similar CLI tools such as **wrk** (https://github.com/wg/wrk).

For more complex use cases, **Apache JMeter**™ (http://jmeter.apache.org/) is a good solution as it also comes bundled up with a GUI.

Client-side testing

So far, we have covered testing the backend functionality of our projects as well as ensuring that the server returns the correct HTTP responses by using supertest. To achieve the holy grail of programming, we can go even further and test our client-side code.

We will not focus on test frameworks or how to write client-side tests and run them step-by-step, but instead, we will see what our toolbox contains so that we have our options clear.

There are different types of tools that can help us in our quest by either spinning up a real browser or simulating their environment, such as the following ones:

- Those that try to emulate a browser, such as the NPM module Zombie.js (`https://www.npmjs.org/package/zombie`), which used jsdom (`https://www.npmjs.org/package/jsdom`) under the hood to simulate a browser environment

- Those that launch headless browsers and have a custom API for interacting with it, such as PhantomJS (`http://www.phantomjs.org`)

- Those that launch native browsers and execute the client-side JavaScript unit test, such as Karma (`http://karma-runner.github.io/`)

- Those that have a built-in browser control mechanism and launch local or remote browsers, such as Selenium Webdriver (`http://docs.seleniumhq.org/projects/webdriver/`)

Most of these tools are designed primarily for end-to-end testing, while others are specifically targeted to run unit tests in the browsers (such as Karma).

It is worth noting that you can also use PhantomJS with Selenium Webdriver starting with Version 1.8 (`http://phantomjs.org/release-1.8.html`). The benefit of this approach is that you can reuse the same tests for executing them locally in the headless browser as well as on a CI server with a more complex setup, for example (which spins up multiple native browsers). On top of that, it is also faster to spin up PhantomJS instead of a real browser, so that would make your local tests run faster too.

In case you choose Selenium Webdriver to run your tests, there are two useful NPM modules you can use:

- `selenium-webdriver`: This module represents the official WebDriver JavaScript bindings from the Selenium project. You can find it at `https://www.npmjs.org/package/selenium-webdriver`.

- `wd`: This module implements the Selenium JsonWireProtocol. You can find it at `https://www.npmjs.org/package/wd`.

There are also commercial solutions available to run both unit tests and functional tests in the cloud, with a variety of web browsers available. You can find examples of such services by visiting the following sites:

- `https://ci.testling.com/`
- `https://saucelabs.com/`
- `http://www.browserstack.com/`

In the end, it's up to you to figure out what tools work best for your project, but the important thing is to have the big picture in mind.

Continuous Integration

Continuous Integration (CI) represents the development practice of pushing code to a shared repository several times a day to identify problems quickly and solve them as early as possible. This has multiple benefits, such as the following:

- Caching bugs quickly
- Supports distributed builds on different operating systems and CPU architectures
- Keeps the build history available
- Sends real-time notifications with the build status
- Automatically generates metrics, such as code coverage and code complexity, among others

CI servers

There are several CI platforms available, whether they are open source, commercial, or self-hosted or not.

One of the most popular CI solutions is Jenkins, an extendable open source continuous integration server written in Java, which you can install on your own servers. Although it is used primarily by the Java community, it can be set up to work with Node projects as well.

 For more details on how to set up your Node project with Jenkins, read the article at `https://blog.dylants.com/2013/06/21/ jenkins-and-node/`.

If you are a Node purist, then StriderCD (`https://github.com/Strider-CD/ strider`) might also be a good option since it's written in Node, and is open sourced and self-hosted.

You can find a more comprehensive list of continuous integration software at `http://en.wikipedia.org/wiki/Comparison_of_continuous_integration_ software`.

Free CI for open source projects

If you are working on an open source project hosted on GitHub, then you can integrate it with the Travis CI continuous integration service for free (`https://travis-ci.com`).

This integration has several benefits; the most important ones are as follows:

- Automatically running builds when pushing to GitHub
- Generating status images that you can include in the project's readme file
- Checking the build status of the pull requests before merging them
- Getting notified of failed builds by e-mail

In fact, Express itself is integrated with Travis CI, as you can integrate it from the project's main page on GitHub or NPM. You can see what the Travis build history looks like for Express in the following screenshot:

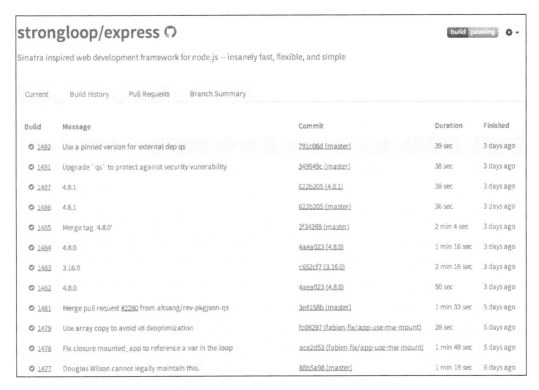

To integrate your open source project with Travis CI, you will first need to sign up for the service. Afterwards, you can use the travisify CLI tool from NPM (`https://www.npmjs.org/package/travisify`) to automatically add Travis CI hooks to your GitHub project and generate a status badge for the readme markdown file. You can see an example of how to do it in the following screenshot:

```
● ○ ○                            1. bash
alexandruvladutu at MBP in ~/www/sample-github-repo
$ travisify
github username: alessioalex
github password:
travis-ci api key:
travis hook added for alessioalex/sample-github-repo with id 2788456
^Calexandruvladutu at MBP in ~/www/sample-github-repo
$ travisify badge
[![build status](https://secure.travis-ci.org/alessioalex/sample-github-repo.png
)](http://travis-ci.org/alessioalex/sample-github-repo)
```

Summary

In this chapter, we have learned about writing tests for Express applications and in the process, explored a variety of helpful modules. We have also integrated static analysis tools into our project to provide meaningful information related to code complexity and linting. To conclude the chapter, we have explored continuous integration and client-side testing.

At the end of our mastering Express journey, we have covered quite a lot of ground and hopefully, you have a better understanding of the ins and outs of developing real-world applications using the framework. More specifically, we have covered the following topics:

- Comparing Express with other web frameworks
- Structuring Express applications
- Understanding the inner workings of the middleware system and building our own
- Creating RESTful APIs using Express
- Express templating
- Reusing NPM modules to keep the codebase dry
- Using efficient strategies for error handling
- Optimizing the performance and throughput of Express web applications
- Monitoring and debugging applications using the latest techniques
- Securing Express web applications against common attacks
- Improving code quality using existing tools
- Testing Express applications

Index

Symbols

A

B

frame-src 287
img-src 287
media-src 287
object-src 287
script-src 287
CSRF protection 278-282
css(value) function 286
csurf module 281
cuid module
about 230
URL 230
custom-err module 168
custom errors
creating 167, 168
custom Express error handler
creating 177-180
custom validation module
creating 88-91

D

database library 18
debug flag
debug module, versus regular logger 263
using 261-263
debugging commands
removing 273
debug module, versus regular logger
benefits 263
DELETE method 76
DRY templates
using, with layouts 130
Dust.js
URL 124
dynamic data, caching
about 215-222
Etag 222-224

E

EJS module 39, 182
environment-based loading,
of middleware 45-47
error
checking 159-161
handling, with middleware 53-57

human errors 169
logging 176, 177
runtime errors 169
error delivery ways, in Node applications
error first callback pattern 171
EventEmitter errors 172
synchronous style 170, 171
error-first callback pattern 171
errorhandler module
adding 256-261
URL 253
error handling, in practical application
about 182
application entry point, creating 183-186
application, running 194, 195
Post model 187
Primus, using 186
routes modules 189-193
static JavaScript file (core.js) 194
User model 188
view files 194
error-handling middleware
about 253, 254
application, for time display in current
time zone 254-256
improved error handler,
adding 256-261
error objects
features 173
errTo module 160
ESLint
URL 323
esprima
URL 273
ETag
about 222-224
URL 116
EventEmitter errors 172, 173
Express
about 12, 13
benchmarking, URL 146
comparing, with frameworks 8
features 7, 8
template engines, integrating with 139-147
used, for serving static resources 197

Thank you for buying
Mastering Web Application Development with Express

About Packt Publishing

Packt, pronounced 'packed', published its first book "*Mastering phpMyAdmin for Effective MySQL Management*" in April 2004 and subsequently continued to specialize in publishing highly focused books on specific technologies and solutions.

Our books and publications share the experiences of your fellow IT professionals in adapting and customizing today's systems, applications, and frameworks. Our solution based books give you the knowledge and power to customize the software and technologies you're using to get the job done. Packt books are more specific and less general than the IT books you have seen in the past. Our unique business model allows us to bring you more focused information, giving you more of what you need to know, and less of what you don't.

Packt is a modern, yet unique publishing company, which focuses on producing quality, cutting-edge books for communities of developers, administrators, and newbies alike. For more information, please visit our website: www.packtpub.com.

About Packt Open Source

In 2010, Packt launched two new brands, Packt Open Source and Packt Enterprise, in order to continue its focus on specialization. This book is part of the Packt Open Source brand, home to books published on software built around Open Source licenses, and offering information to anybody from advanced developers to budding web designers. The Open Source brand also runs Packt's Open Source Royalty Scheme, by which Packt gives a royalty to each Open Source project about whose software a book is sold.

Writing for Packt

We welcome all inquiries from people who are interested in authoring. Book proposals should be sent to author@packtpub.com. If your book idea is still at an early stage and you would like to discuss it first before writing a formal book proposal, contact us; one of our commissioning editors will get in touch with you.

We're not just looking for published authors; if you have strong technical skills but no writing experience, our experienced editors can help you develop a writing career, or simply get some additional reward for your expertise.

Express Web Application Development

ISBN: 978-1-84969-654-8 Paperback: 236 pages

Learn how to develop web applications with the Express framework from scratch

1. Exploring all aspects of web development using the Express framework.

2. Starts with the essentials.

3. Expert tips and advice covering all Express topics.

Advanced Express Web Application Development

ISBN: 978-1-78328-249-4 Paperback: 148 pages

Your guide to building professional real-world web applications with Express

1. Learn how to build scalable, robust, and reliable web applications with Express using a test-first, feature-driven approach.

2. Full of practical tips and real-world examples, and delivered in an easy-to-read format.

3. Explore and tackle the issues you encounter while commercially developing and deploying an Express application.

Please check **www.PacktPub.com** for information on our titles

Node Web Development
Second Edition

ISBN: 978-1-78216-330-5   Paperback: 248 pages

A practical introduction to Node.js, an exciting server-side JavaScript web development stack

1. Learn about server-side JavaScript with Node.js and Node modules.

2. Website development both with and without the Connect/Express web application framework.

3. Developing both HTTP server and client applications.

Mastering Node.js

ISBN: 978-1-78216-632-0   Paperback: 346 pages

Expert techniques for building fast servers and scalable, real-time network applications with minimal effort

1. Master the latest techniques for building real-time, big data applications, integrating Facebook, Twitter, and other network services.

2. Tame asynchronous programming, the event loop, and parallel data processing.

3. Use the Express and Path frameworks to speed up development and deliver scalable, higher quality software more quickly.

Please check **www.PacktPub.com** for information on our titles